IMAGES
of America

AROUND AUBURN
VOLUME II

IMAGES
of America

AROUND AUBURN
VOLUME II

Stephanie E. Przybylek

ARCADIA
PUBLISHING

ISBN 978-0-7385-6371-8

Published by Arcadia Publishing
Charleston, South Carolina

Printed in the United States of America

Library of Congress Catalog Card Number: 2005930853

For all general information contact Arcadia Publishing at:
Telephone 843-853-2070
Fax 843-853-0044
E-mail sales@arcadiapublishing.com
For customer service and orders:
Toll-Free 1-888-313-2665

Visit us on the Internet at www.arcadiapublishing.com

This book is dedicated to the memory of Isabel "Izzie" Chase,
who showed me that some of the personal stories
entwined with Auburn's history are the richest.

Acknowledgments

I would like to express my sincere thanks to the following individuals and organizations for help with this project: Jim Richerson, Jessica Kline, and Lynn Palmieri, Cayuga Museum; Lou and Myrtle Chomyk; Charles Schaeffer; Mr. and Mrs. Albert Gatto; Wayne Mason; Susan Lorenc; Rev. Mihai Dubovici; Rose Marie Gauthier; Hollywood Restaurant; Lydia Rosell; Phil Simone; Pearl O'Brien; Bob Orman; Laura Grauer, Philadelphia Toboggan Coasters, Inc.; Tom Eldred and Malcom Godelle, Cayuga County Historian's Office; Judy Lee, Community Preservation Committee; Jim Courtney and Dixie Warner-Webert, YMCA-WEIU; Sharon Middleton and Peg Gollnick, Cayuga County Chapter of the American Red Cross; the Cayuga County legislature; the residents of the Boyle Center; and everyone who graciously and patiently answered my repeated requests for identification of persons, places, and things.

Contents

Foreword

Photographic collections, such as the one presented in this book, play much the same role as a museum. Both are reference points for the familiar and the forgotten, and both act as a repository for a dynamic collective memory.

Images, like objects in a collection, are signposts marking the way through the past for those that have been there and for later generations that will only know these places through such memorabilia. Searching through these frozen moments in time, the viewer is swept up in a variety of emotions and personal reflections.

At a quick glance, such photographs seem static. But with the passing of time, they reveal a great deal about the people and places captured in those illuminated instances. Through such images, we are reminded that with experience and age our perception is constantly evolving, hence nothing is static.

The objects in the photographs—people, hairstyles, clothing, machines, signs, and buildings—are each seemingly singular points on a timeline. For an instant, a multitude of things are captured together. The limits of the photograph's edge, like a museum exhibit, makes us more conscious of relationships that are otherwise lost in the rush of daily routines.

The images shine through to us today like stars whose light sources are at unthinkable distances. The light we see is decades old. The point of origin, like the moment the image is captured, is a place we know we can never physically be in. Yet, they stimulate wonder and awe. Are such sights so different from what our parents viewed? Will they be different to us only a few decades down the road?

This collection of photographs plays on memory, both personal and shared. Its seemingly casual role as a momento should not be taken for granted. Such collections change with each look and each person, especially those who choose to return and reflect on the past as a way of seeing a richer present and future.

The thought-provoking and subtle selections and chapter groupings of the photographs enhance each image's power to stimulate memory and emotion. In *Around Auburn, Volume II*, the Cayuga Museum's Curator, Stephanie Przybylek, clearly blends her expert skills as a researcher and a keeper of collections. Her work, in Arcadia's classic, winning format, delivers to viewers a dynamic succession of moments that shall become a point of reference onto itself.

Jim Richerson,
Executive Director, Cayuga Museum

INTRODUCTION

As the companion volume to *Around Auburn*, published by Arcadia in 1995, *Around Auburn, Volume II* chronicles the history of Auburn, New York from the late nineteenth century into the 1970s. The photographs included in this collection convey the boom years of Auburn, from expanding commercial opportunities and industrial enterprises, to the men and women who manned the machines throughout the city. These images also address the transition of later years, when the industrial climate declined, but community character remained strong. Many of the photographs are from the collections of the Cayuga Museum and the Community Preservation Committee. Other images came from generous individuals in the community. Several collecting projects, related to major exhibitions in 1997 and 1998, uncovered wonderful, seldom-seen photographs of industries, neighborhood stores, social organizations, musical pursuits, and local amusement parks. It is a pleasure to include these images in this record of Auburn's history.

The nature of Auburn as a community is one of constant change and reinvention. By the early 1880s, the city had been transformed by industrial development from a quiet, tree-lined community into a thriving manufacturing center. The diverse product base included agricultural machinery, wagons, carriages, carpets, woolen and other textile goods, shoes, and buttons. Massive brick factory complexes dominated the landscape. Older structures, built to take advantage of power gained by the convenient water supply of the Owasco Outlet, lined both sides of the outlet as it wound its way through the heart of the city. Advances in transportation networks and available power sources in the late 1870s enabled other factories to be built farther away from the outlet, and industrial complexes, like the one which housed Auburn Button Works and Logan Silk Mills on Logan Street, stood in residential neighborhoods.

The industrial community relied on human labor to operate the machines and produce the goods shipped throughout the world, and the shifting demands of the local work force often fueled social and political reform. In Auburn's early years, many local industries utilized prison labor, although the system was never without controversy. In the late nineteenth century, the development of labor unions and shifting opinions of the surrounding community resulted in an increasingly negative view of prison labor for private enterprise, and the outside contract system ended in 1890.

Women began appearing in employment roles by the 1860s, and by the 1880s they constituted a sizable percentage of the work force. Many of the women, as young as 12 and 13, came from the surrounding rural areas, and took up temporary residence as boarders in the neighborhoods surrounding the factories. They worked in the button, textile, and paper box factories, and as seamstresses, clerks, and teachers. Often, men and women intermingled informally in these work environments, a fact of great concern to middle and upper-class women reformers, who feared the results of such casual contact. Reformers campaigned for better working conditions, livable housing, and educational and entertainment opportunities for Auburn's young working women, both as a means of ensuring their moral welfare and preserving the decorum of the community.

The early twentieth century brought another transformation to Auburn's work force, and to its cultural landscape. Italian, Jewish, Polish, Russian, and Ukrainian immigrants arrived in large numbers, brought by relatives previously settled in the area and plentiful employment opportunities in the city's booming industries. By 1915, census figures show that Auburn's population had expanded from 18,000 to 35,000 people, many of them foreign-born. The new arrivals settled in the northwest end of the city, as established residents moved to Auburn's more fashionable southeastern neighborhoods.

The immigrants chose to live in close-knit ethnic neighborhoods, located near the factories where many of them worked, especially Columbian Rope Company and McIntosh and Seymour Company. Auburn's "Little Italy" was centered along South Division Street (now Columbus Street), while sections of State Street catered to the Polish and Ukrainian communities. The fragrant aromas of fresh bread and imported cheeses, the pungent smell of sauerkraut, tastes of pastries, pierogies, and kapusta, and the voices of many nationalities mingled in these streets. Neighborhood saloons functioned as community gathering spots when factory shifts let out. Immigrants worshipped in newly established churches that reflected their respective nationalities and faiths.

Auburn, in the 1910s and 1920s, was a thriving, bustling city, with Genesee Street being the focus of attention. The factories fueled the local economy, and local shops featured an endless array of the finest in goods. Streetcars provided easy transportation to many sections of the city, and stores remained open into the evening hours. Theaters such as the Jefferson, Grand, Strand, and Universal provided the latest in entertainment opportunities. The sounds of whistles from the factories echoed throughout the city, serving as a background counterpoint to day-to-day activities.

Through the 1930s and 1940s, Auburn survived the Great Depression and World War II by the same means that many other communities did—through determination, neighborhood camaraderie, and a stubborn willingness to pull together in hard times. Many local residents recall getting dressed up and going "downtown" to walk along Genesee Street and window shop at a time when few people could afford to buy. Auburn men and women of many nationalities served overseas, worked long hours in factories converted to wartime production, and volunteered to serve as zone wardens in the civil defense of the city.

Celebrations, including festivals and parades, marked important anniversaries, commemorated the close of military conflicts, and served as showcases for diverse elements of the community. Music of all kinds was played and sung, by musicians running the gamut from amateur enthusiasts to professional headliners. Amusement parks on the shores of nearby Owasco Lake provided a summer playground for many residents. Even during the Depression, residents remember hitchhiking to the park to listen to the big bands in the inexpensive shade of the pavilion porch, or climbing under the stairs of the old Deauville Hotel to scrape together enough coins for a ride on the roller coaster.

What is most striking in these images is the rich sense of character and resilience which runs through Auburn's history. It is reflected in the faces of factory and railroad workers, in residents persevering in the midst of disasters both man-made and natural, and in the landscape itself in the face of urban renewal and economic transitions. Auburn's colorful history strongly suggests a community that will continue to adapt to changing times in the future.

Stephanie E. Przybylek, Curator

One

The Turn of the Century

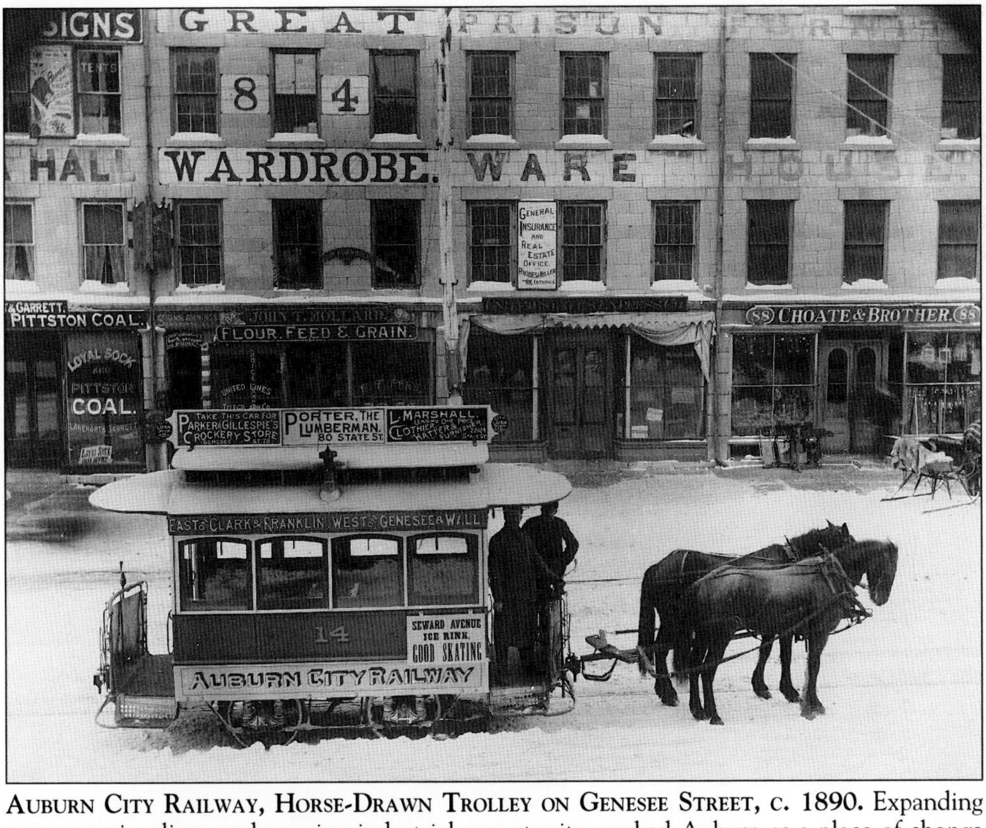

Auburn City Railway, Horse-Drawn Trolley on Genesee Street, c. 1890. Expanding transportation lines and growing industrial opportunity marked Auburn as a place of change near the end of the nineteenth century.

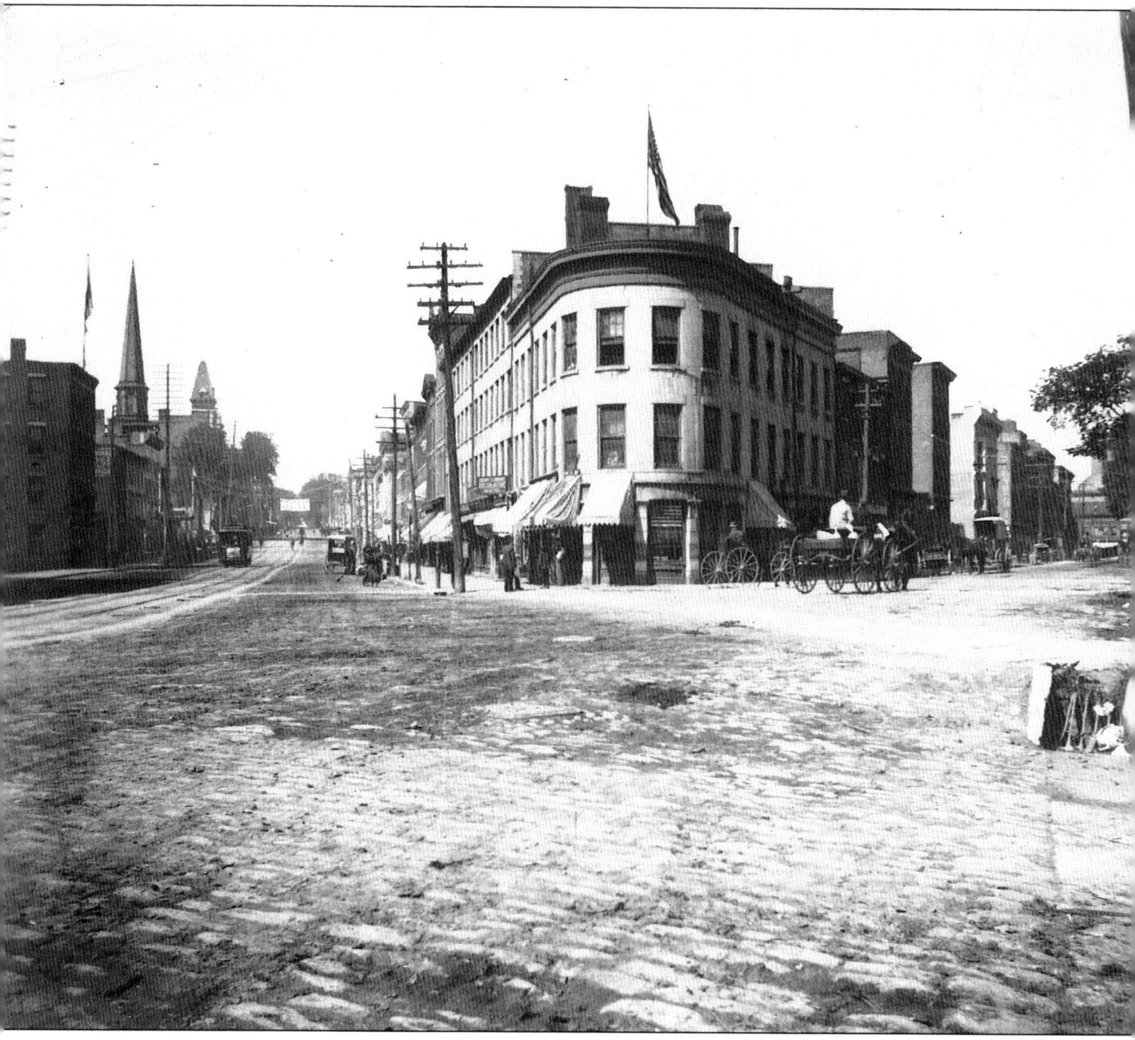

Flat Iron Building, Corner of Genesee and Market Streets, Late Nineteenth Century. This building, constructed in 1849 on the site of Center House Tavern, was one of many commercial stone structures in Auburn's business district. It housed various enterprises, including a tavern, music store, meat market, and tailor shops before falling to urban renewal in the 1970s.

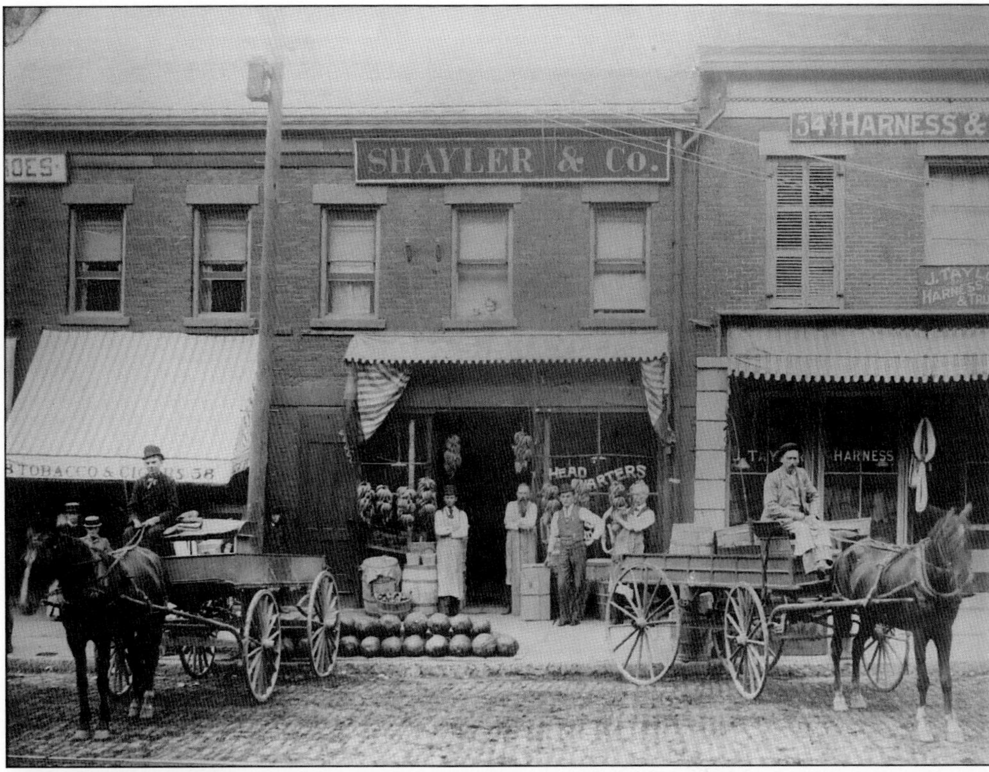

SHAYLER AND COMPANY STORE FRONT ON STATE STREET, c. 1895. Delivery wagons and employees with fresh produce posed proudly for this portrait of George and William Shayler's wholesale fruit business.

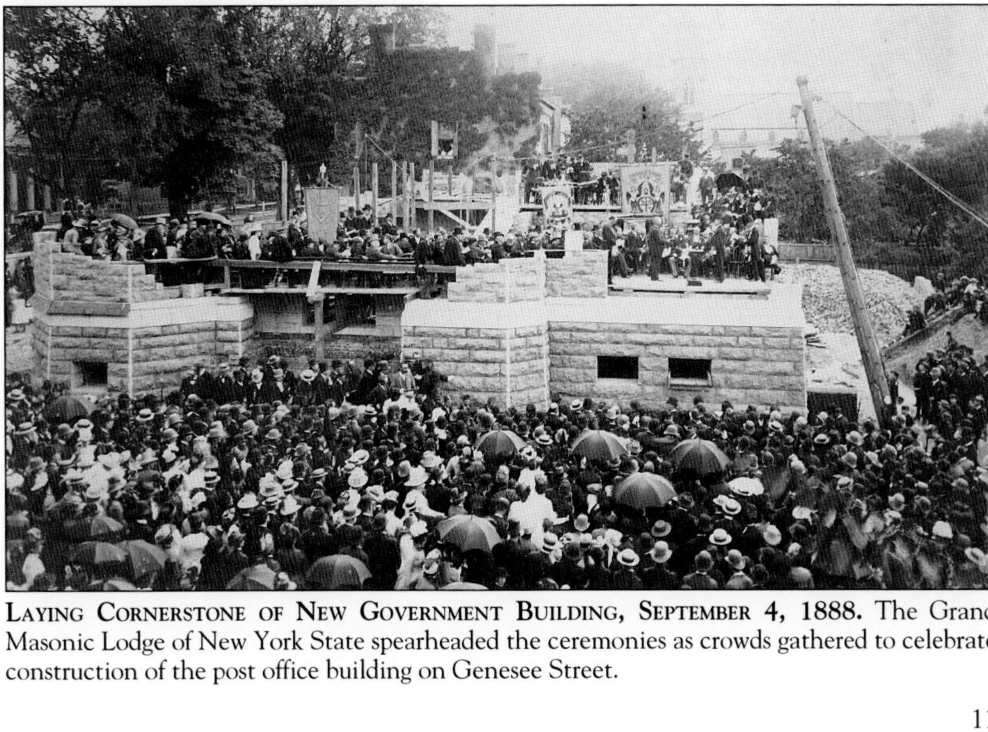

LAYING CORNERSTONE OF NEW GOVERNMENT BUILDING, SEPTEMBER 4, 1888. The Grand Masonic Lodge of New York State spearheaded the ceremonies as crowds gathered to celebrate construction of the post office building on Genesee Street.

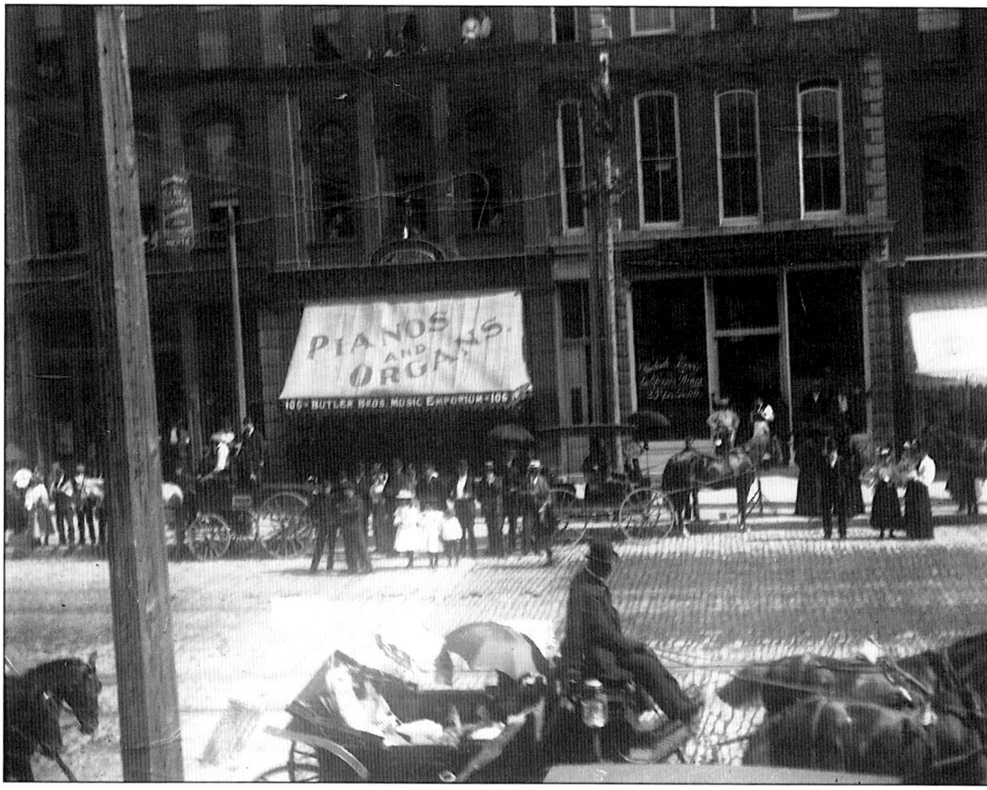

BUTLER BROTHERS MUSIC EMPORIUM, C. 1900. T.J. Butler sold pianos, organs, and other musical accessories in his store on Genesee Street.

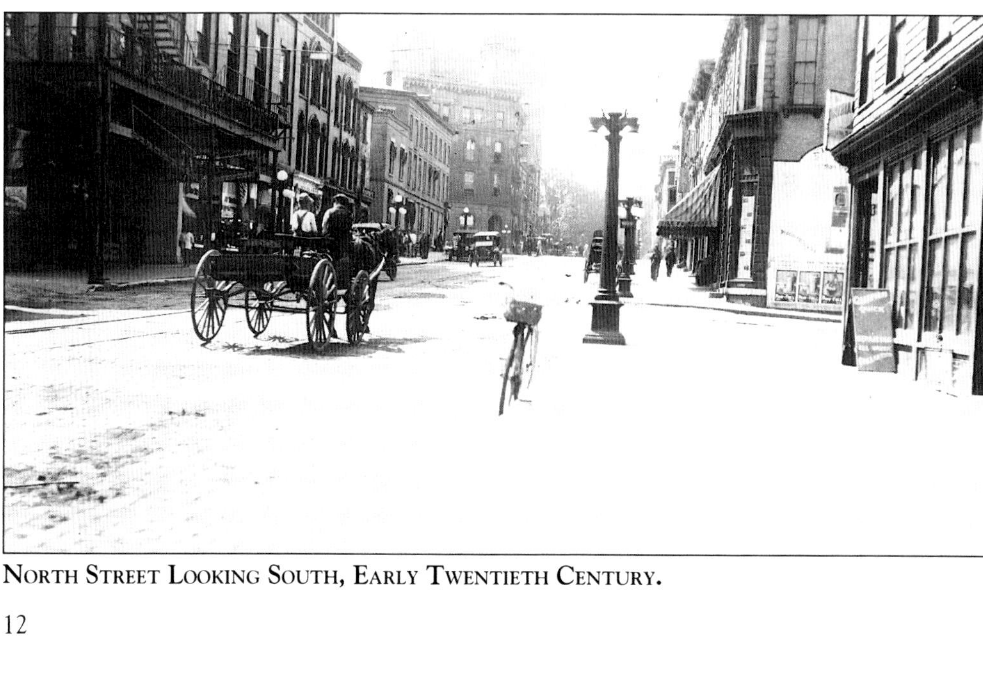

NORTH STREET LOOKING SOUTH, EARLY TWENTIETH CENTURY.

NATIONAL BANK OF AUBURN BUILDING, GENESEE STREET, LATE NINETEENTH CENTURY. This structure, which faced State Street, also briefly housed Auburn Business College.

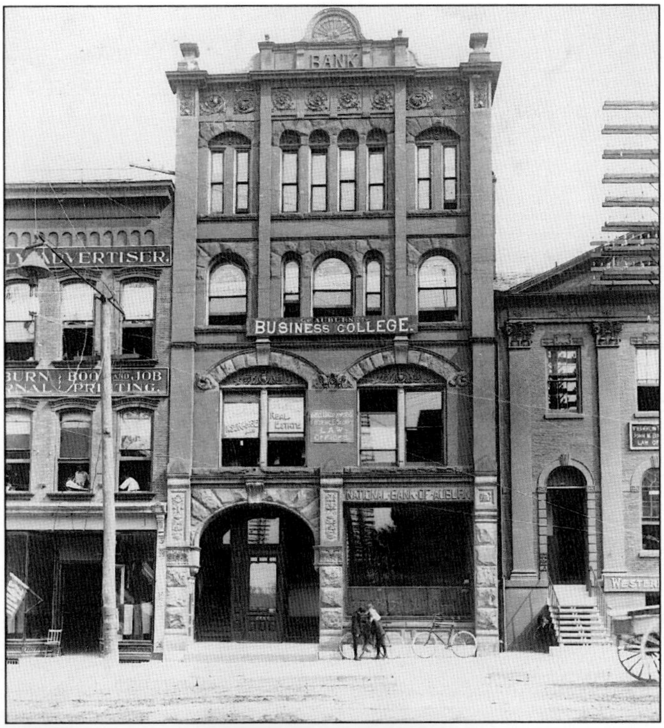

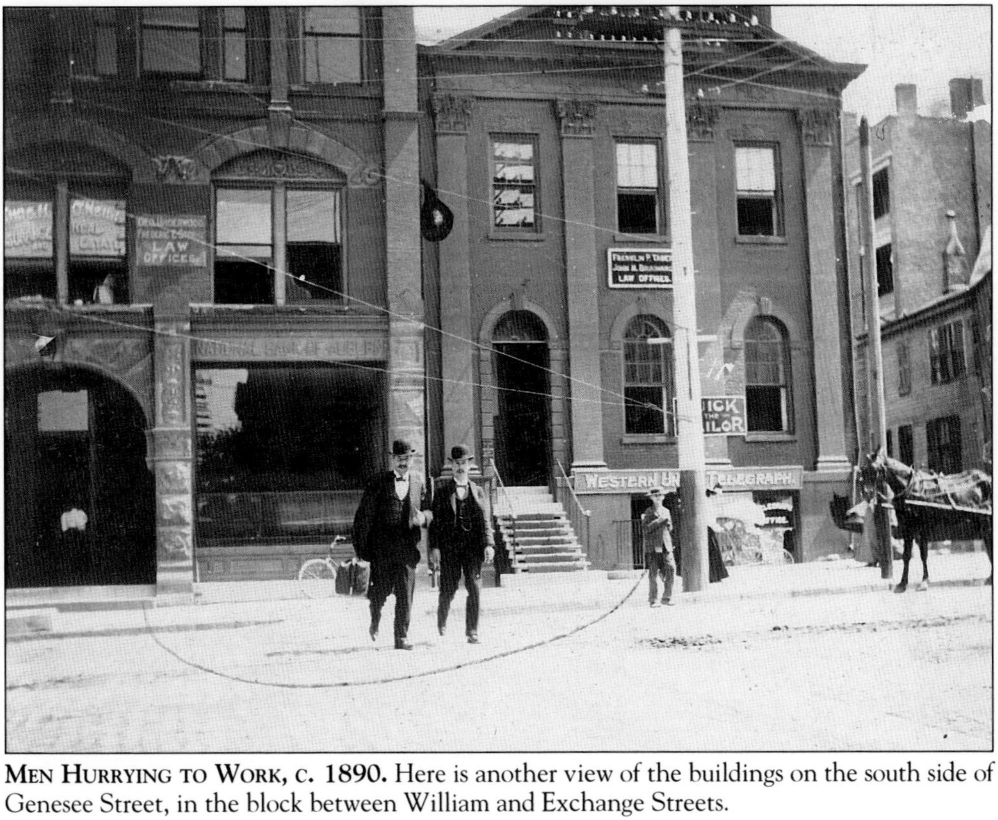

MEN HURRYING TO WORK, C. 1890. Here is another view of the buildings on the south side of Genesee Street, in the block between William and Exchange Streets.

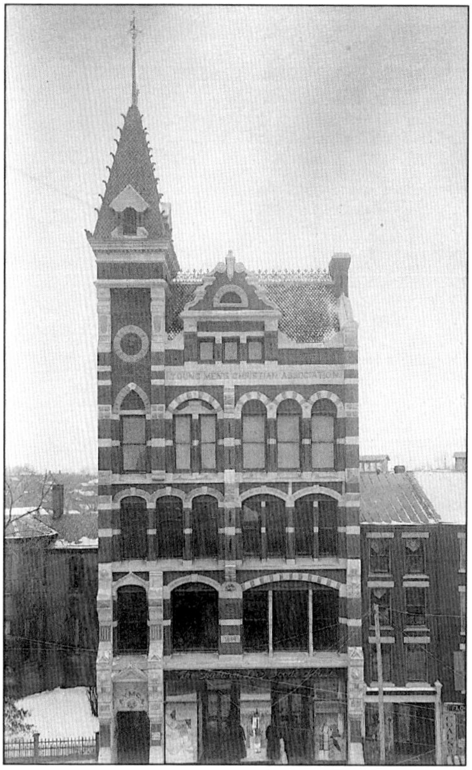

YMCA, GENESEE STREET, C. 1885. This building of boldly contrasting stonework housed the YMCA of Auburn until the late 1930s, when the organization moved to its current location on William Street.

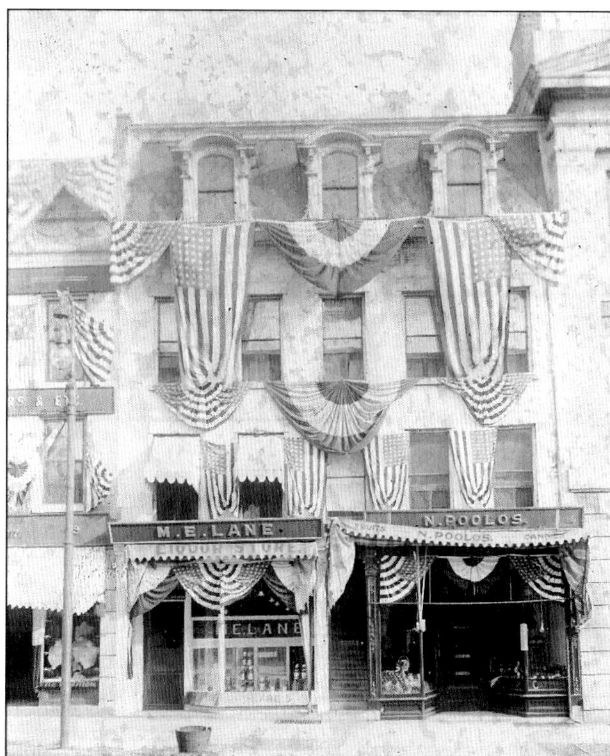

M.E. LANE LIQUOR STORE AND POOLOS CANDY STORE, LATE NINETEENTH CENTURY. The Poolos family, well known to generations of local residents, ran a candy store on Genesee Street into the 1970s.

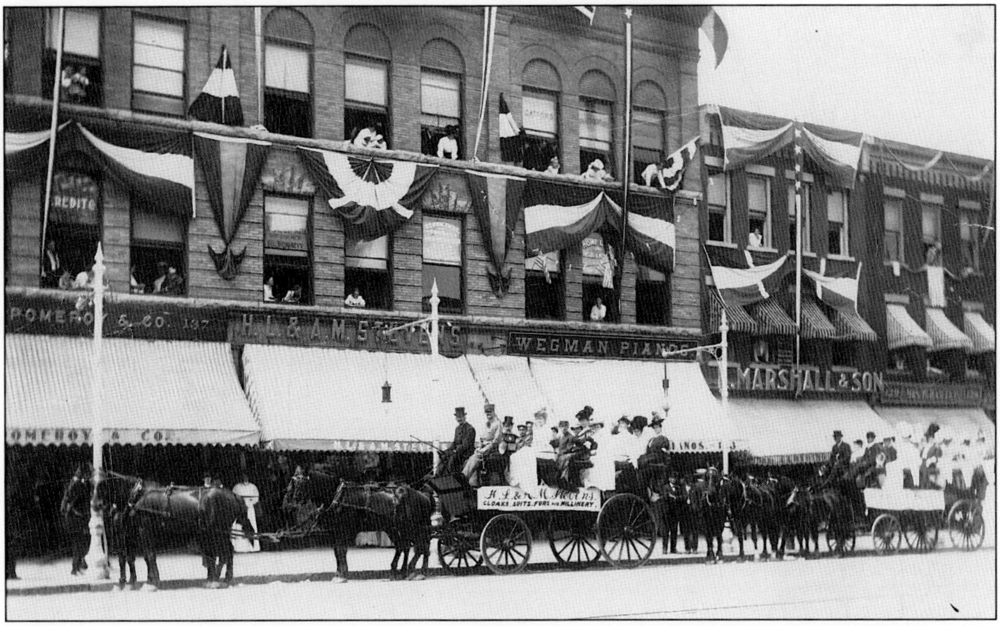

PARADE FLOAT ALONG GENESEE STREET, C. 1906. The wagon and riders with the float for H.L. and A.M. Stevens paused in front of their clothing and millinery store on Genesee Street.

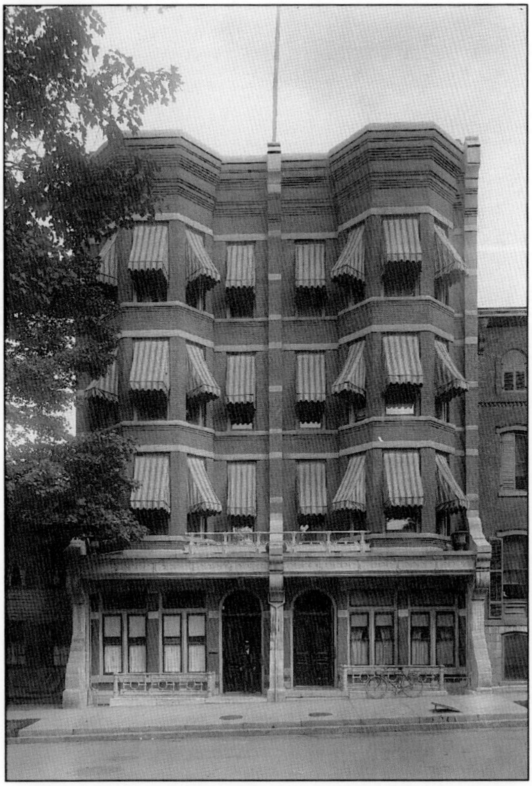

WHEELER BLOCK, WILLIAM STREET, C. 1884. Mayor Cyrenus Wheeler authorized construction of this apartment complex in 1882. The building was ready for tenants by 1884, then the epitome of urban dwelling.

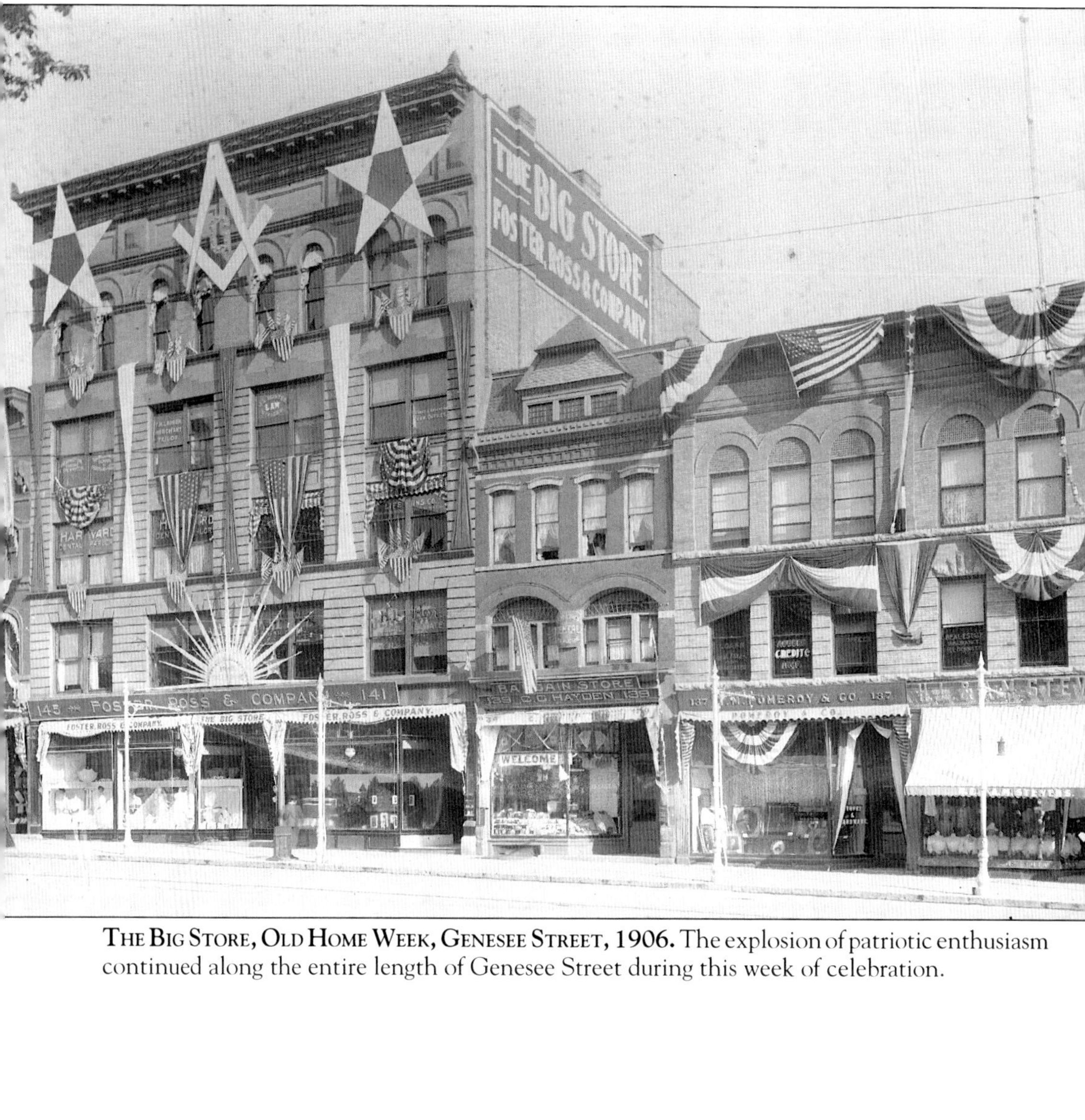

THE BIG STORE, OLD HOME WEEK, GENESEE STREET, 1906. The explosion of patriotic enthusiasm continued along the entire length of Genesee Street during this week of celebration.

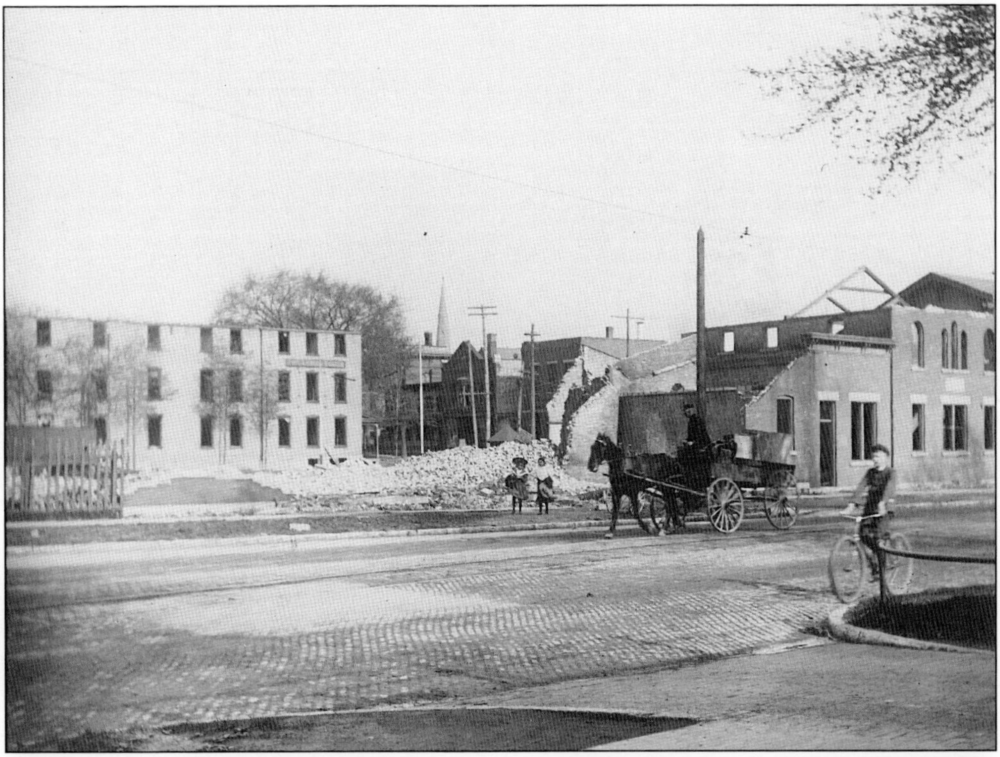

CONSTRUCTION IN PROGRESS, 1903. These buildings near Chapel and State Streets came down to make way for construction of the Central New York Railroad depot.

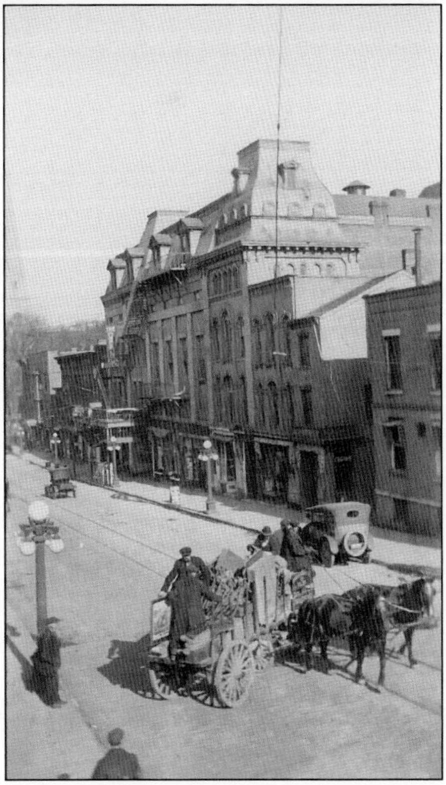

MOVING DAY, 1917. The Auburn Draying Company wagon parked on North Street while employees emptied the first load from the loft of 67 and 69 Genesee Street. (Image from Collection of Community Preservation Committee.)

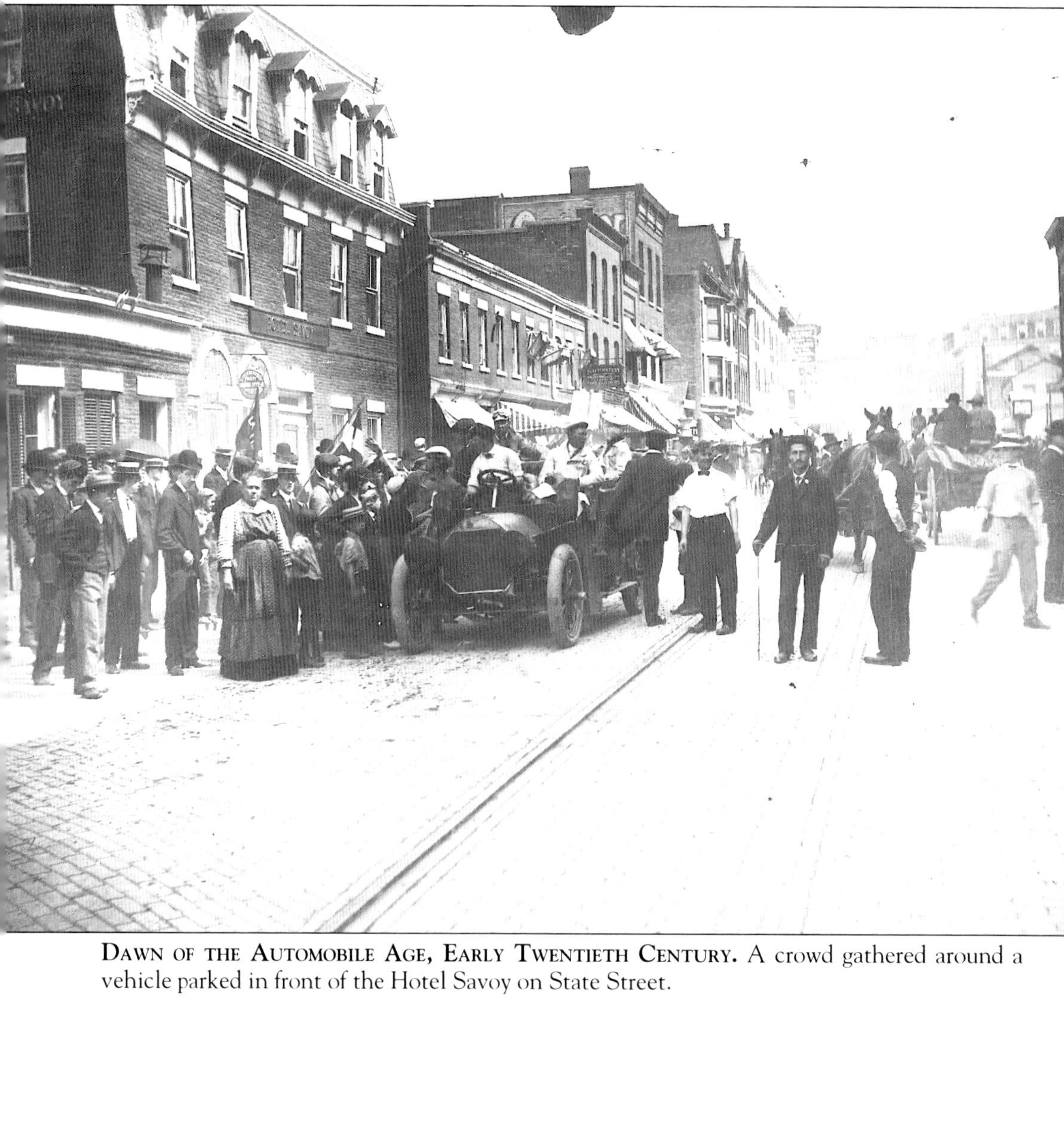

DAWN OF THE AUTOMOBILE AGE, EARLY TWENTIETH CENTURY. A crowd gathered around a vehicle parked in front of the Hotel Savoy on State Street.

Two

AUBURN COMES OF AGE

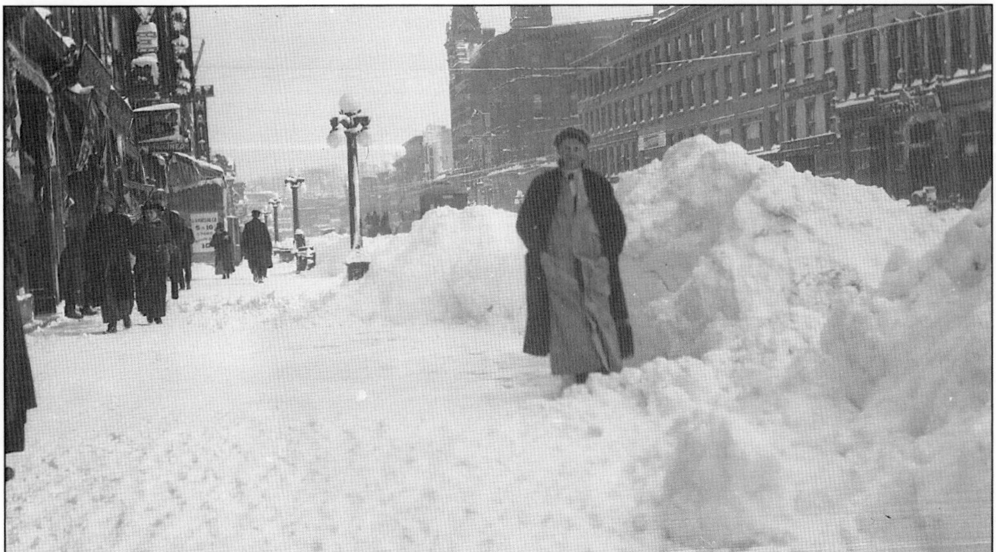

AFTERMATH OF SNOWSTORM, GENESEE STREET, 1916. This hearty resident's demeanor in the midst of a Central New York winter typified the character of the booming city in the early twentieth century.

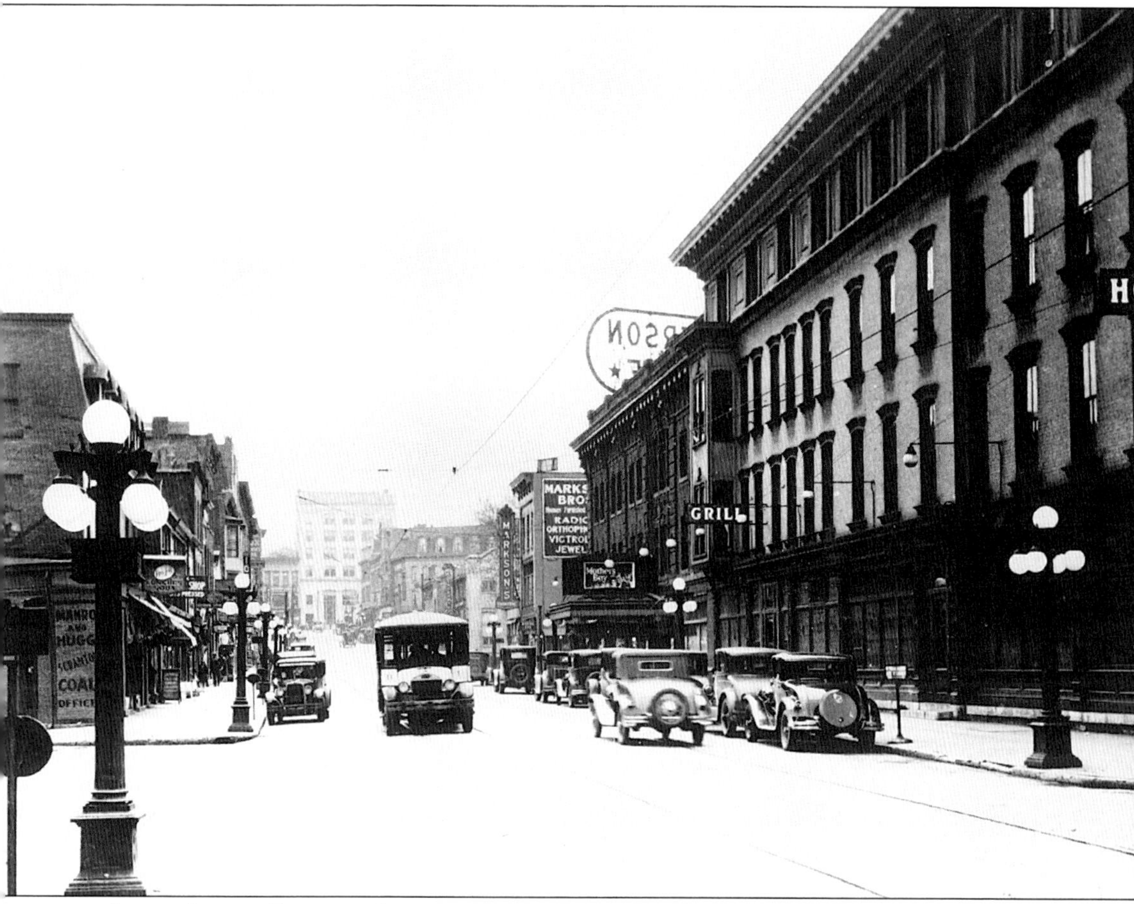

STATE STREET LOOKING SOUTH, 1920s. Businesses, hotels, restaurants, and entertainment venues vied for patrons' attention on State Street, one of Auburn's main thoroughfares. The Osborne Hotel and the rear of the Jefferson Theater marquee are visible on the right.

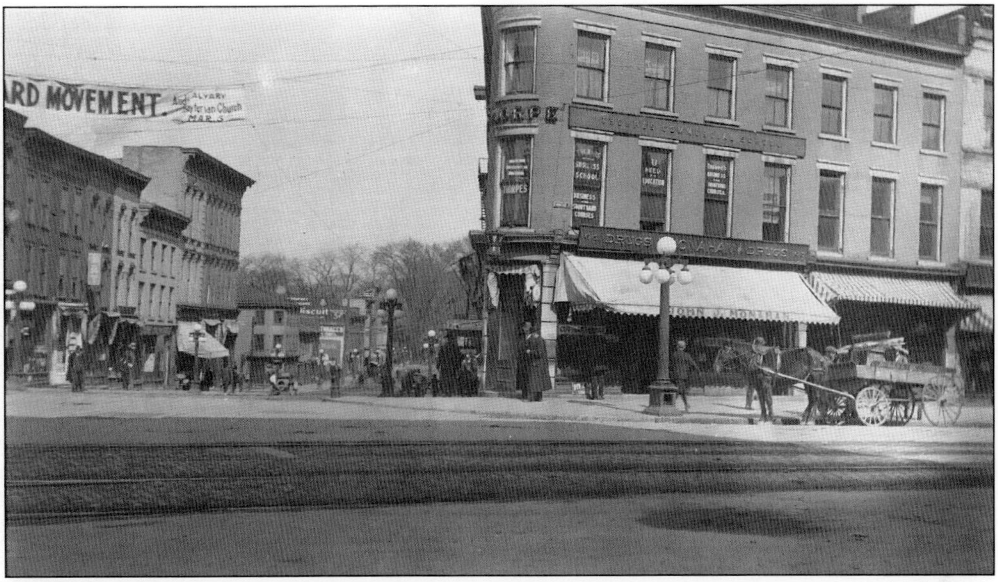

Corner of Genesee and North Streets, 1916. Monahan Drug Company and Thorpe's Commercial Store occupied this stone building on the site of the Auburn Trust Company (later Marine Midland Bank).

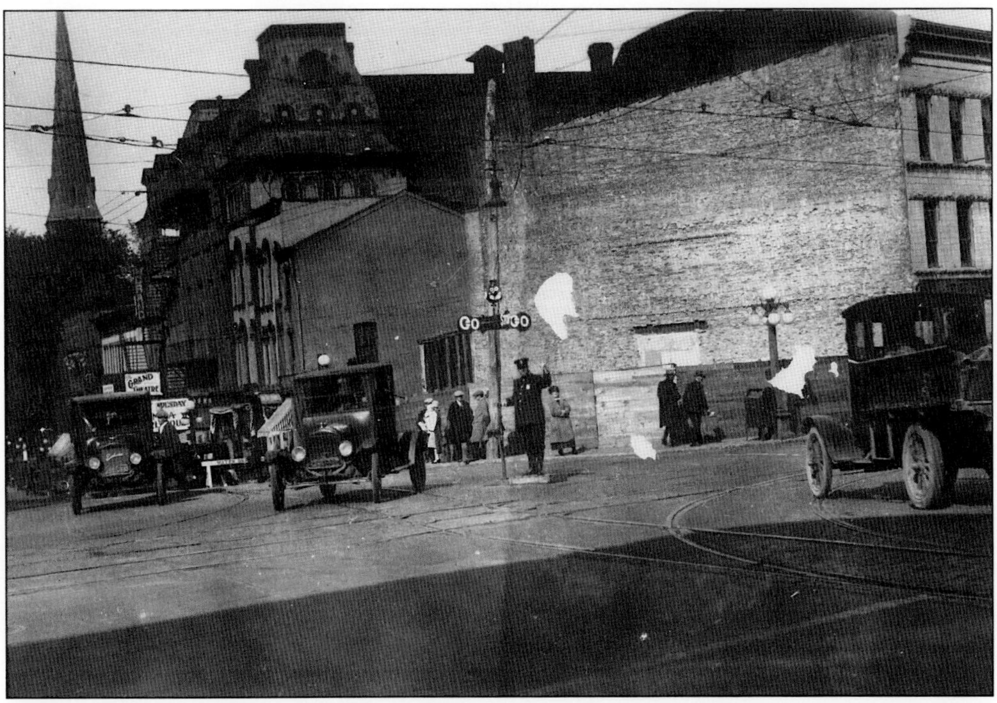

Making Way for Progress, 1922–1923. A policeman directed traffic as the Auburn Trust Company building went up at the corner of North and Genesee Streets.

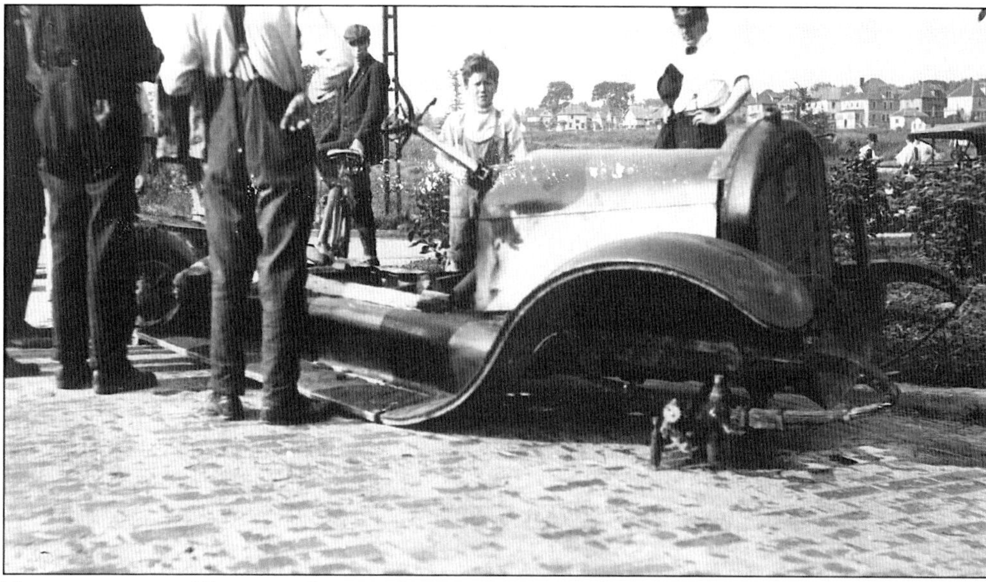

TRANSPORTATION HAZARDS, GENESEE STREET, 1920s. Onlookers gathered to survey the damage to a car stuck by a trolley near Morris Street.

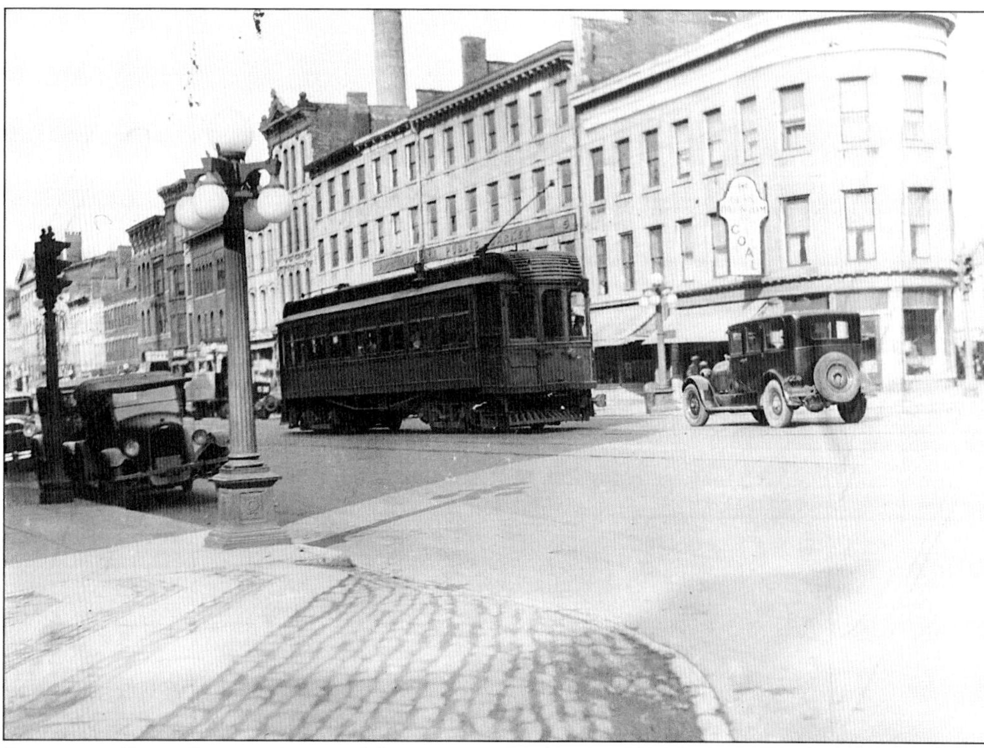

END OF THE LINE, GENESEE STREET, MAY 15, 1930. The arrival of the automobile marked the end of the trolley age. This image was taken the day the last Auburn and Syracuse Electric Railroad trolley completed its run to Auburn. The Flat Iron building is visible in the background.

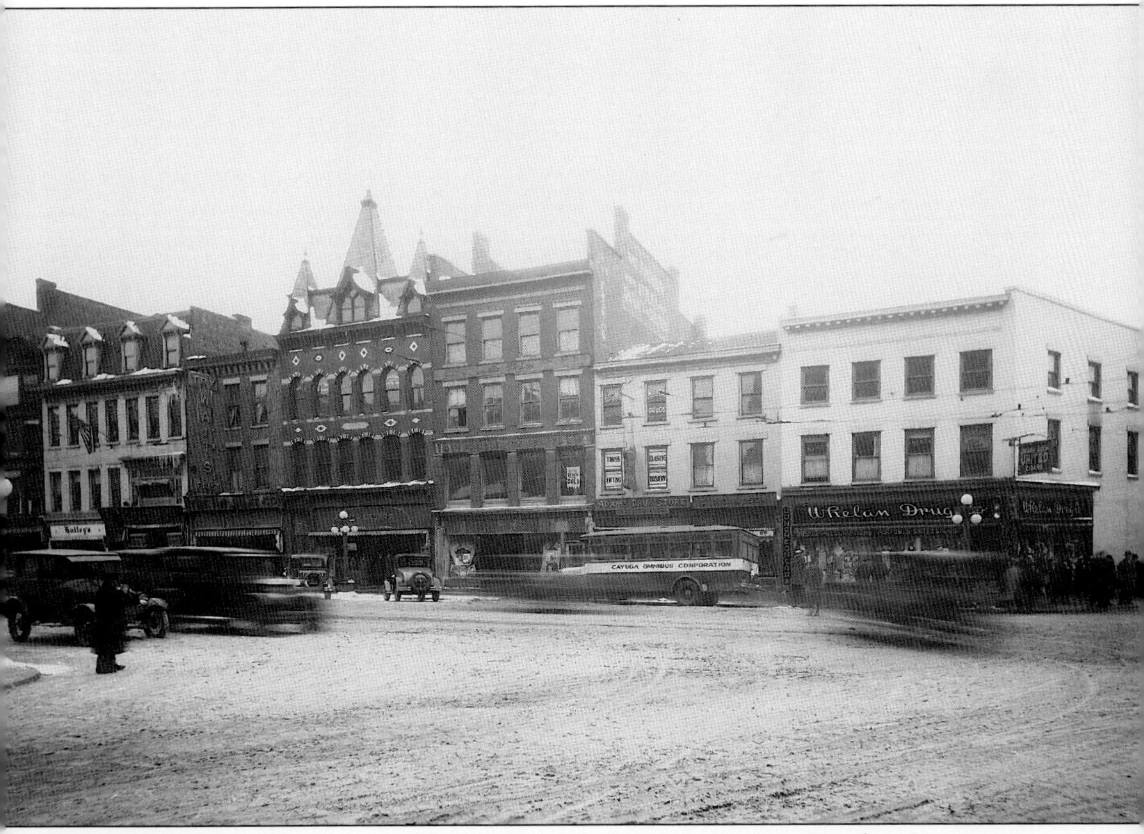

CITY IN MOTION, 1930s. Automobiles, trucks, and a bus from Cayuga Omnibus Corporation approached the intersection of Genesee and South Streets. Cayuga Omnibus Corporation offered regular service between Auburn and Syracuse, and included a terminal at the Osborne Hotel. (Image from collection of Community Preservation Committee.)

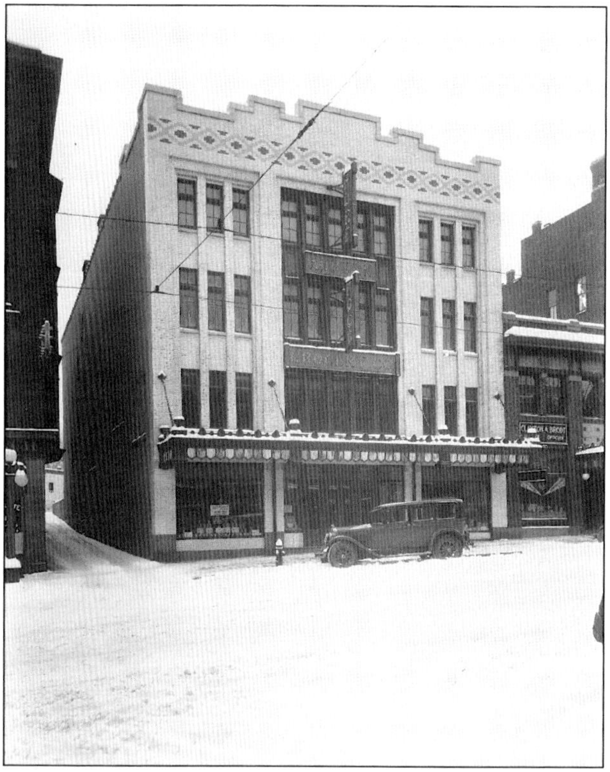

Pure Food, Genesee Street, 1930s. Sun Grocery operated this store on Genesee Street, which later became part of Auburn Grocery Company, a division of C.G. Meaker and Company. (Image from collection of Community Preservation Committee.)

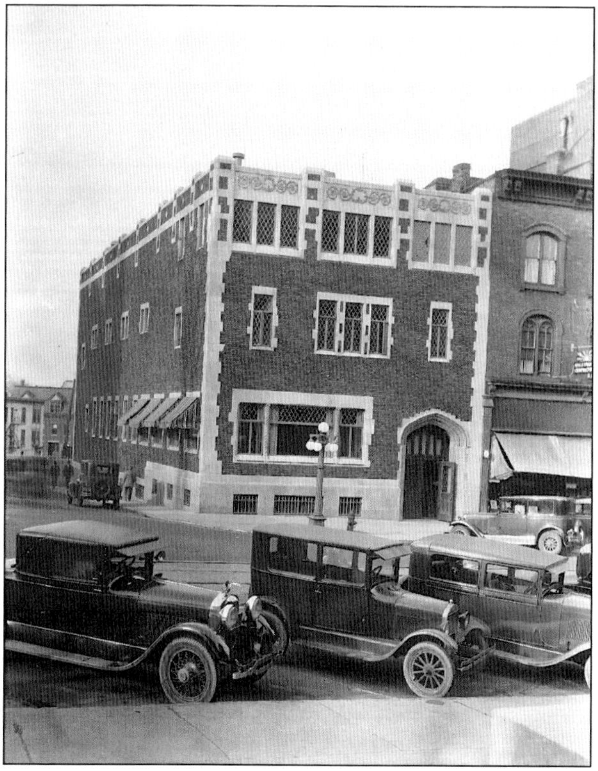

All Parking Spaces Filled, 1930s. This building at 149 Genesee Street later housed the Elks Club. (Image from collection of Community Preservation Committee.)

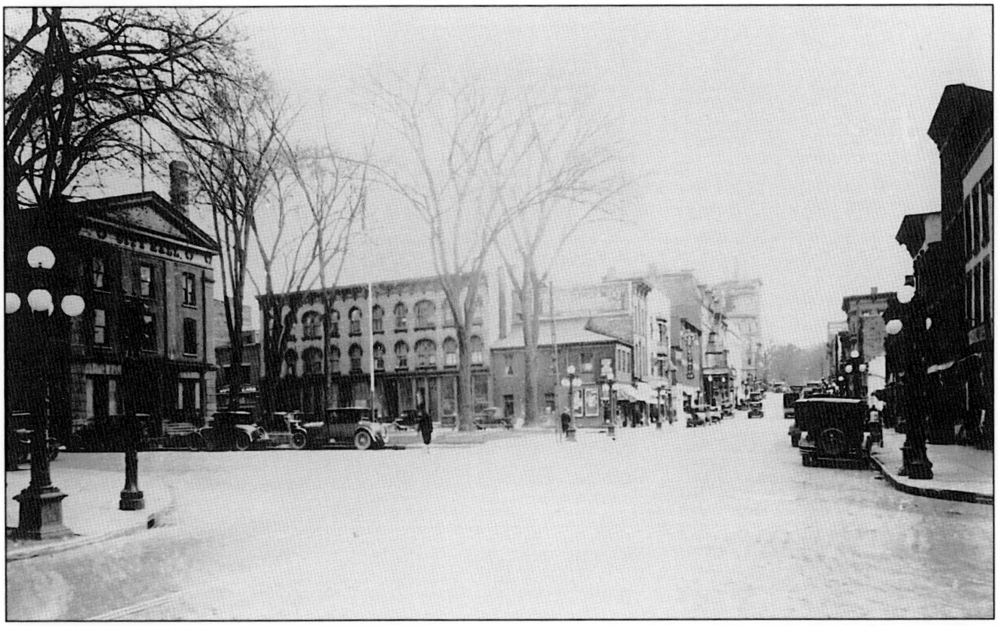

North Street Looking Toward Genesee Street, 1920s. The old city hall at the corner of Franklin and North Streets, built in 1837, once included a market house in its basement.

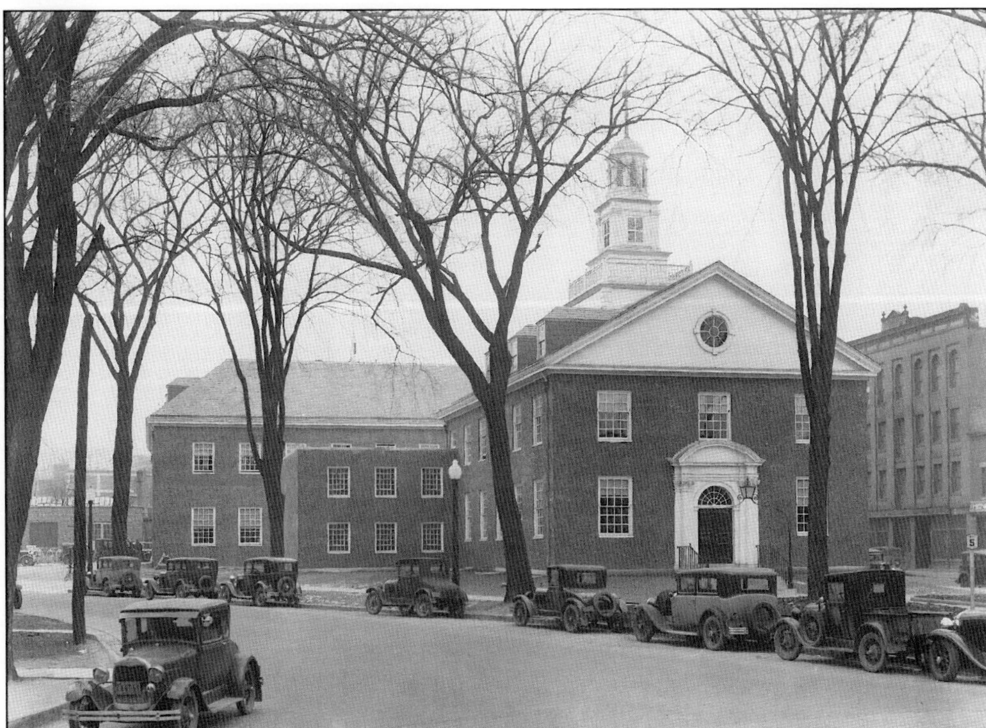

Police Station, Franklin and North Streets, 1930s. The old city hall building came down in 1930, and was replaced by this more modern structure. (Image from collection of Community Preservation Committee.)

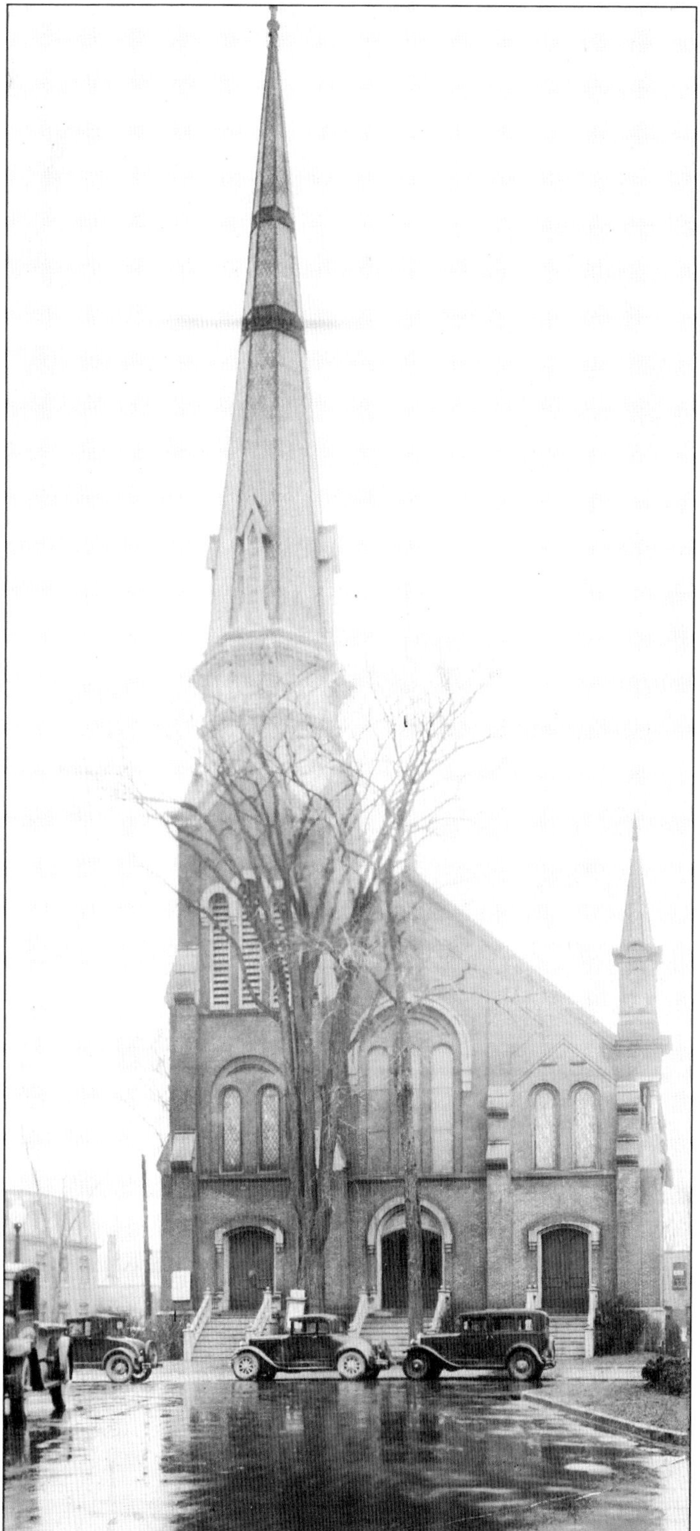

First Universalist Church, 1930s. Built in 1847, this striking, elongated, gothic structure stood at the corner of South and Lincoln Streets until it was razed in 1964.

THOMPSON MEMORIAL AME ZION CHURCH, PARKER STREET, 1960s. This church, an institution rich with history for the Auburn African-American community, held its first meeting in 1840 in the First Methodist Church. The new congregation built a wooden chapel on Washington Street in 1845, and moved to Parker Street in 1891. They now worship in a church on Wall Street.

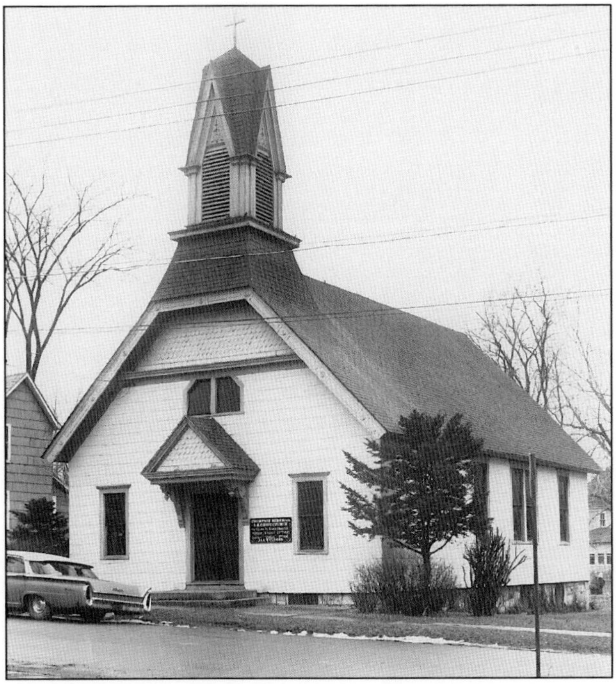

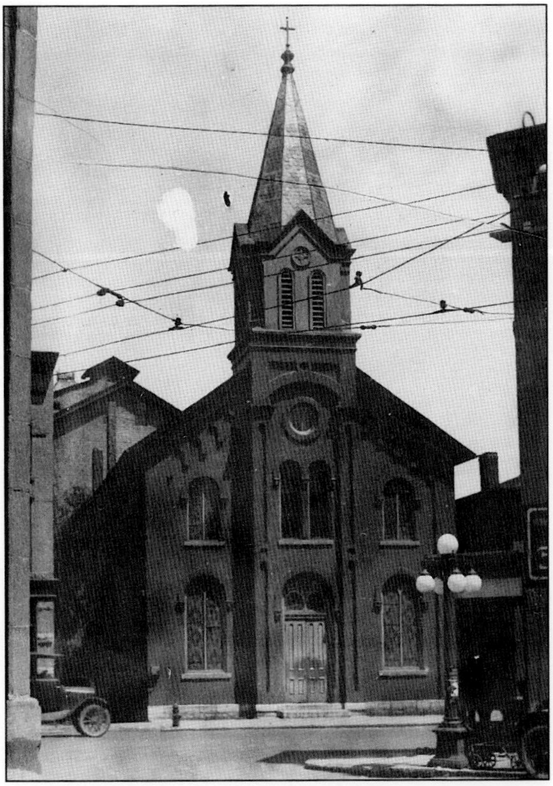

SAINT ALPHONSUS ROMAN CATHOLIC CHURCH, WATER STREET, 1922–1923. Members of the local German community founded this parish in 1853. The Water Street edifice was built in the 1920s.

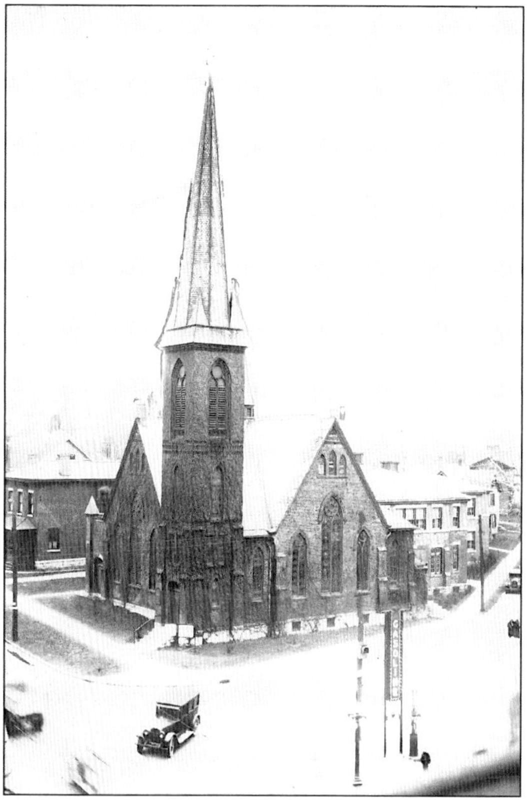

SECOND BAPTIST CHURCH, GENESEE AND OWASCO STREETS, C. 1930. In 1869, the First Baptist Church conducted missionary work from a building at the corner of Lizette and Owasco Streets. In 1879, the mission incorporated as the Second Baptist Church, and built this structure at the corner of Genesee and Owasco Streets in 1884.

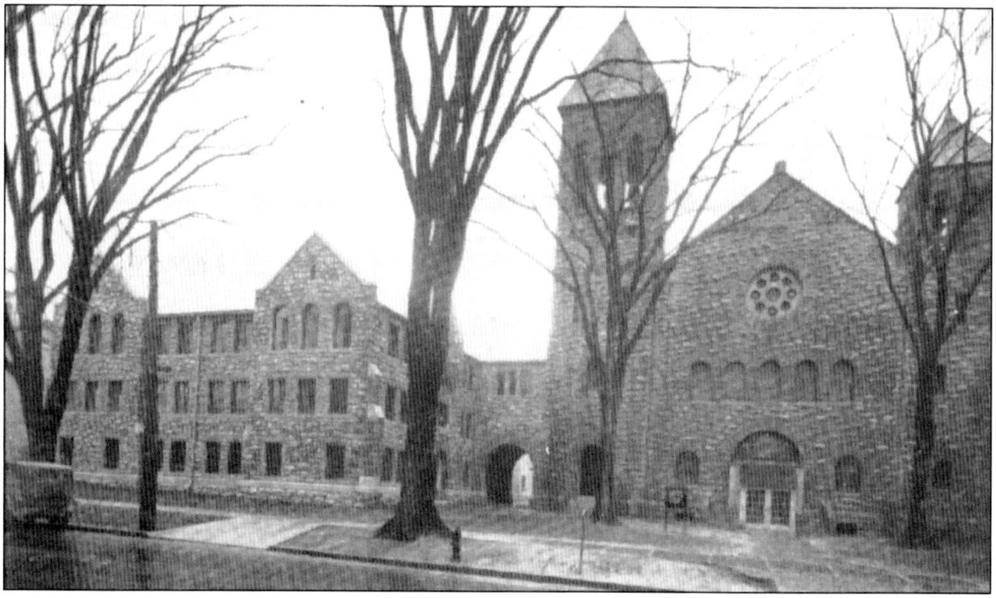

SECOND PRESBYTERIAN CHURCH, WILLIAM STREET, 1920S. This stone church was built between 1869 and 1870, with an addition constructed in 1885. Today, these buildings, now Westminster Presbyterian, still welcome worshippers.

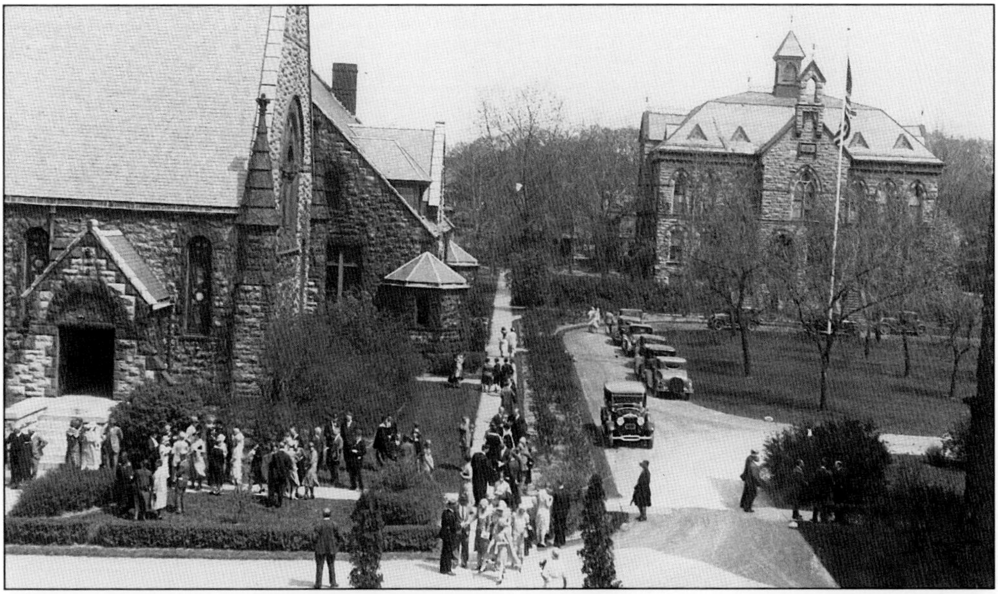

AUBURN THEOLOGICAL SEMINARY GROUNDS, C. 1930. Founded in 1819, the seminary held considerable influence in Auburn's history until it merged with Union Seminary in New York City in 1939. Presbyterian by denomination, it accepted divinity students of many faiths.

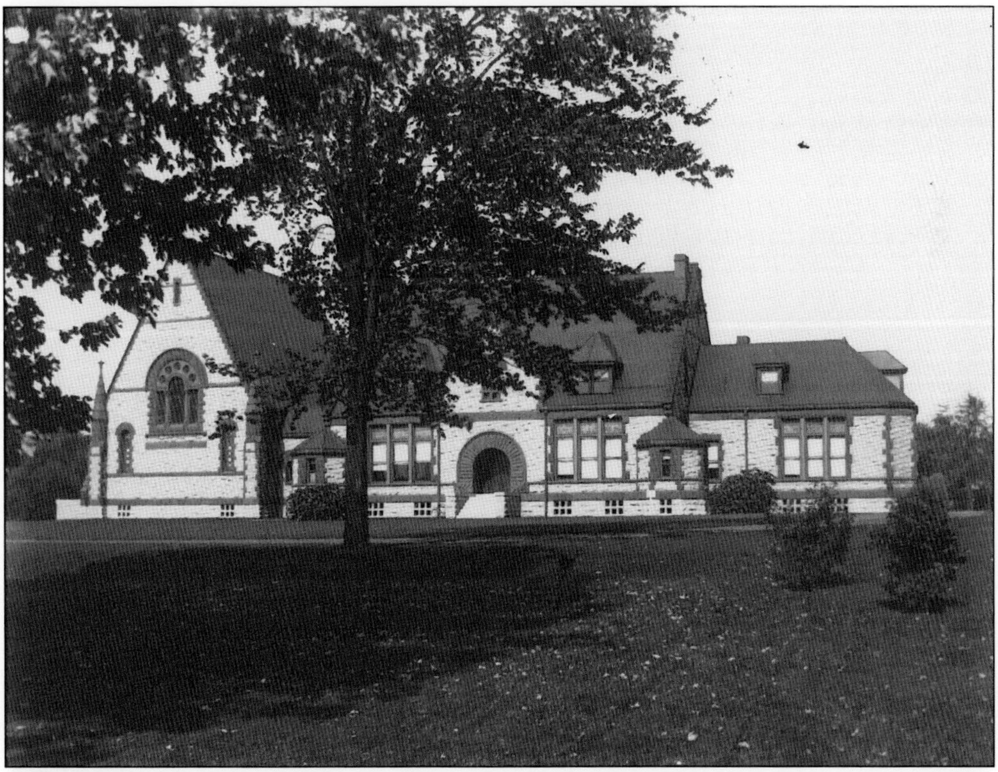

WILLARD CHAPEL AND ADJOINING WELCH BUILDING, 1920S. This structure, with its chapel interior crafted by Tiffany Glass and Decorating Company, is all that remains of Auburn Theological Seminary.

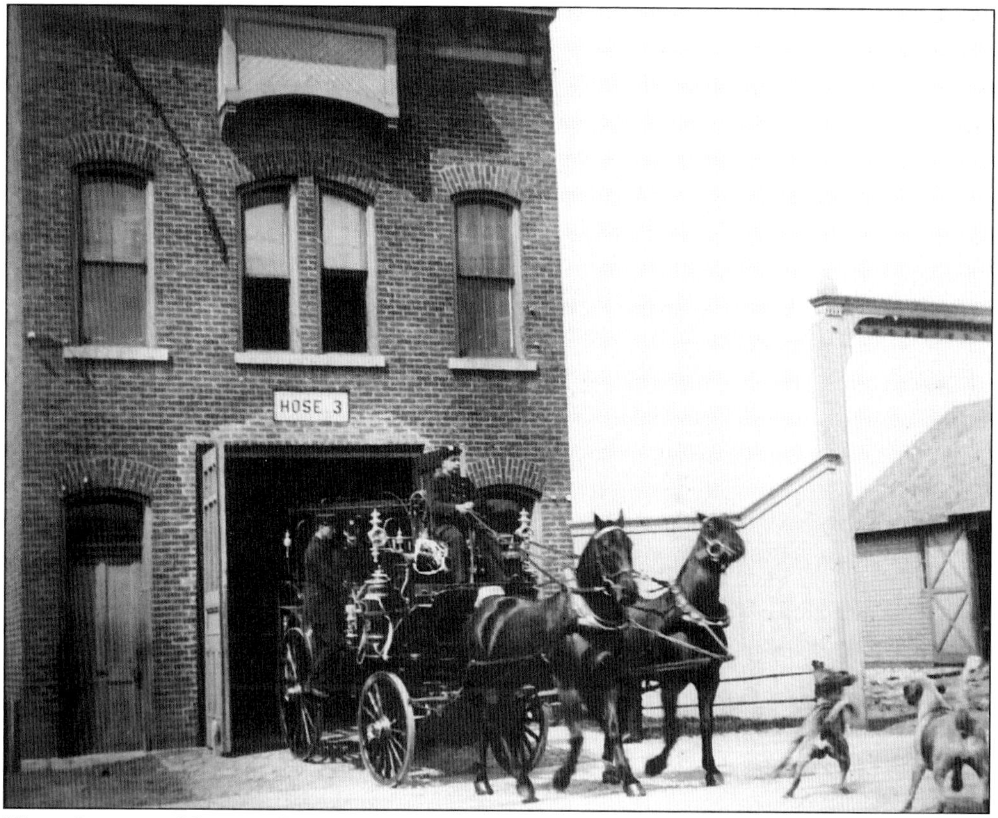

Hose Company Number Three Station, Clark Street, July 1864. Horses Dan and Joe pulled the engine in the race to the fire, while dogs Strike and Veney barked in excitement.

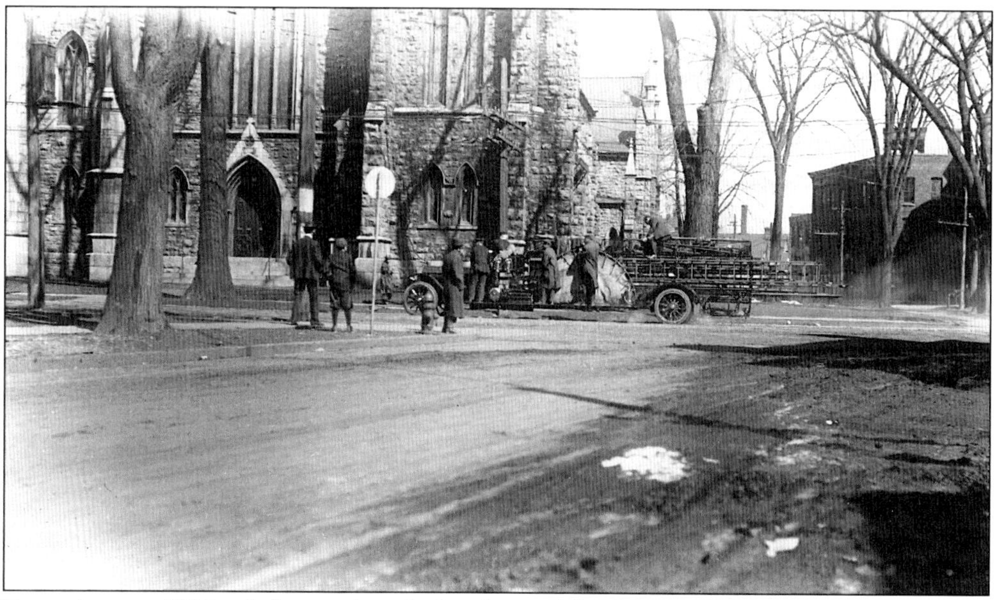

False Alarm, 1920s. A fire truck parked in front of the First Presbyterian Church on North Street while onlookers watched.

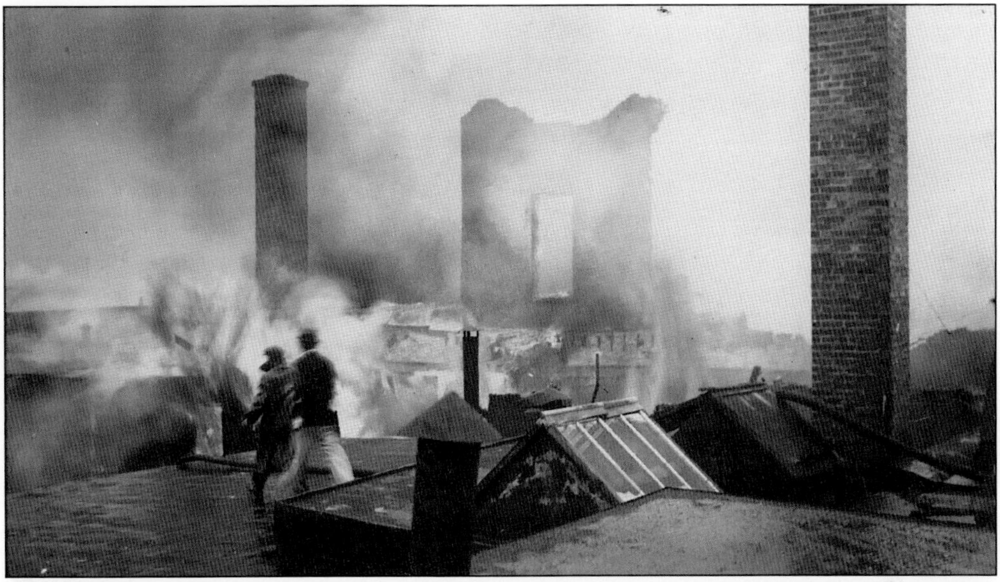

Fire at Hislops Department Store, Genesee Street, 1931. Fire has been a constant scourge to life in Auburn.

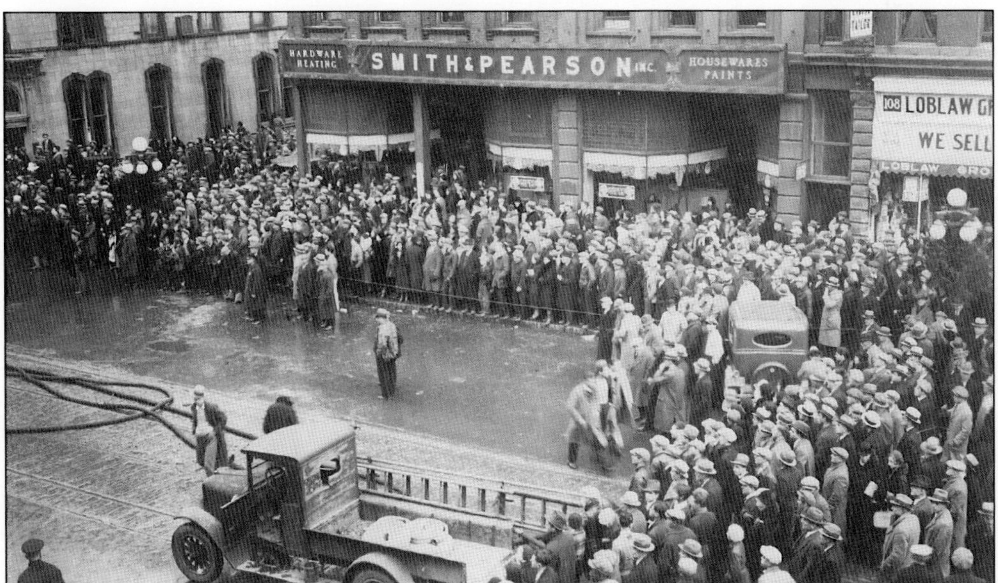

The Hislops Fire, 1931. A crowd gathered on Genesee Street to watch the fire at Hislops Department Store.

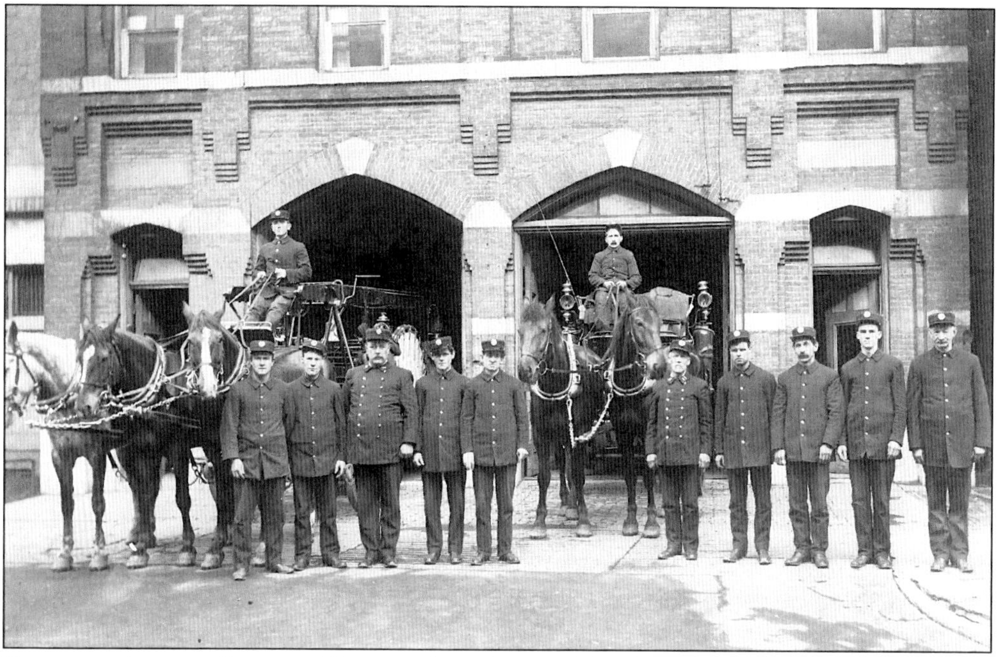

Hook and Ladder Company Number One, Auburn Fire Department, c. 1904. The men, horses, and equipment of Company Number One proudly posed for a portrait at the Market Street station house near city hall.

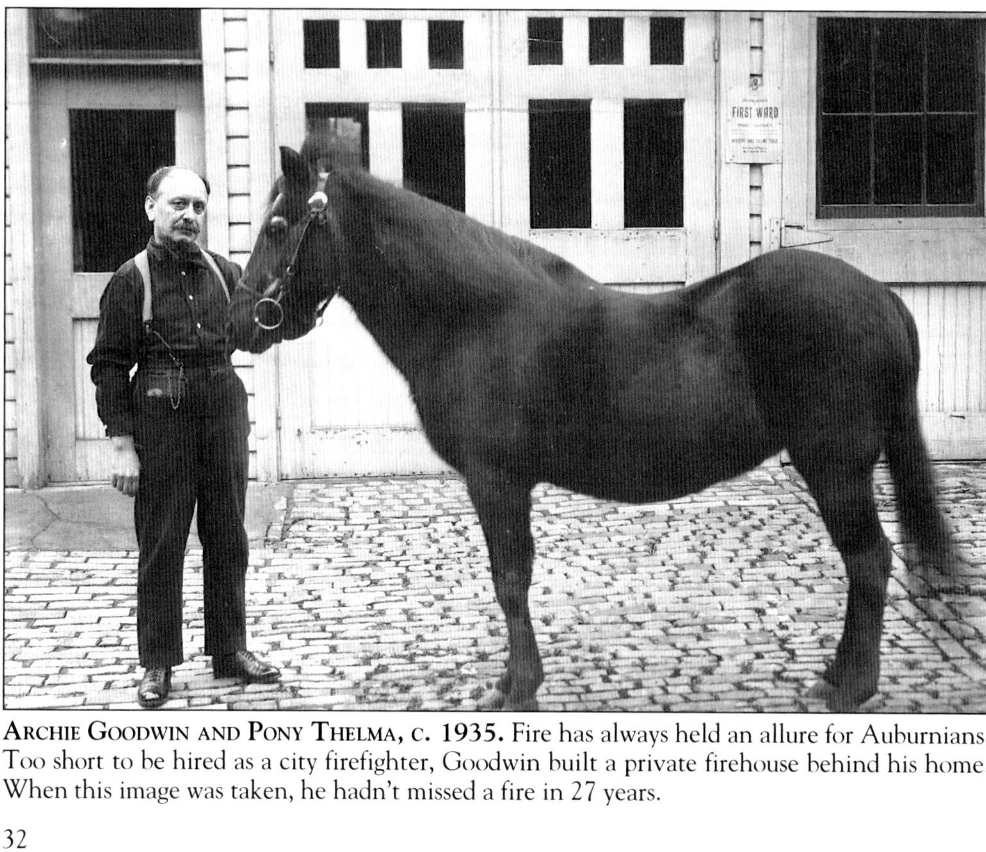

Archie Goodwin and Pony Thelma, c. 1935. Fire has always held an allure for Auburnians. Too short to be hired as a city firefighter, Goodwin built a private firehouse behind his home. When this image was taken, he hadn't missed a fire in 27 years.

Three

Both Sides of the Wall

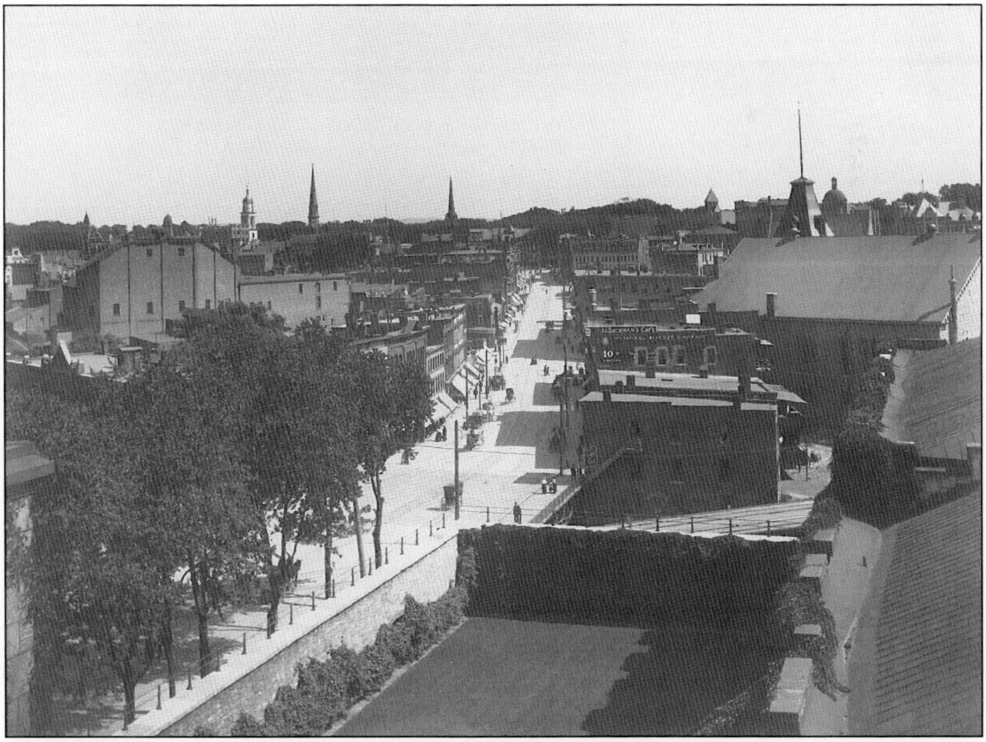

State Street Business District, View from Auburn Prison, c. 1900. The prison has profoundly impacted Auburn's development since its founding in 1816.

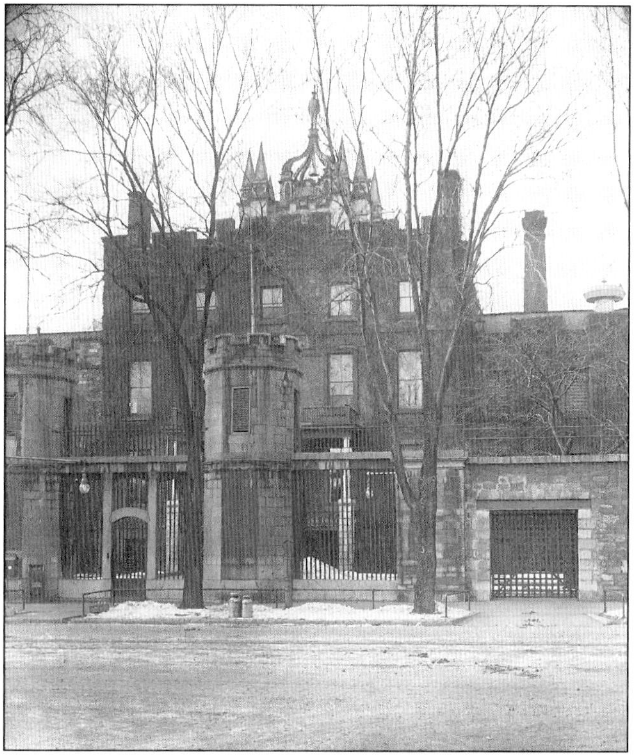

PRISON FRONT GATE AND ADMINISTRATIVE BUILDING, STATE STREET, EARLY TWENTIETH CENTURY. Winter lent a stark, somber air to these imposing prison structures.

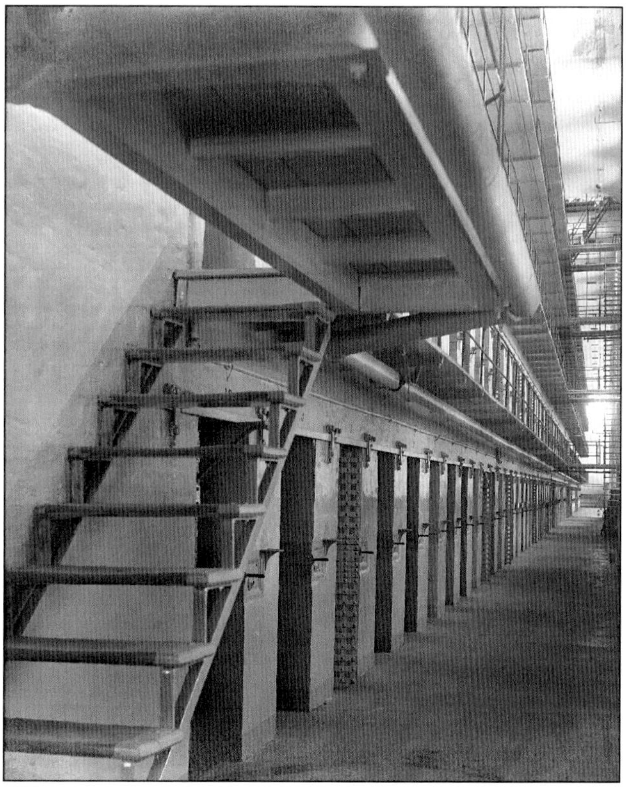

NORTH WING CELL BLOCK, C. 1900. Completed in 1821, this forbidding wing of the prison included only solitary cells. The official policy of silence in the prison ended in its entirety only in 1910.

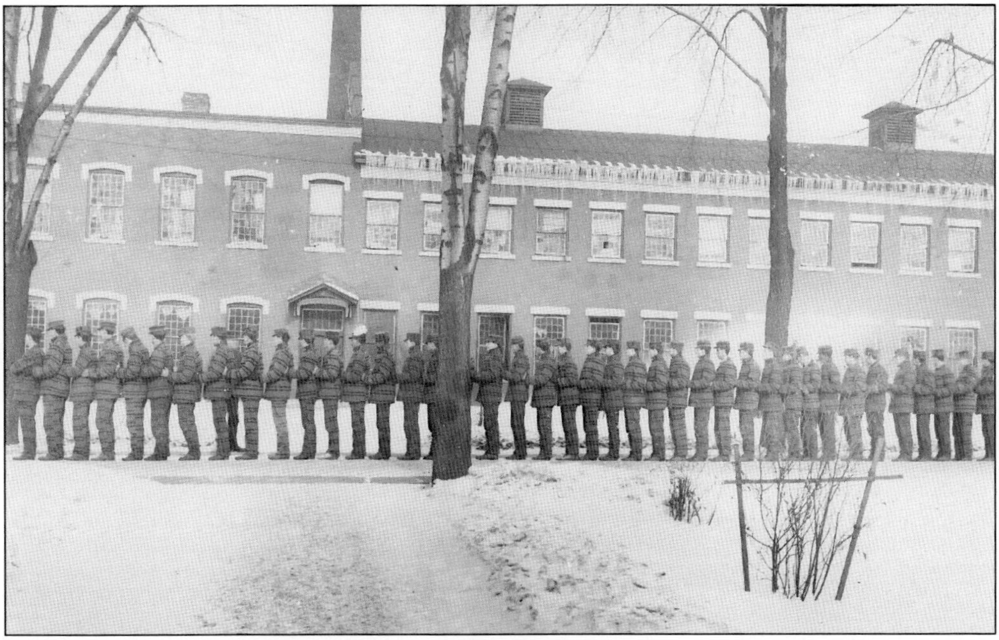

PRISONERS IN LOCKSTEP FORMATION, C. 1900. Striped uniforms, such as these winter outfits worn by prisoners in the yard, were abolished throughout the New York State system in 1904.

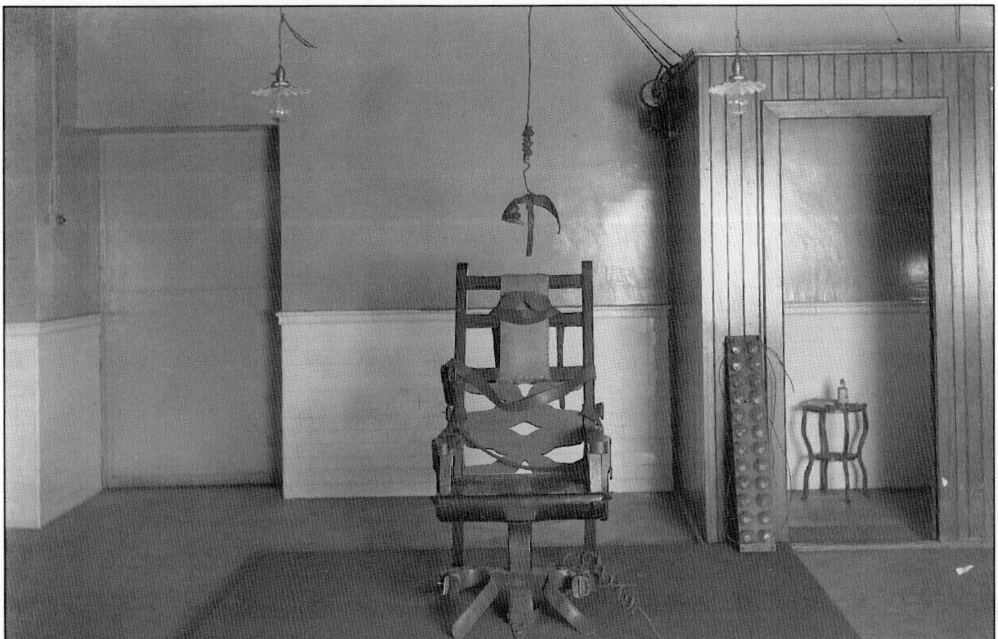

ELECTRIC CHAIR AND DEATH CHAMBER, C. 1900. Auburn Prison witnessed the first execution by electric chair, ushering in the modern age of capital punishment. William Kemmler of Buffalo was executed on August 6, 1890, for bludgeoning Tillie Ziegler with a hatchet.

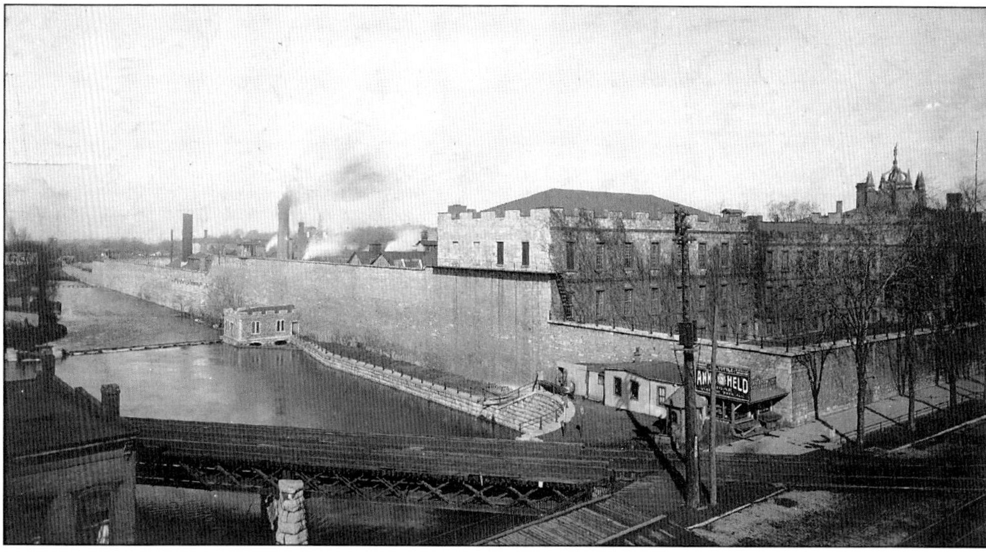

PRISON WALL ALONG OWASCO OUTLET, EARLY TWENTIETH CENTURY. Waterpower, developing transportation systems, and labor—including the prison population—contributed to Auburn's rise as a manufacturing center.

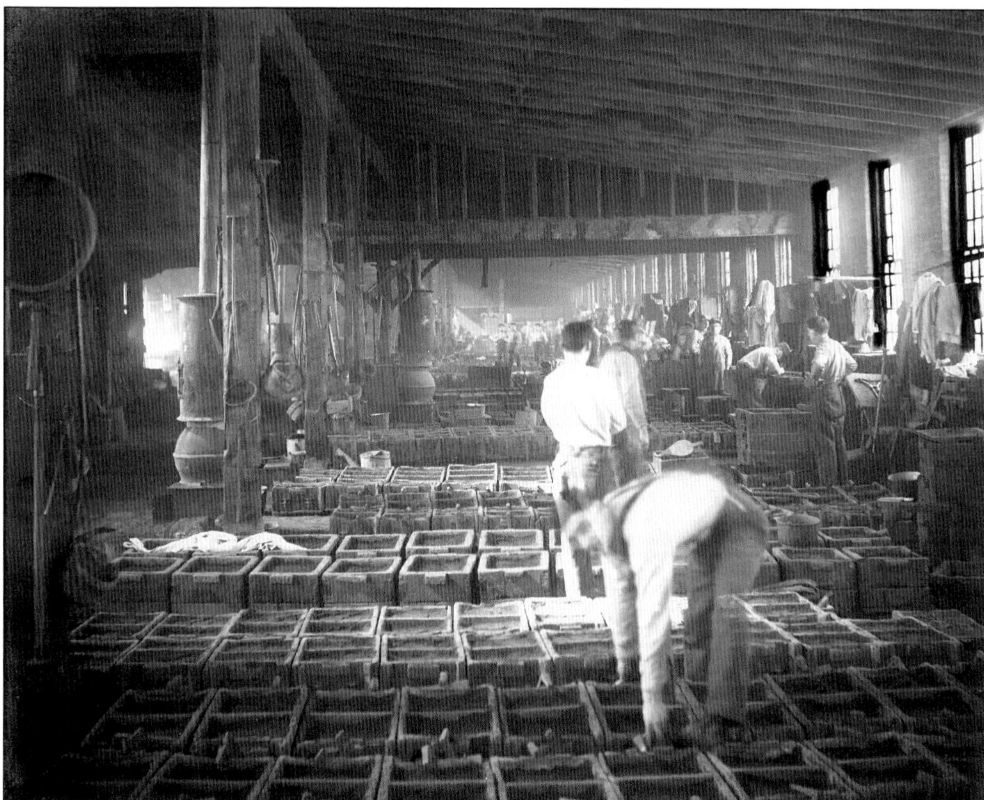

MOLDING SHOP, AUBURN PRISON, C. 1890. The Auburn prison system in the nineteenth century was designed to be self-supporting through convict labor. Prison labor shops produced tools, shoes, furniture, clocks, barrels, and blinds under contract to outside manufacturers.

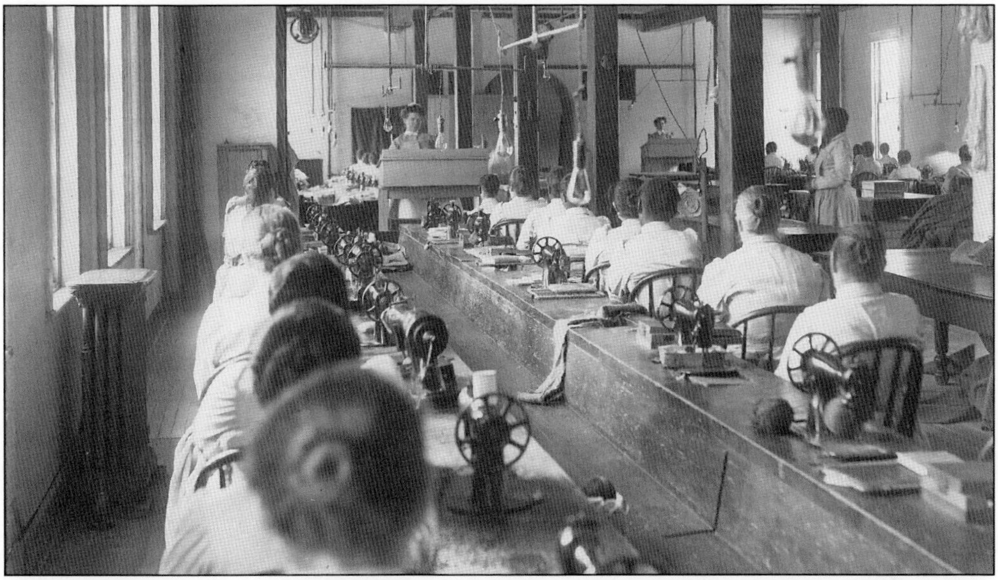

Sewing Shop in Prison for Women, Late Nineteenth Century. Auburn Prison housed women at two different intervals in its history. The last women convicts were transferred from the facility in 1934.

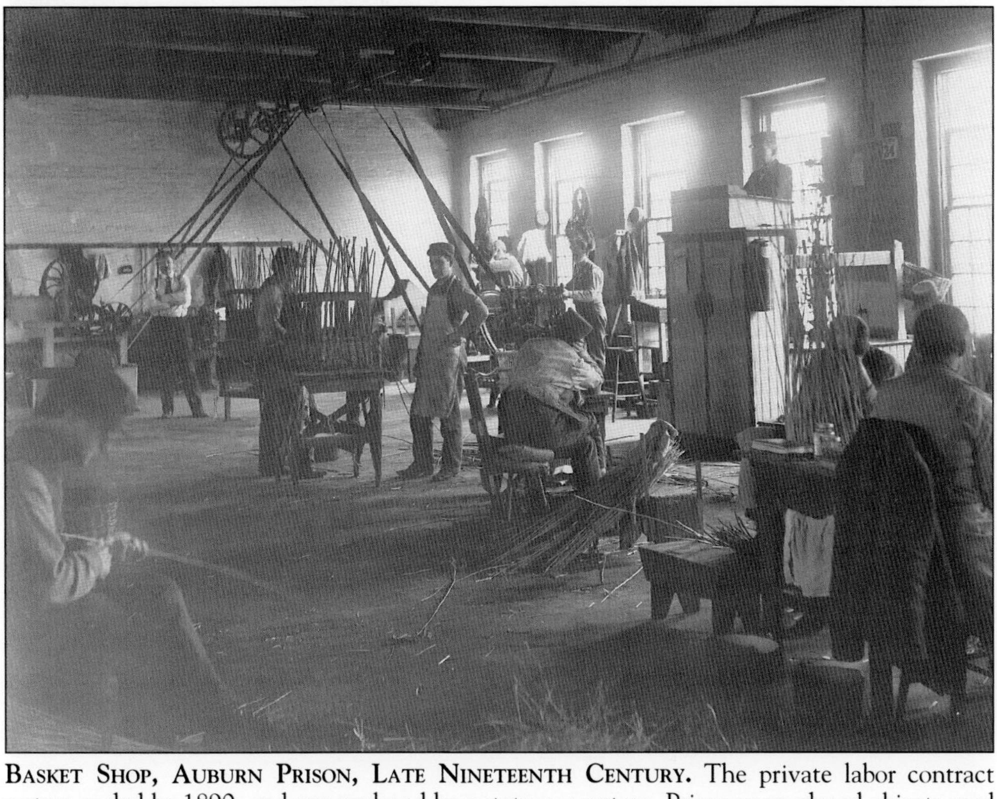

Basket Shop, Auburn Prison, Late Nineteenth Century. The private labor contract system ended by 1890, and was replaced by a state-use system. Prisoners produced objects used within the state system, including woolen cloth for prison uniforms and brooms for state and school property.

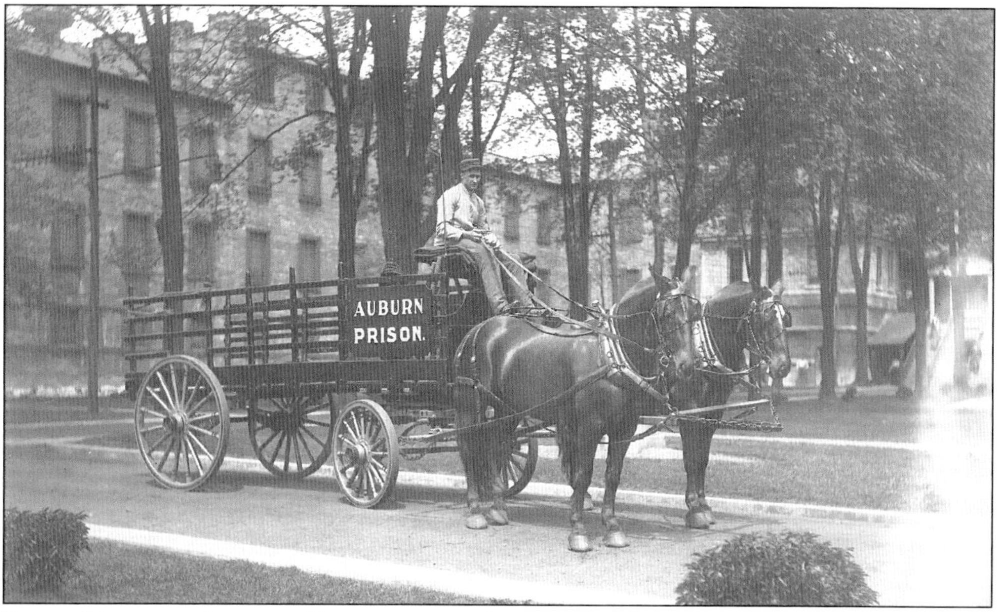

PRISON WAGON IN INTERIOR YARD, C. 1900. Operation of the prison required basic services of all manner. To this day, the prison remains one of Auburn's primary employers.

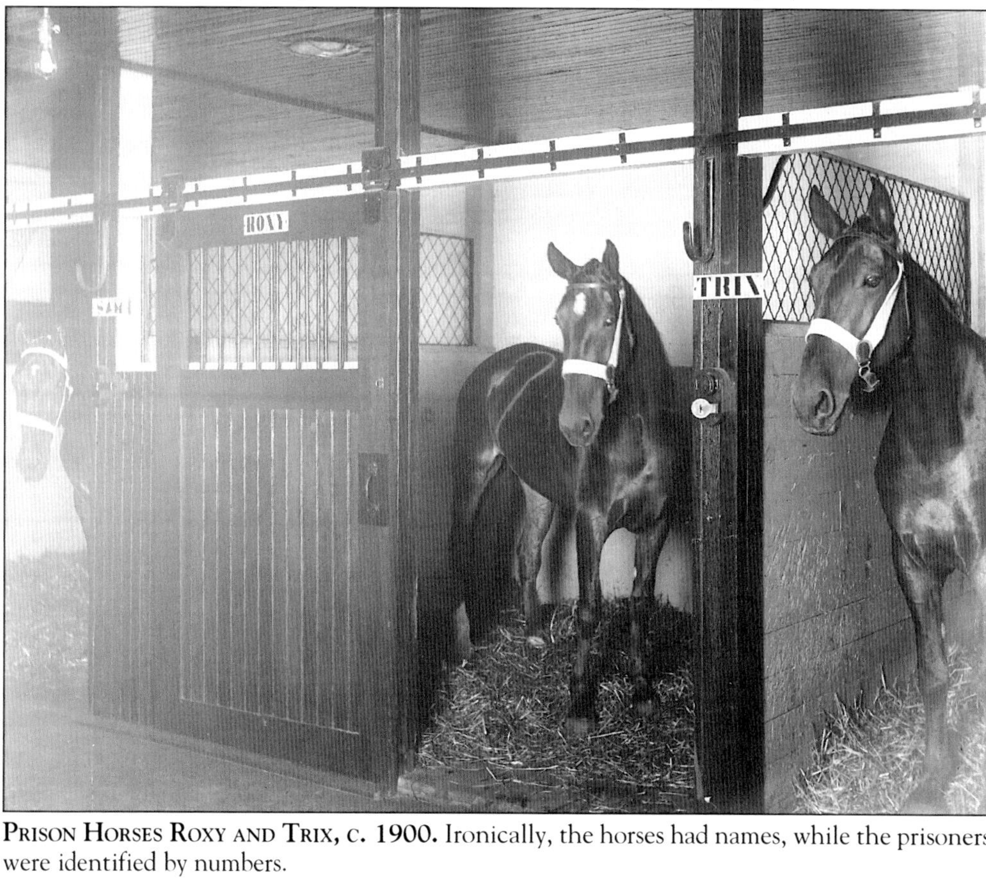

PRISON HORSES ROXY AND TRIX, C. 1900. Ironically, the horses had names, while the prisoners were identified by numbers.

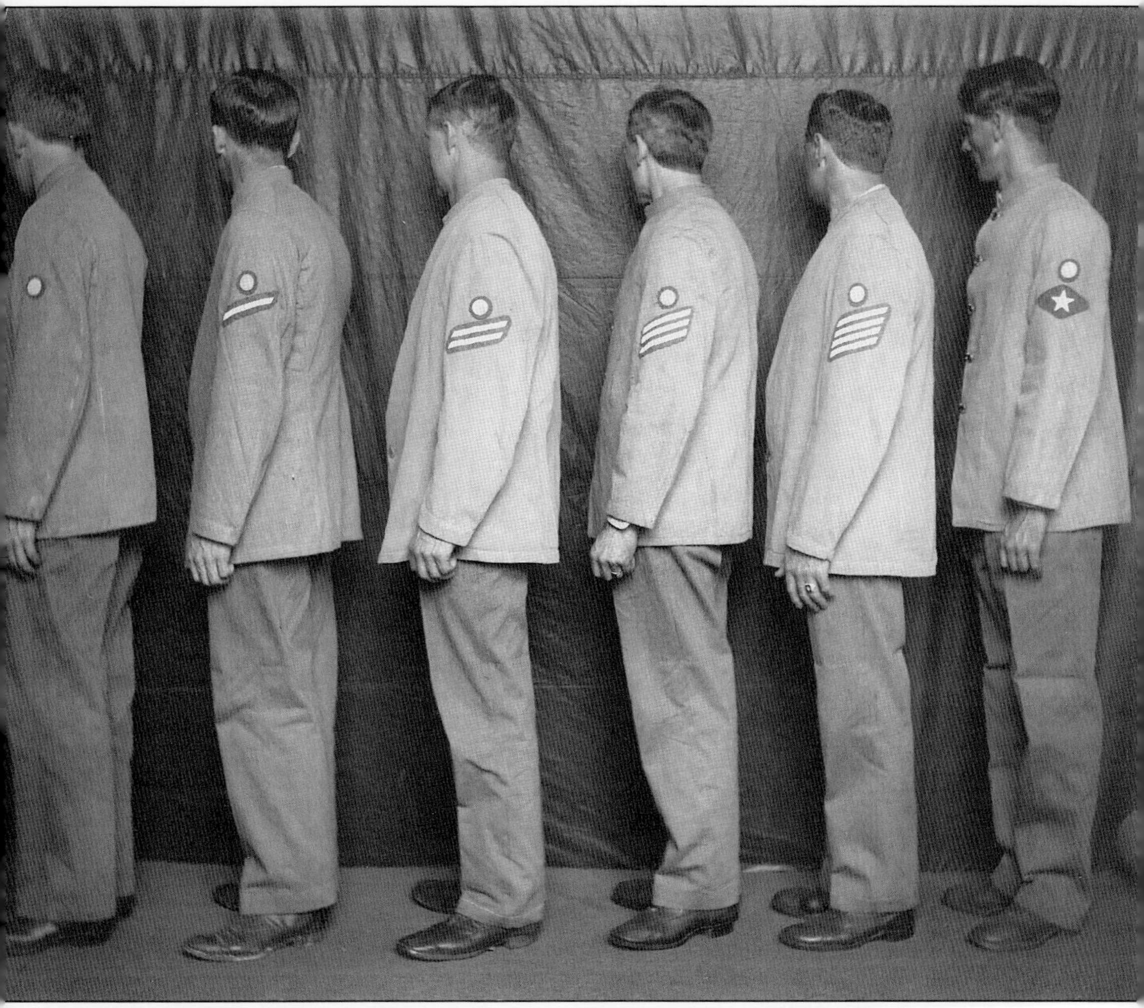

PRISONERS SHOWING MUTUAL WELFARE LEAGUE HONOR BARS, C. 1914. The formation of the Mutual Welfare League in 1913 allowed prisoners some self-government within the prison system. Championed by noted prison reformer Thomas Mott Osborne, the league ideally promoted education and cooperation instead of punishment. These prisoners, faces turned anonymously, revealed honor bars given for good conduct. The dot represented less than one year of good conduct. Each successive bar stood for one full year, and the star was for five years of perfect conduct.

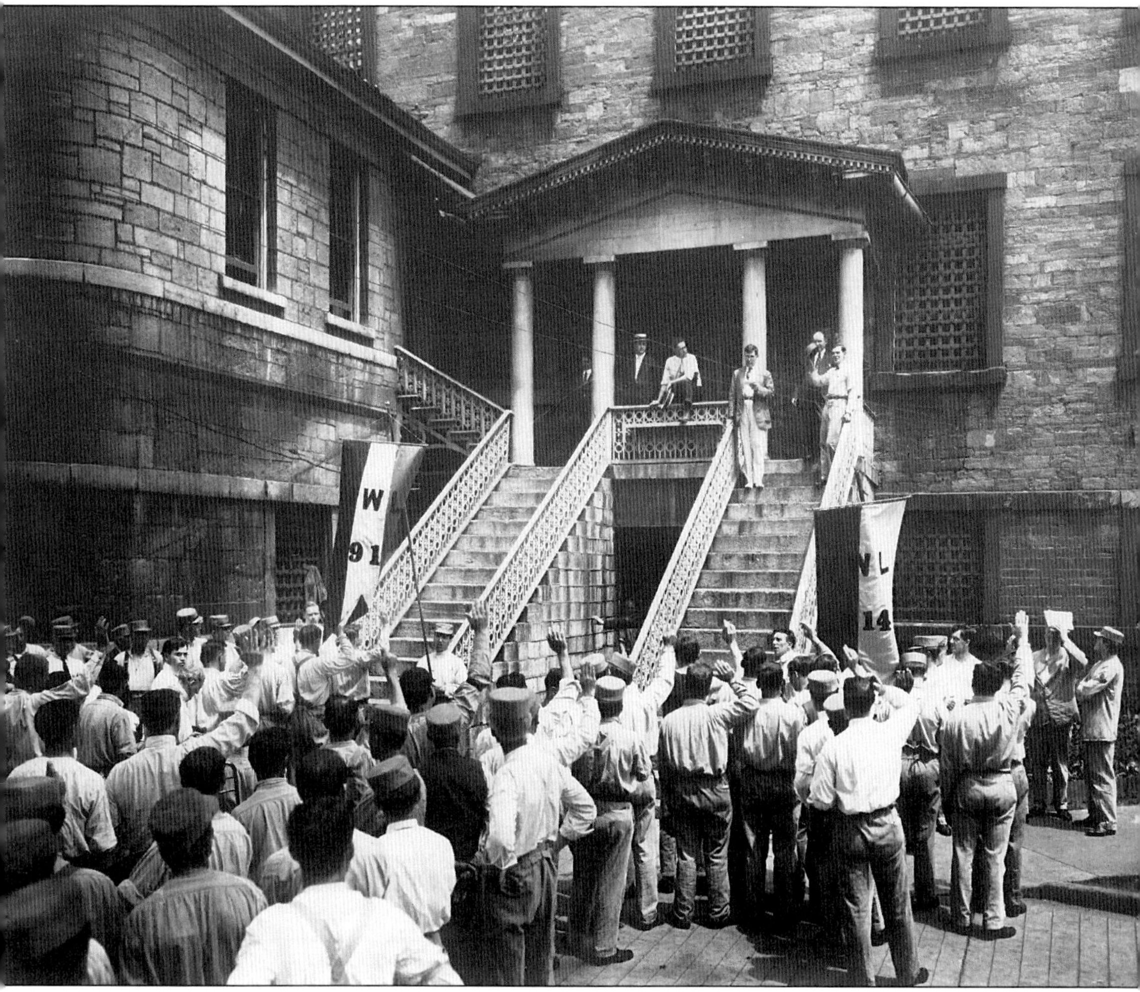

DELEGATES TAKING THE OATH OF OFFICE FOR THE MUTUAL WELFARE LEAGUE, 1914. In the early years of the Mutual Welfare League, reform initiatives successfully transformed the prison system.

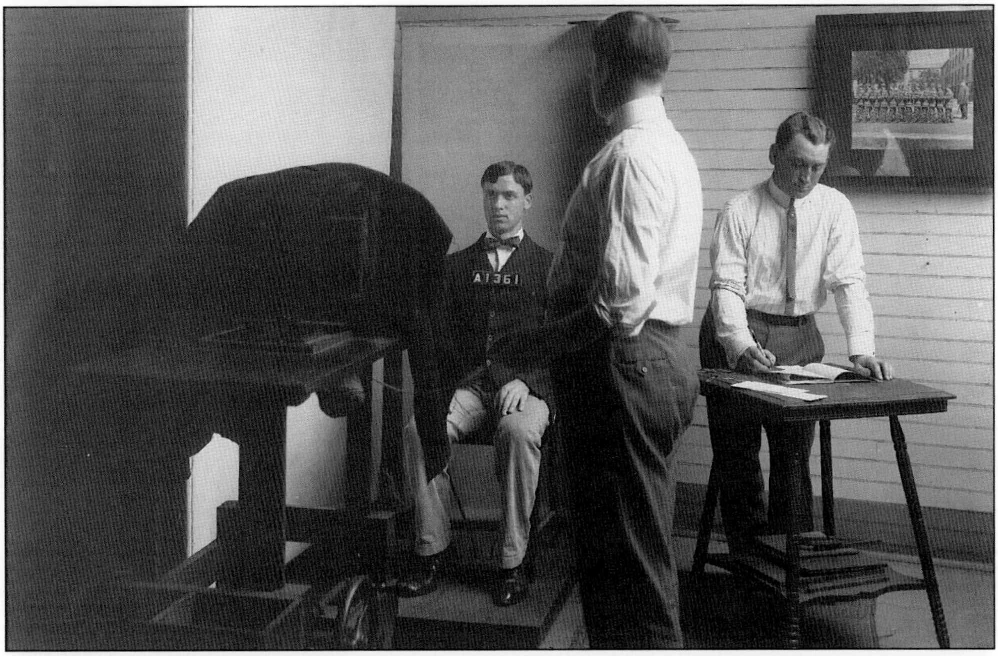

NEW PRISONER BEING PROCESSED, C. 1914. In a display of self-referential history, a photograph of prisoners in lockstep and striped uniforms hung on the wall.

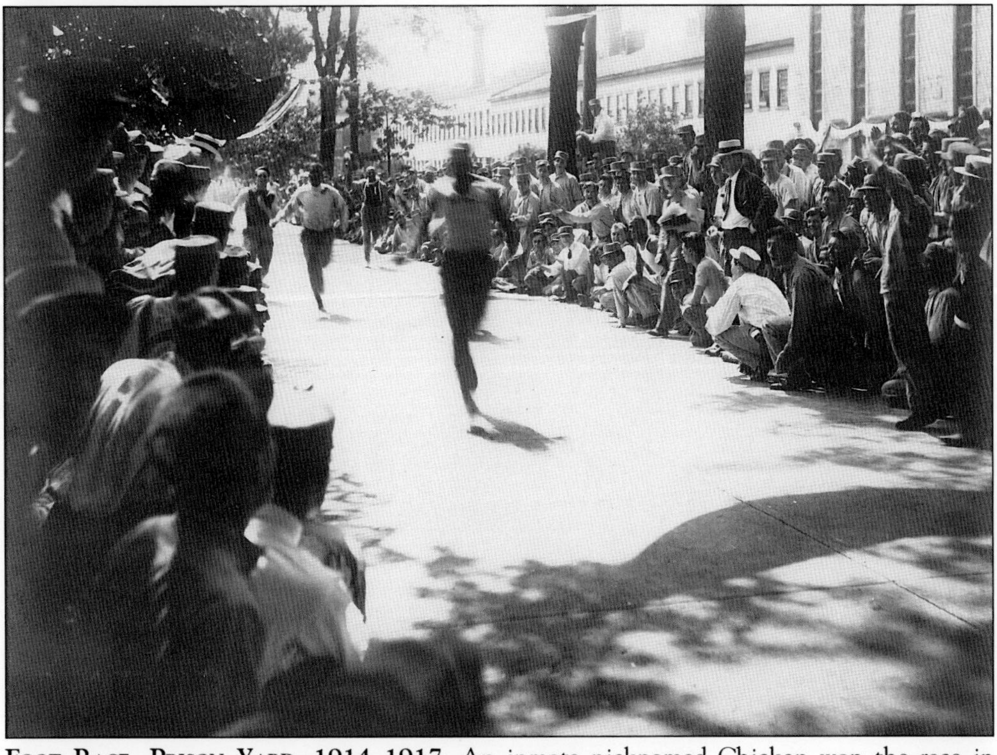

FOOT RACE, PRISON YARD, 1914–1917. An inmate nicknamed Chicken won the race in record time. Onlookers included prisoners and prison officials. Recreation such as foot races and baseball games were part of Mutual Welfare League reforms.

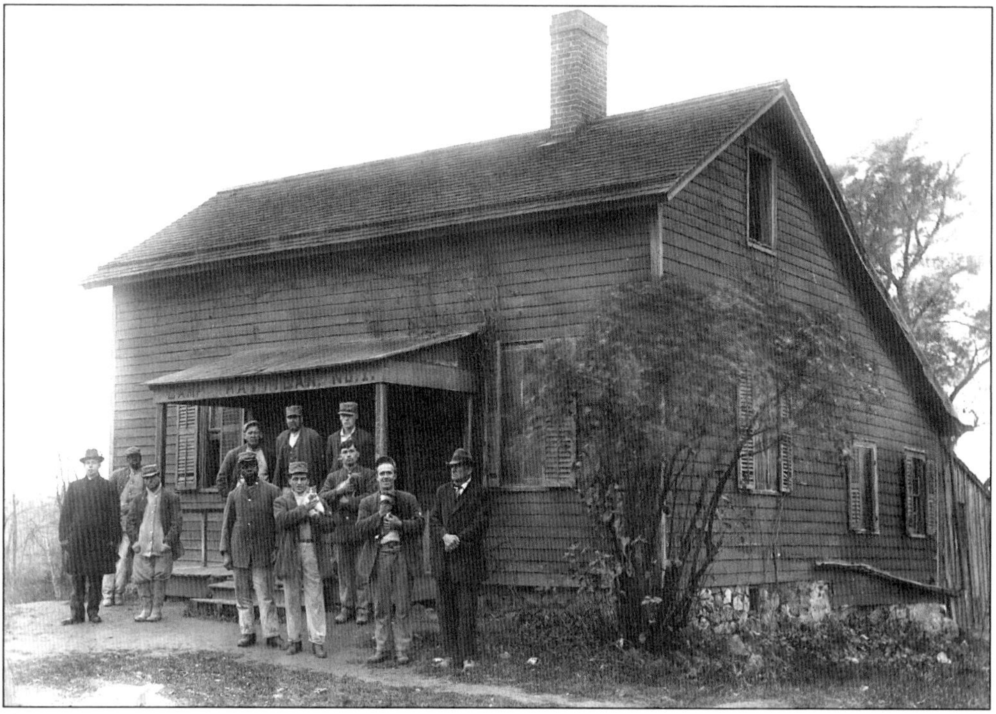

Camp Rattigan, Road Work Camp, c. 1914. Prison road crews, sent out throughout Cayuga County, were housed in farmhouses furnished by local townships. Crews consisted of about 20 men each. This camp was named for Charles F. Rattigan, then the warden of the prison.

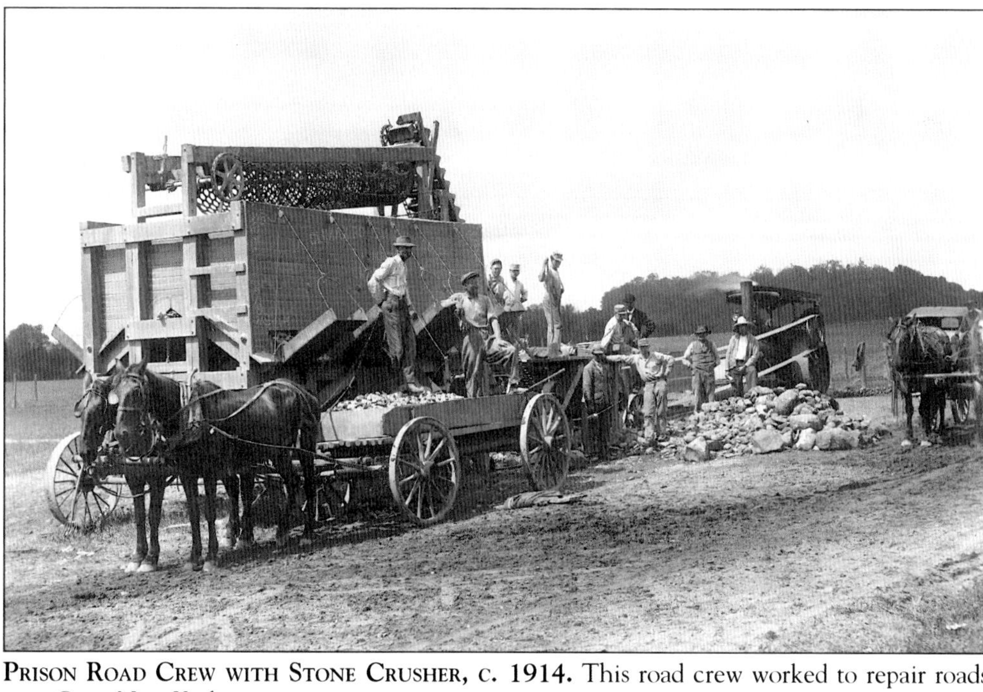

Prison Road Crew with Stone Crusher, c. 1914. This road crew worked to repair roads near Cato, New York.

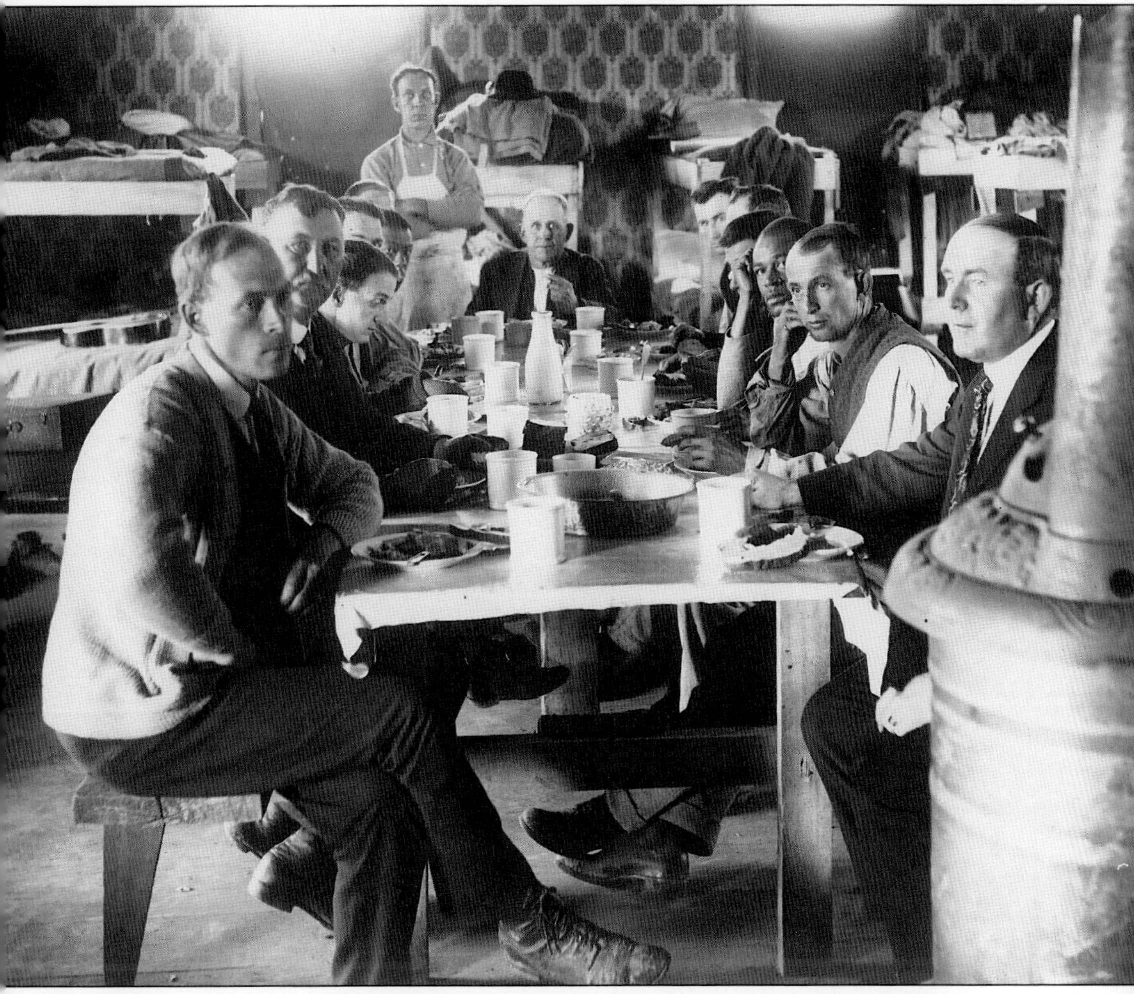

MEAL TIME, C. 1914. Members of a prison road camp and wardens gathered for a meal. Sleeping and eating were done in the same quarters. For men accustomed to antiquated cells in the prison, such accommodations probably seemed a luxury.

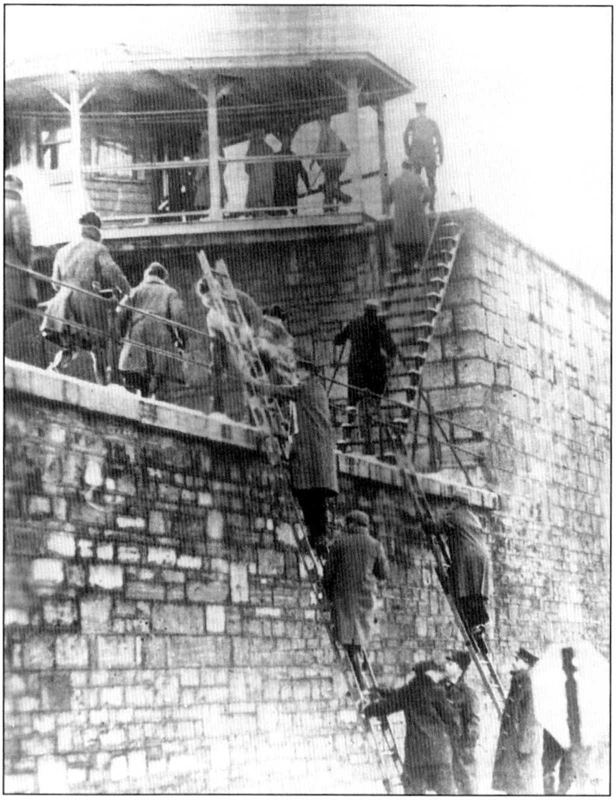

NATIONAL GUARD STORMING PRISON DURING RIOT, DECEMBER 1929. Crowded conditions, inadequate food, and the eventual failure of the ideals established by the Mutual Welfare League were identified as factors in two prison riots which rocked Auburn in 1929.

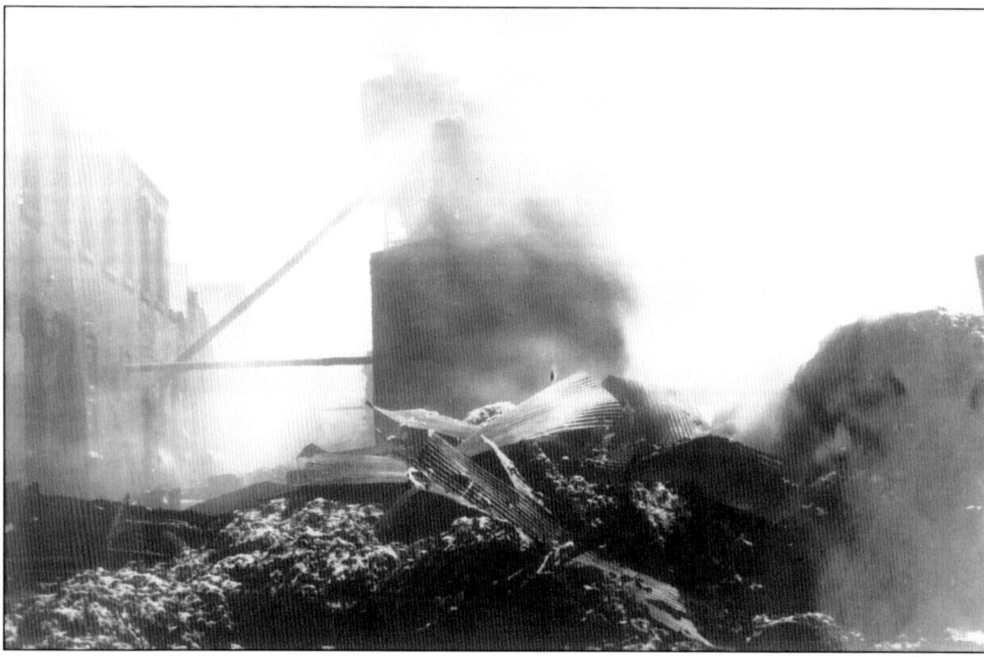

PRISON RUINS AFTER RIOT, 1929. Some Auburn residents vividly remember the fire, confusion, and fear during the riots. Although debate ensued concerning moving the prison outside city limits, it was ultimately decided to rebuild on the original site.

Four

Industry and Commerce

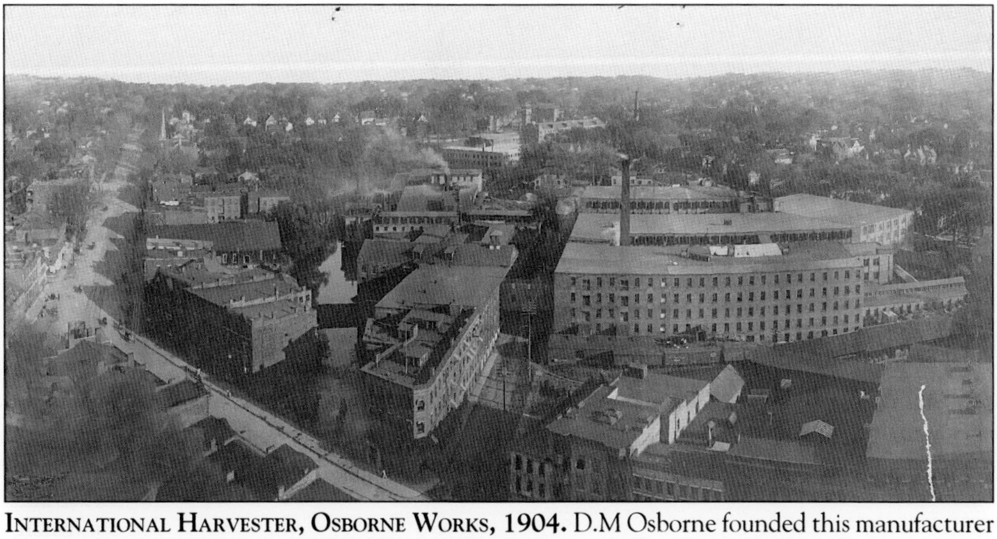

International Harvester, Osborne Works, 1904. D.M Osborne founded this manufacturer of agricultural machinery in 1858. The massive factory complex, located along Genesee Street, dominated the central business district of Auburn.

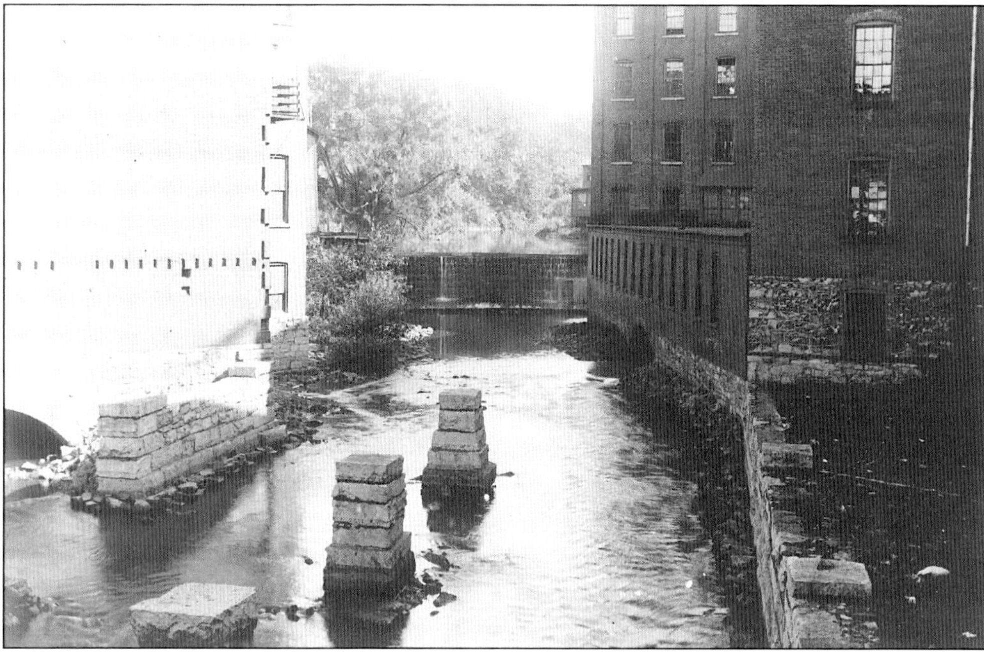

Owasco Outlet, c. 1900. The outlet ran through the Osborne Works in this view looking south, taken from Genesee Street.

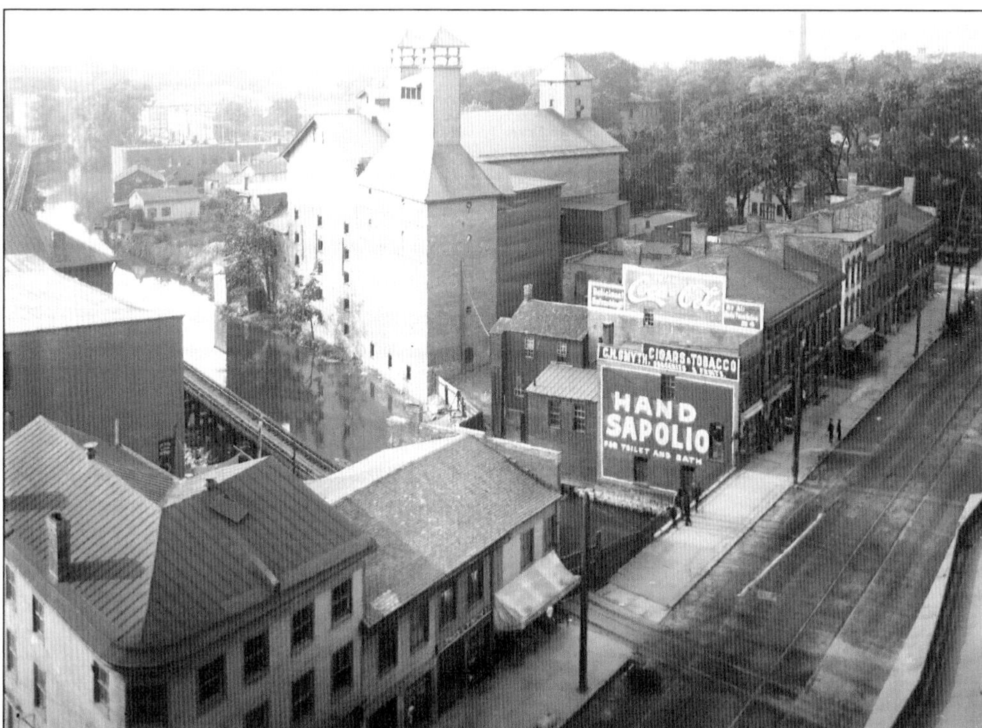

Aerial View of Owasco Outlet, North Street, c. 1900. The North Street landscape near the intersection of Water Street clearly conveyed the gritty, industrial quality of Auburn in the early twentieth century.

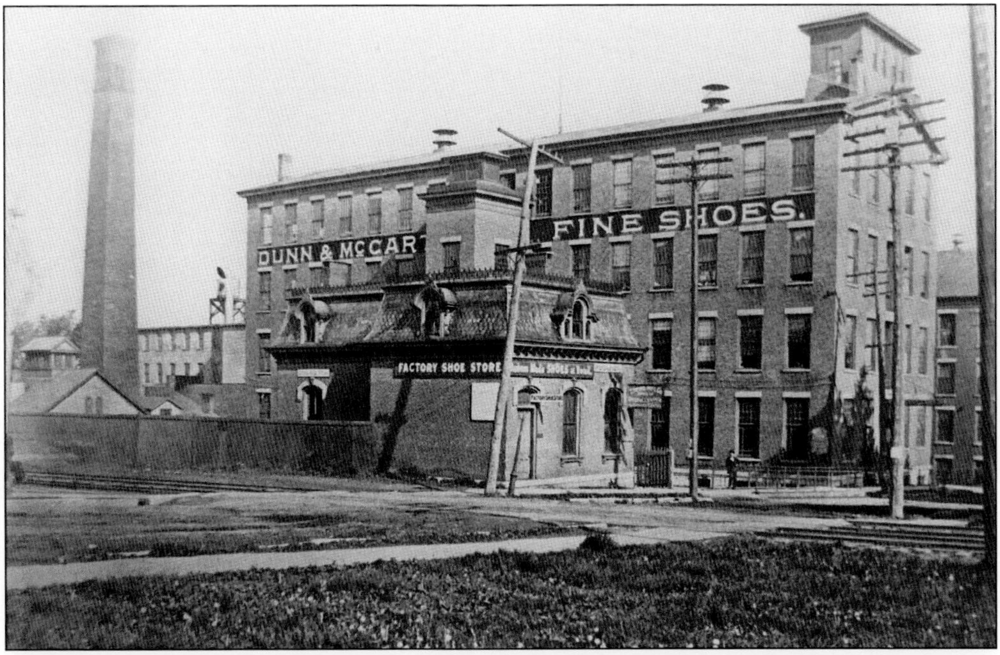

Dunn and McCarthy Company, c. 1900. The factory complex for this shoe manufacturer stood along the Owasco Outlet and the New York Central Railroad.

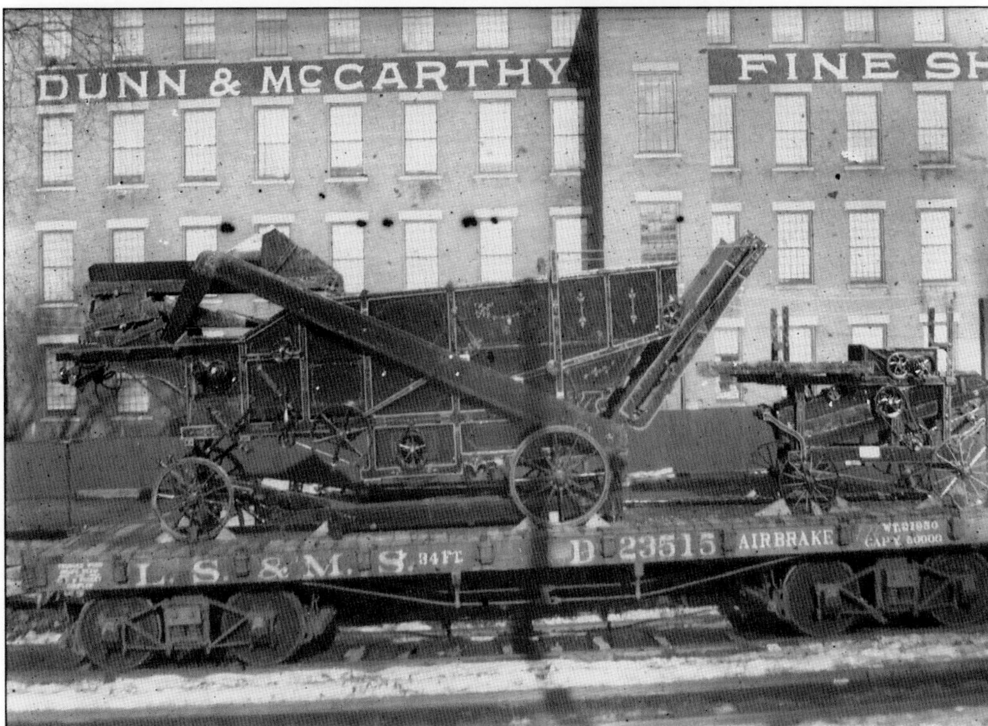

A.W. Stevens Hay Bailer on Rail Line in Front of Dunn and McCarthy, c. 1900. Stevens began his business in Genoa, New York. When fire destroyed his original factory, he moved to Auburn in 1878.

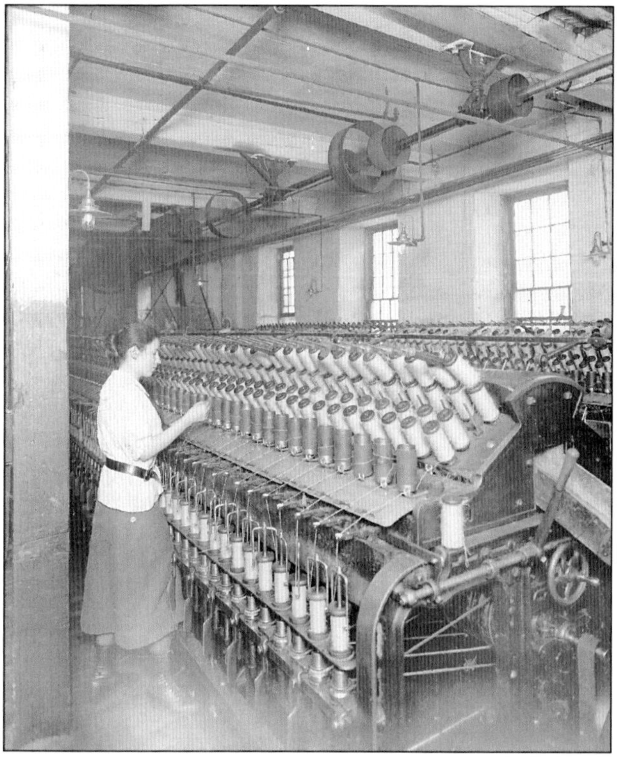

TEXTILE WORKER, LATE NINETEENTH CENTURY. This young woman worked in an unidentified Auburn factory, one of many women employed by the city's booming industries.

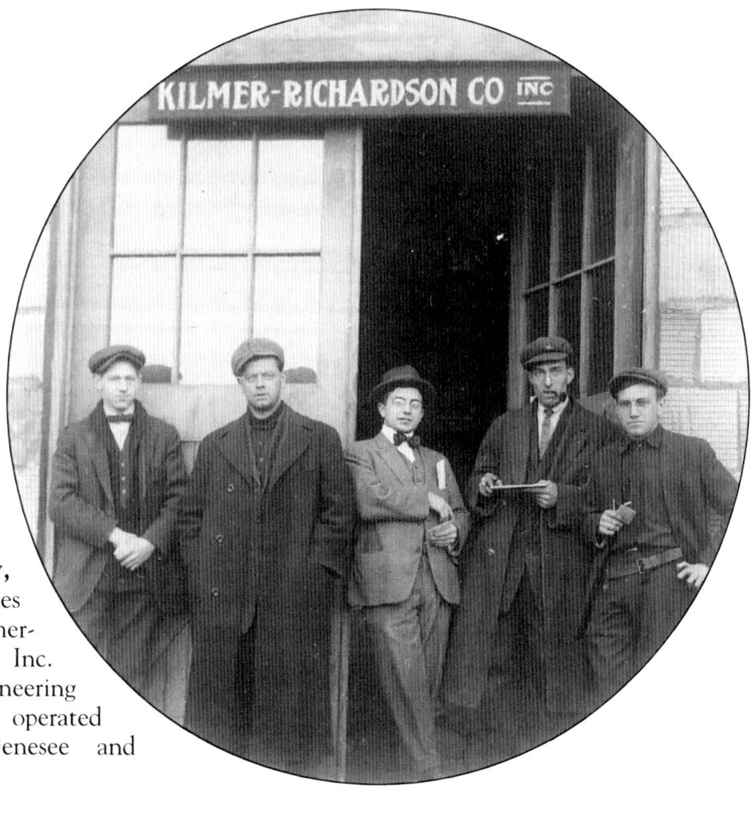

ROGUE'S GALLERY, C. 1918. Employees posed in front of Kilmer-Richardson Company, Inc. The electrical engineering and contracting firm operated in buildings on Genesee and Garden Streets.

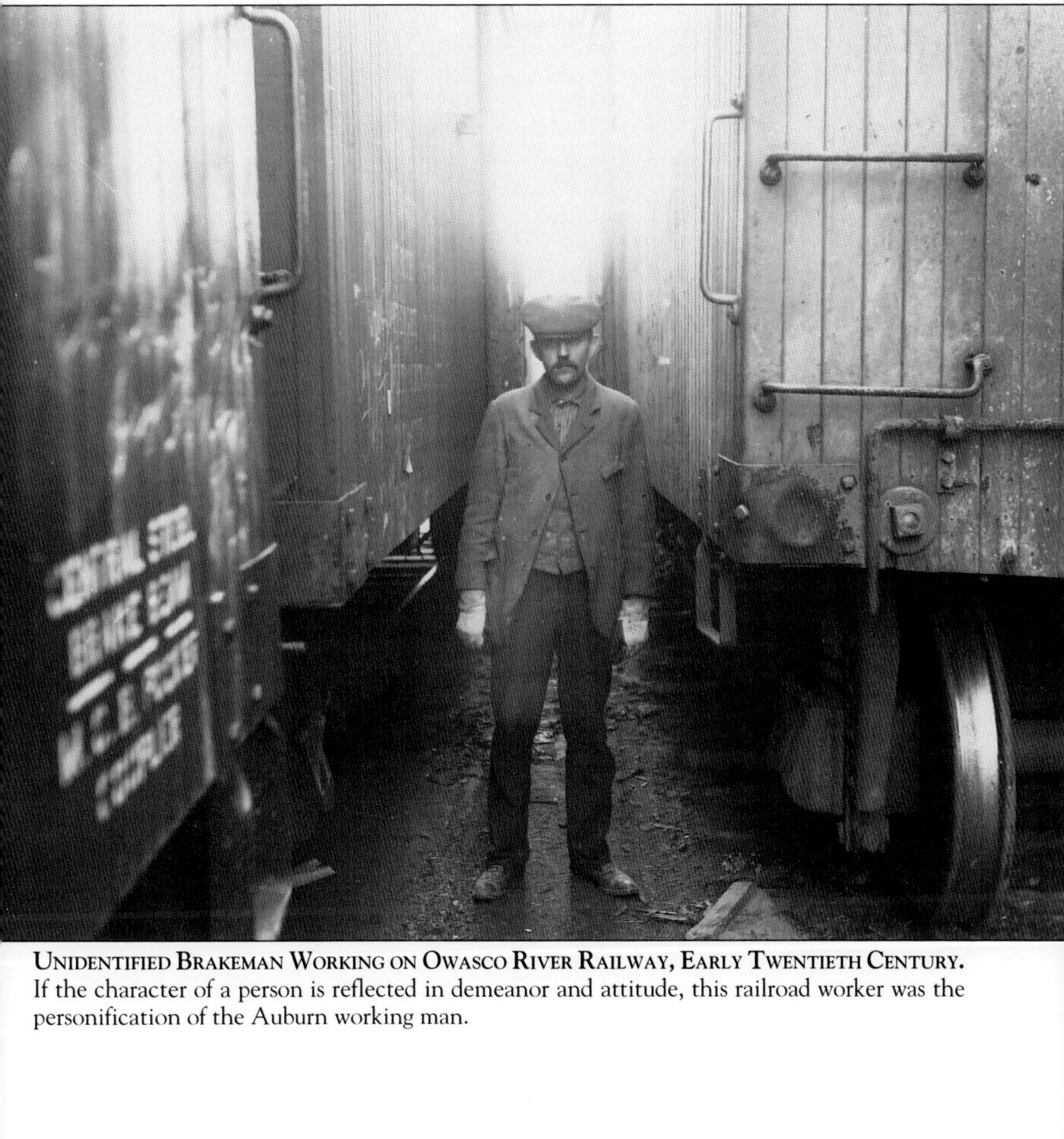

UNIDENTIFIED BRAKEMAN WORKING ON OWASCO RIVER RAILWAY, EARLY TWENTIETH CENTURY. If the character of a person is reflected in demeanor and attitude, this railroad worker was the personification of the Auburn working man.

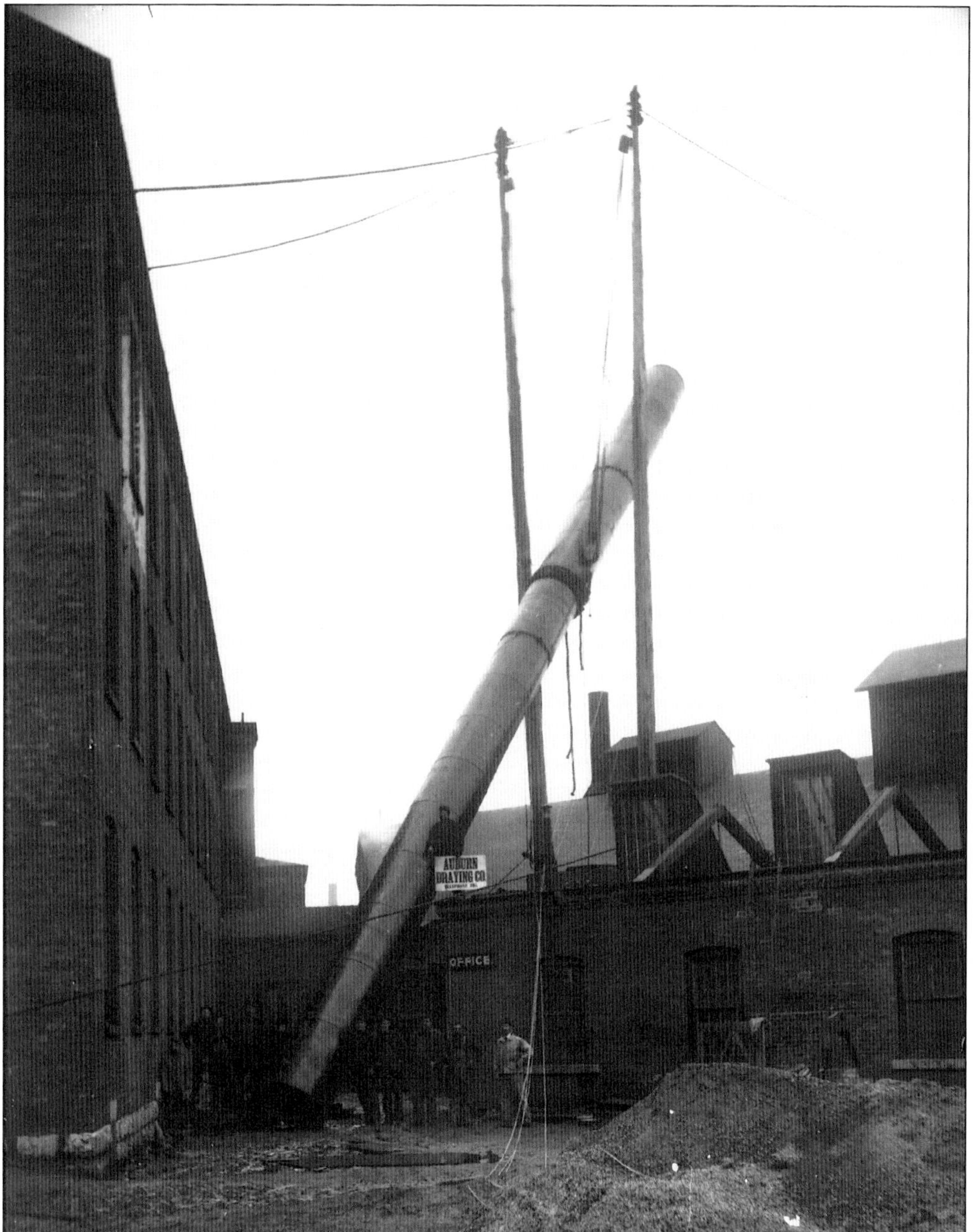

RAISING SMOKESTACK, C. 1900. Men from the Auburn Draying Company completed the tough job of lifting a smokestack into place for an unidentified Auburn factory.

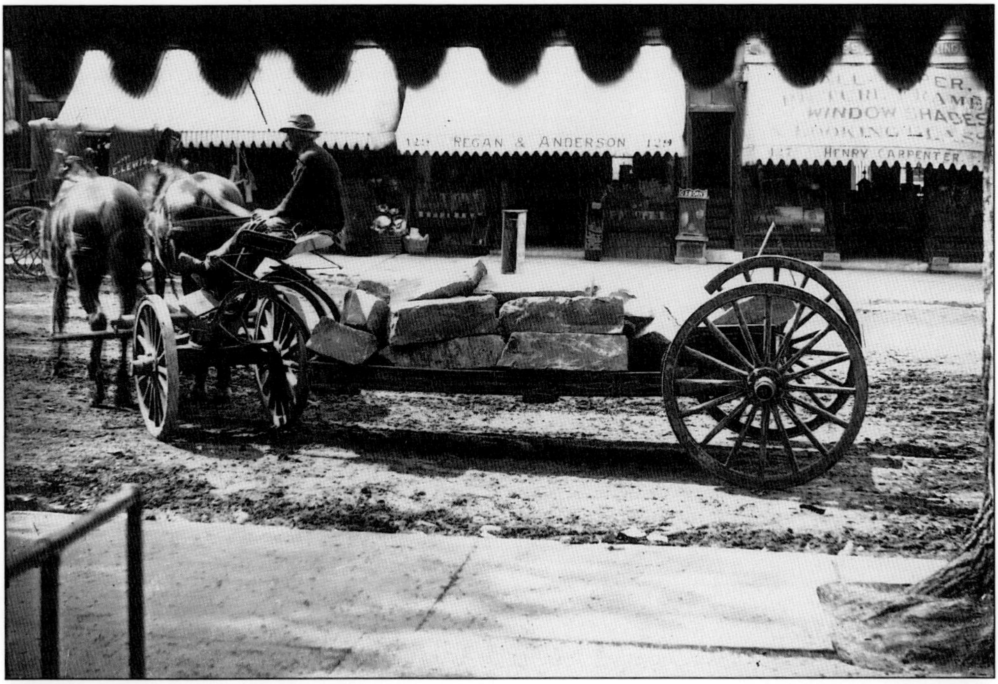

HAULING STONES, C. 1900. This image taken along Genesee Street advertised wagons manufactured by E.D. Clapp and Company. Appropriately enough, the wagons carried the trademark name, "The Auburn."

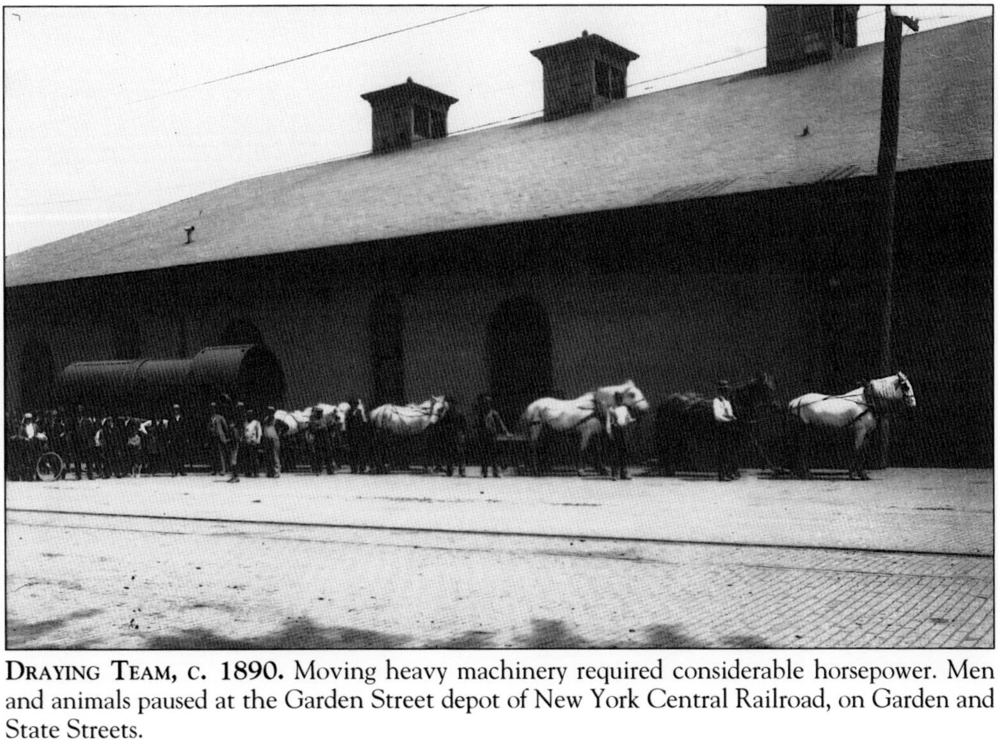

DRAYING TEAM, C. 1890. Moving heavy machinery required considerable horsepower. Men and animals paused at the Garden Street depot of New York Central Railroad, on Garden and State Streets.

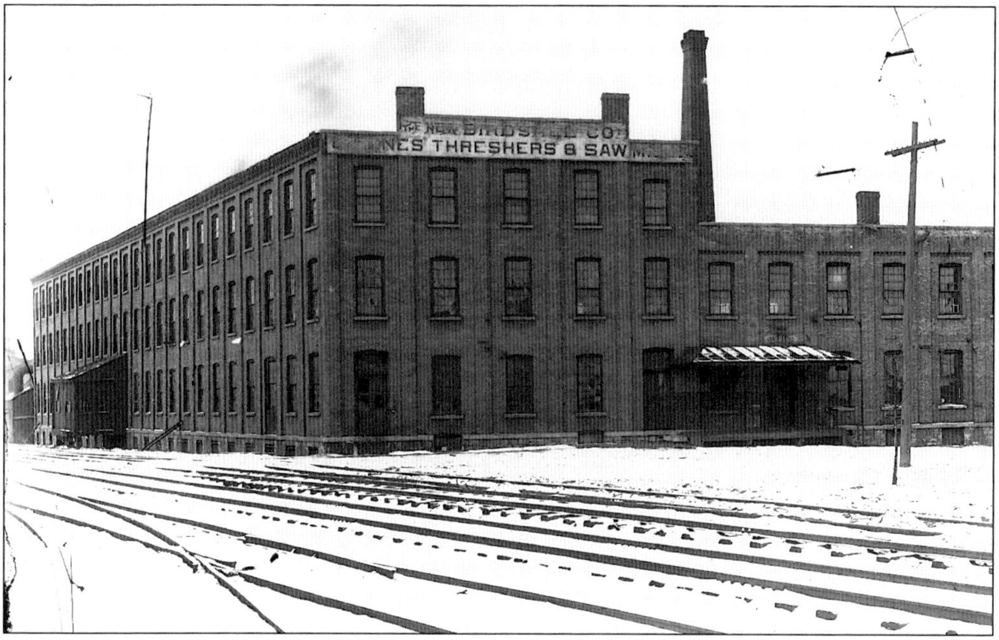

New Birdsall Factory, McMaster Street, c. 1900. New Birdsall manufactured steam traction engines, threshers, and sawmills. This building is one of the few brick factory complexes which still stands in Auburn.

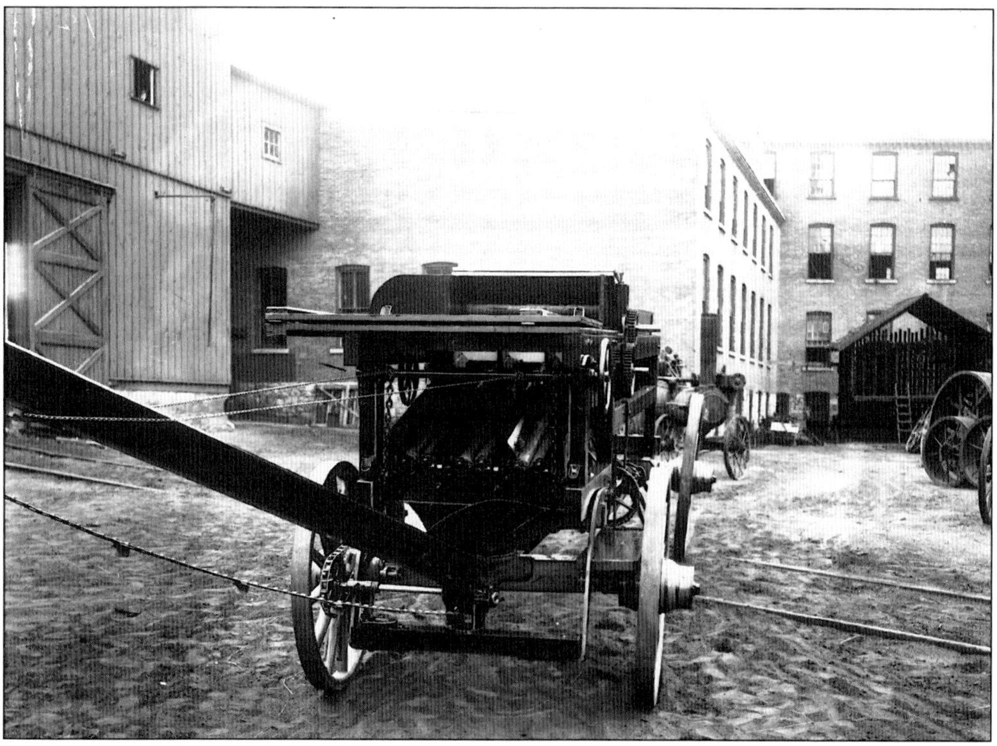

Machinery View, c. 1900. This image from an unidentified Auburn factory, possibly New Birdsall, shows a rail line heading into the factory complex.

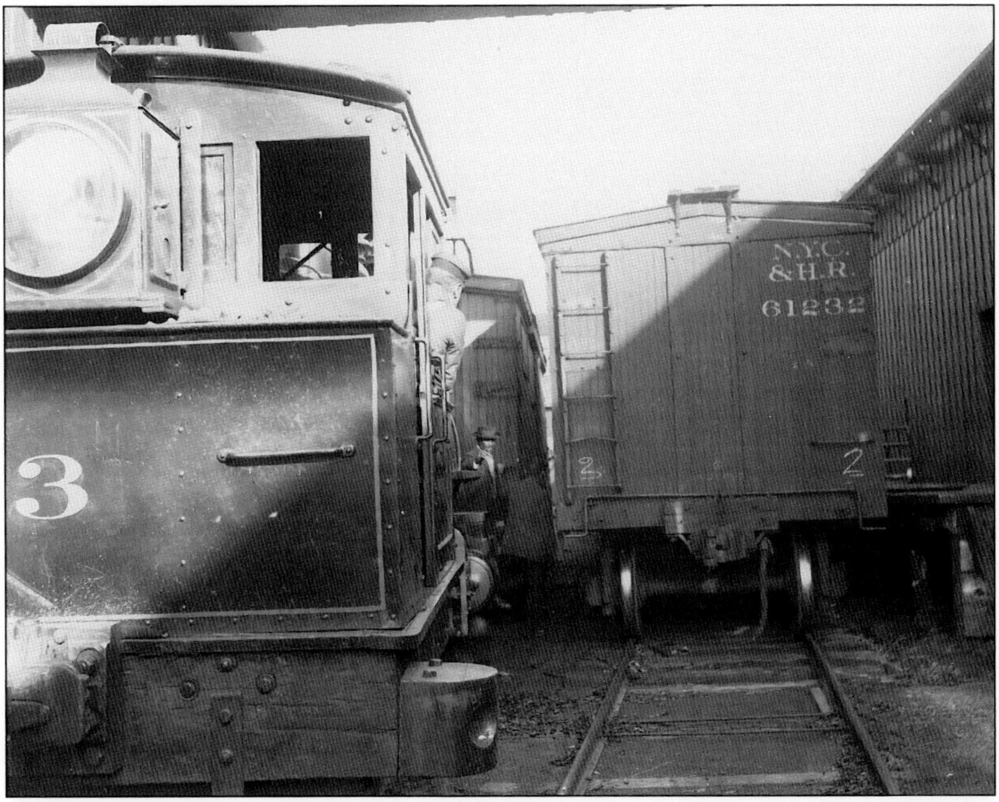

No Room to Pass, c. 1900. Owasco River Railway locomotive number three edged into position on the tracks serving the Osborne Works.

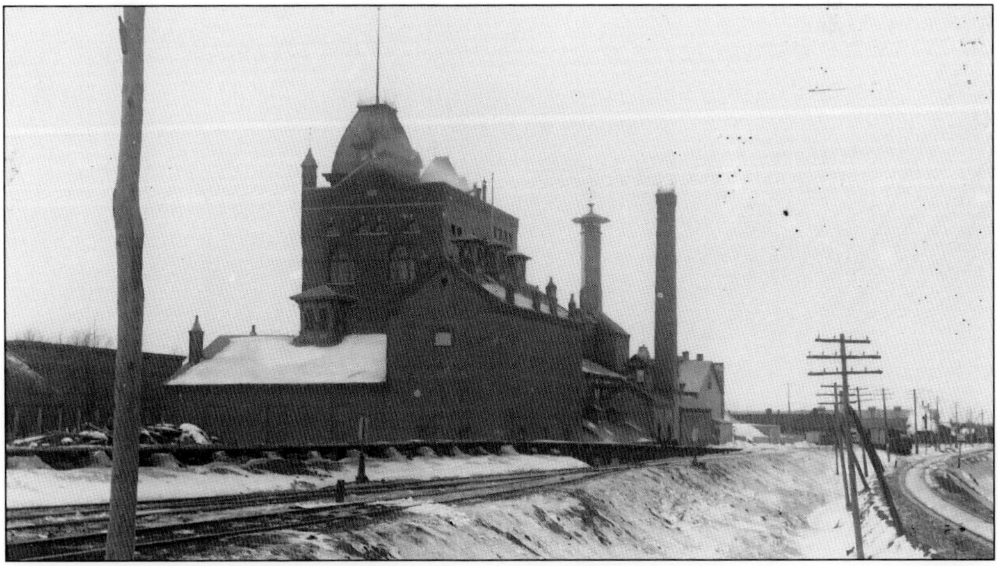

Independent Brewery, Clark Street, Early Twentieth Century. The brewery produced lager beers, Indee ale, and porters until the age of Prohibition. The factory was demolished in the early 1930s to provide a site for the Dairymen's League milk plant.

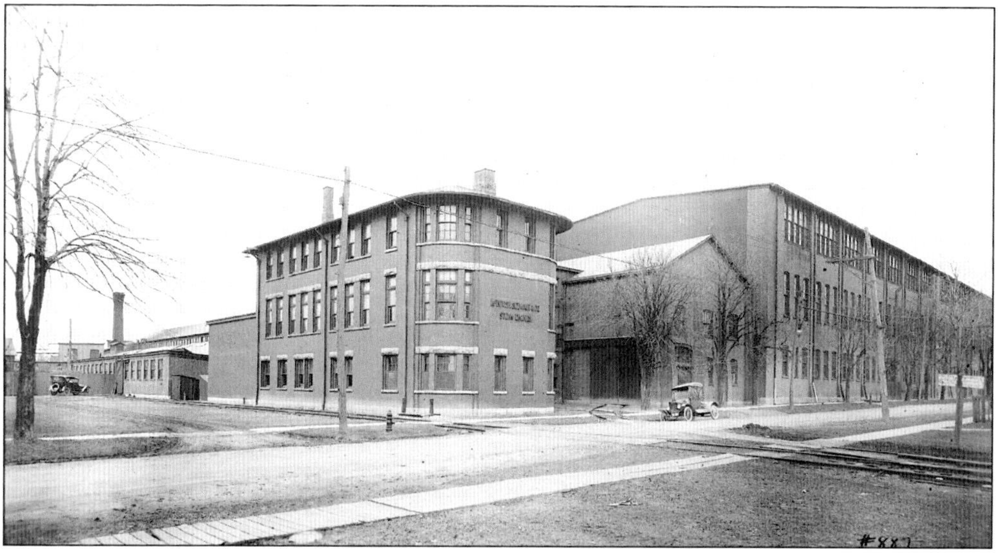

McIntosh and Seymour Company, Orchard Street, c. 1900. McIntosh and Seymour was founded in 1886 for the manufacture of stationary steam engines.

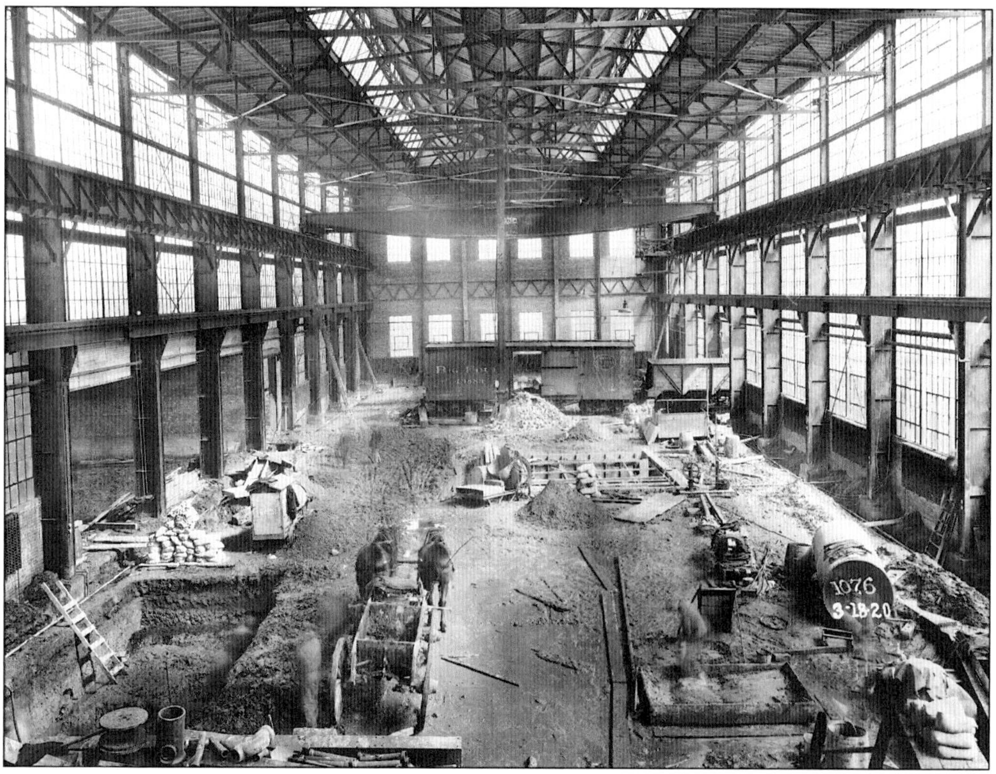

Interior Construction, McIntosh and Seymour Company, c. 1900. The railroad boxcar in the background provides an indication of scale.

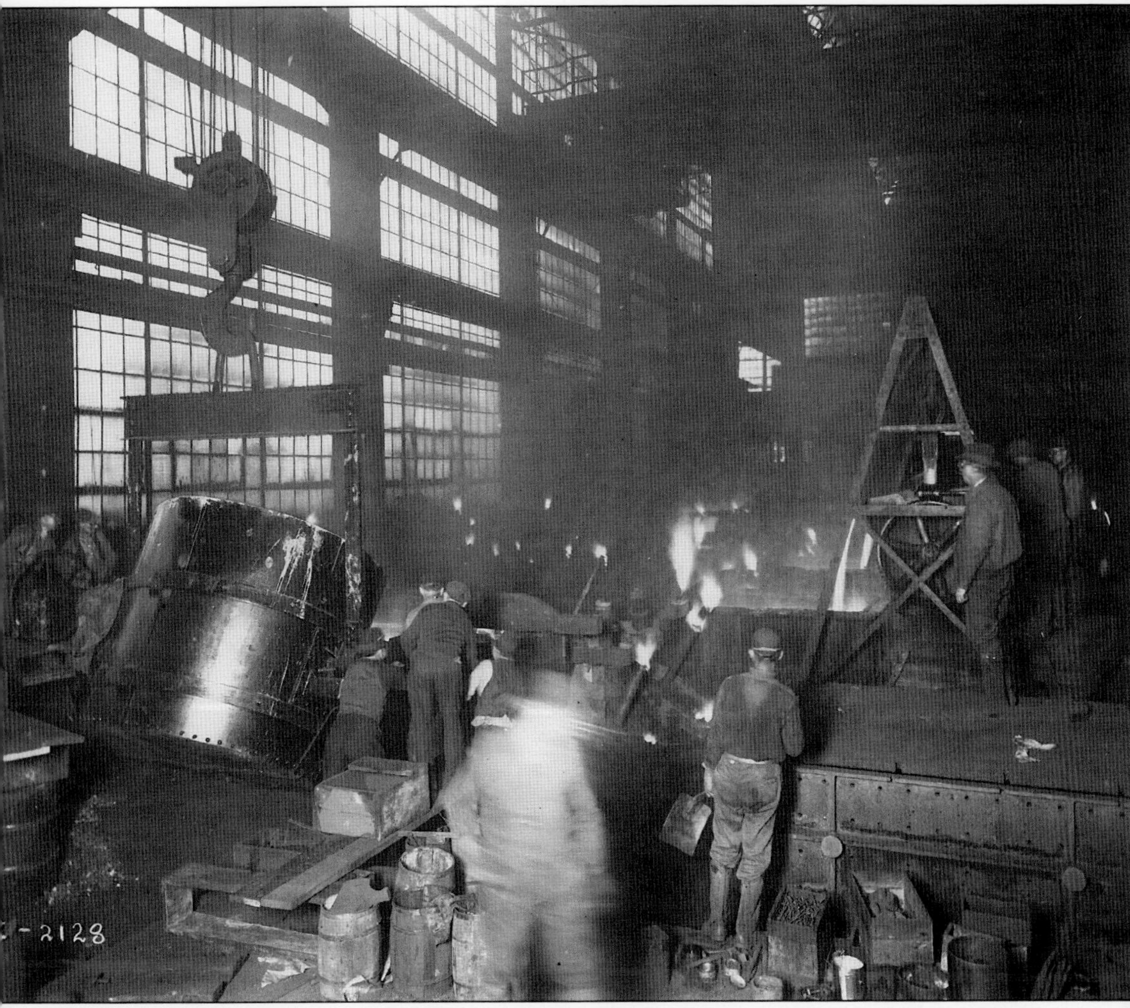

POURING THE BASE, MCINTOSH AND SEYMOUR COMPANY, c. 1900. Manpower and firepower combined to begin the process of manufacturing a massive stationary engine. Engines produced in this factory were shipped throughout the world.

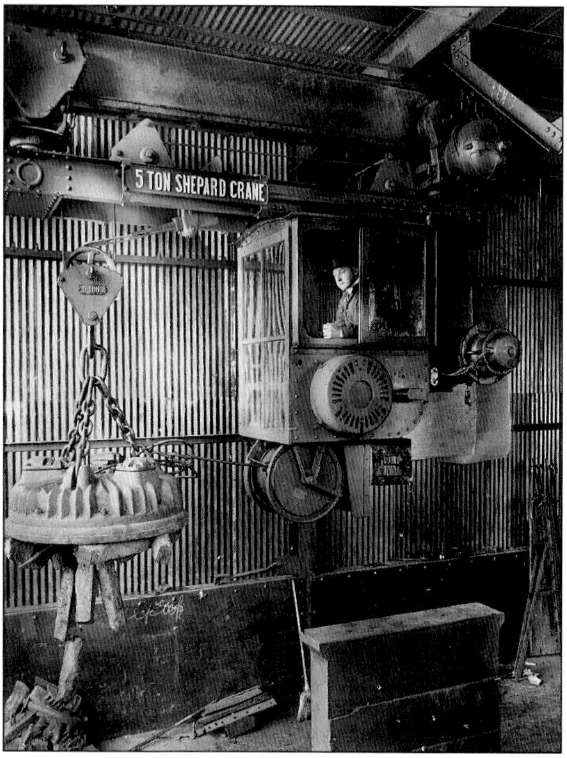

MAN OPERATING CRANE, MCINTOSH AND SEYMOUR COMPANY, C. 1900.

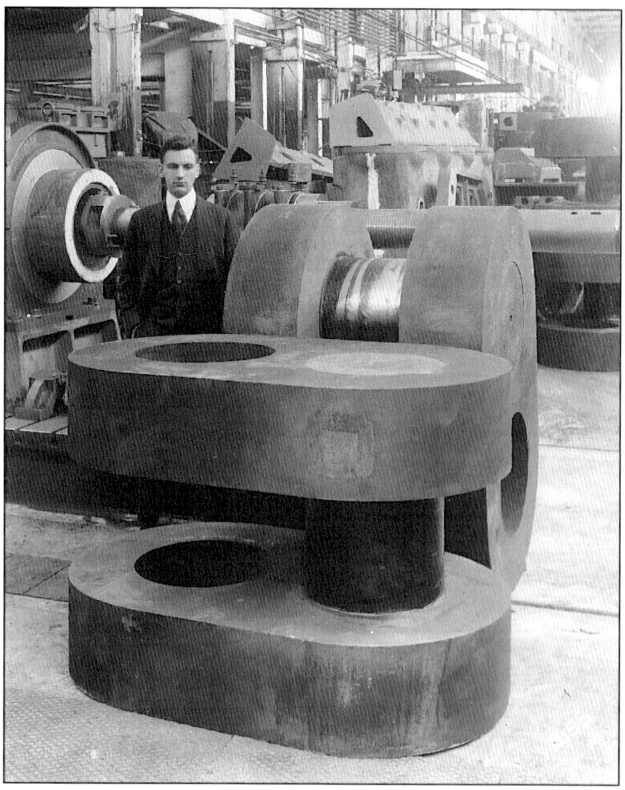

EMPLOYEE WITH ENGINE PARTS, MCINTOSH AND SEYMOUR COMPANY, EARLY TWENTIETH CENTURY.
In 1929, Alco purchased McIntosh and Seymour and began manufacturing engines for internal combustion locomotives.

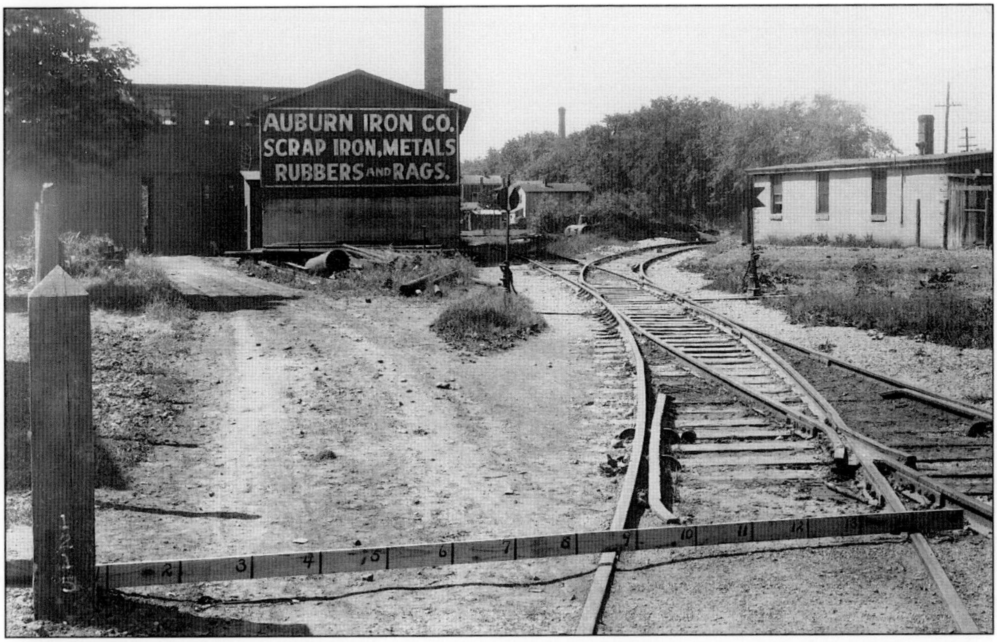

AUBURN IRON COMPANY, C. 1920.

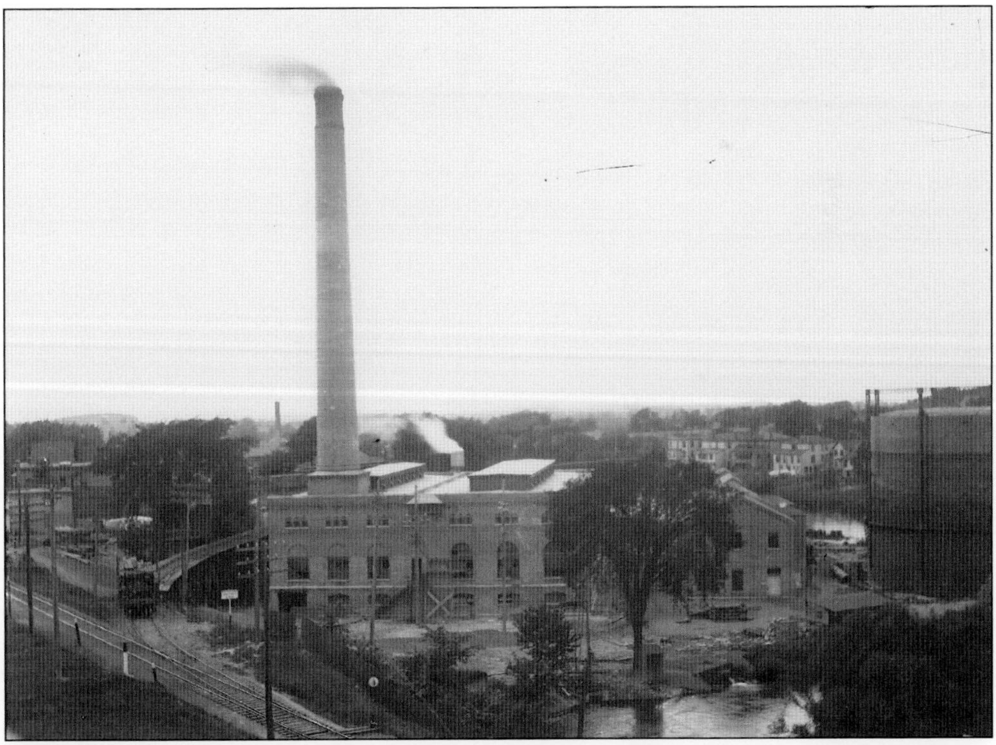

STEAM ELECTRIC GENERATING PLANT, CLARK STREET, C. 1910. Owned by Niagara, Lockport, and Ontario Power Company, the plant generated power for the Auburn and Syracuse Electric Railroad.

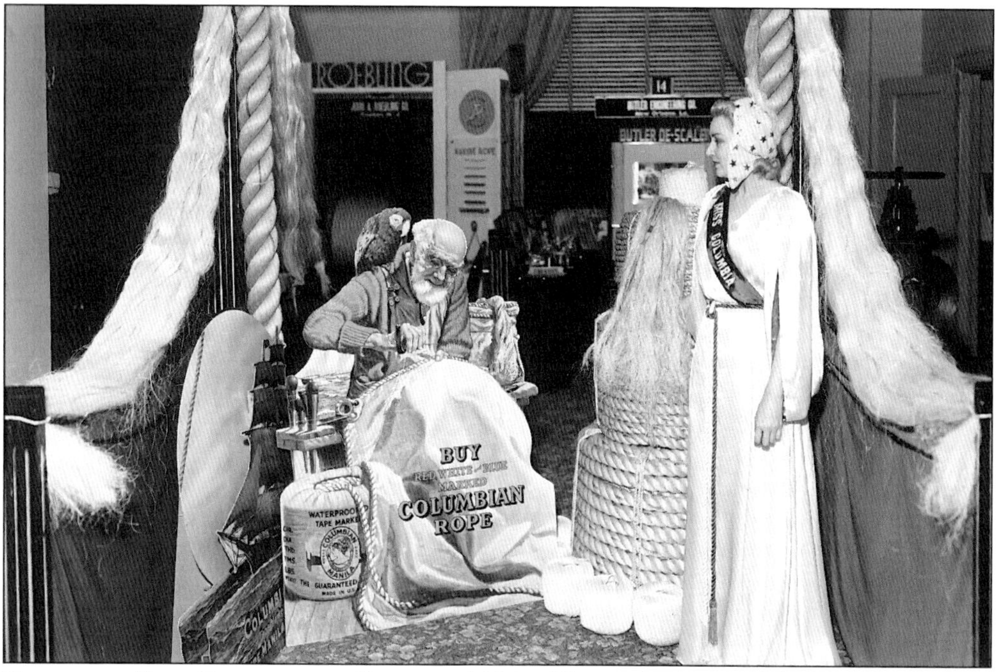

COLUMBIAN ROPE PROMOTIONAL DISPLAY, 1930S. This trade show exhibit in New Orleans included product samples and familiar Columbian Rope advertising images.

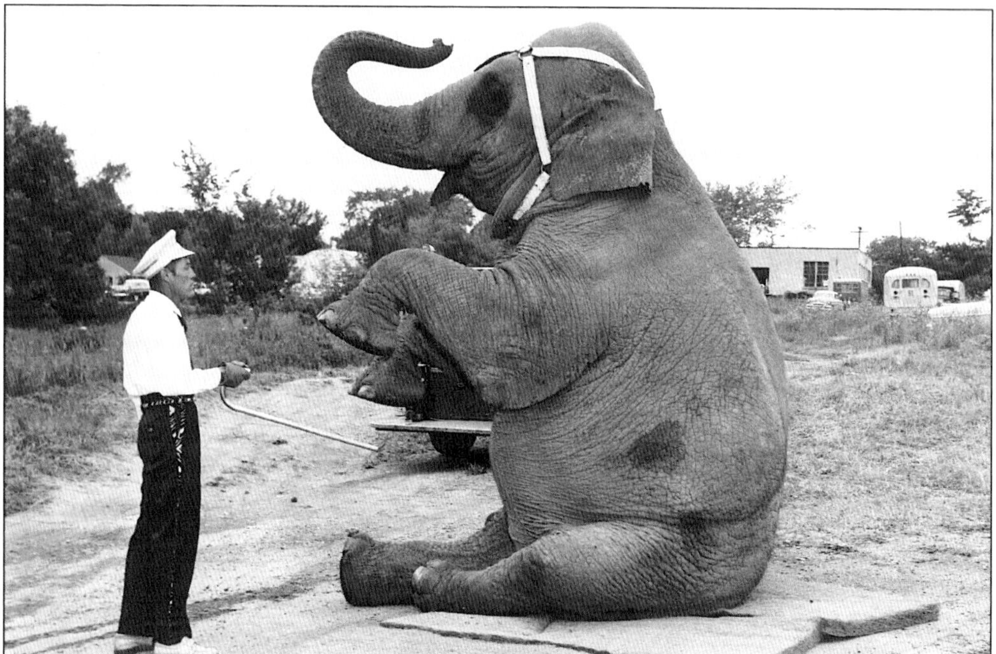

"ELEPHANT COULDN'T DAMAGE IT!" PROMOTION FOR COLUMBIAN ROPE, C. 1946. In a test to augment laboratory findings, Colombian Rope invited a circus elephant to try and crush its new cushioning product, Co-Ro-Text, a latex impregnated coil material. Co-Ro-Text withstood the elephant challenge. (Image from collection of Community Preservation Committee.)

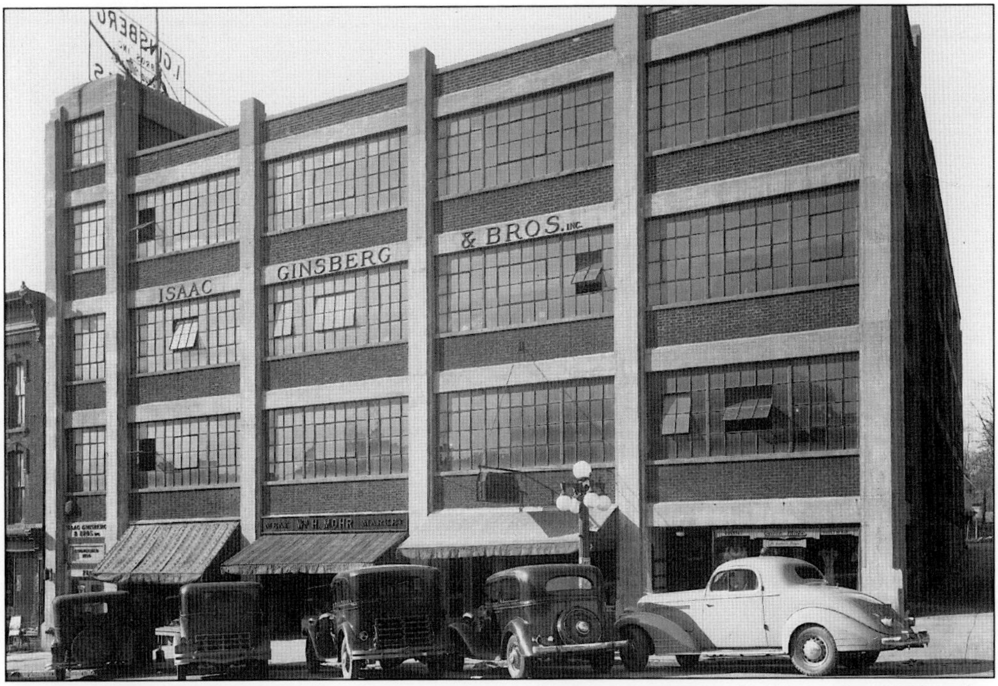

GINSBERG BROTHERS BUILDING, EAST GENESEE STREET, C. 1940. Built in the 1920s, this building served as a dress factory for Isaac Ginsberg & Brothers of New York City.

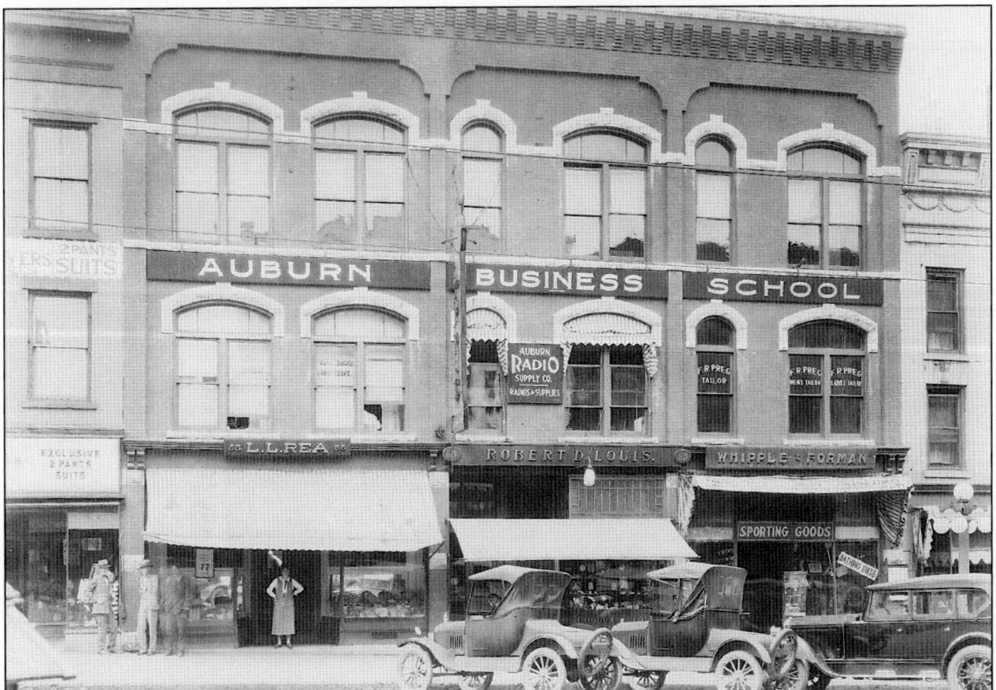

AUBURN BUSINESS SCHOOL, 1920S. Founded in 1889, Auburn Business School shortly thereafter moved to this location at 53 Genesee Street and remained there until it closed in 1952.

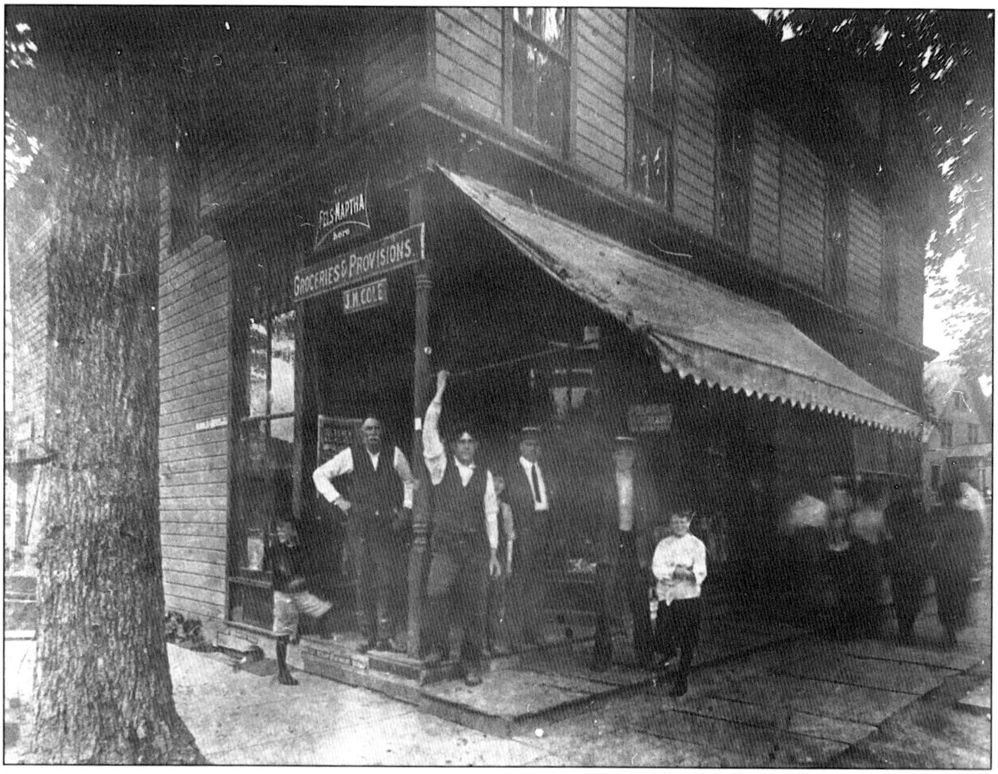

Cole Grocery Store, 191 State Street, 1915. J.M. Cole operated a local grocery at several locations on State Street before moving to Moravia in 1916.

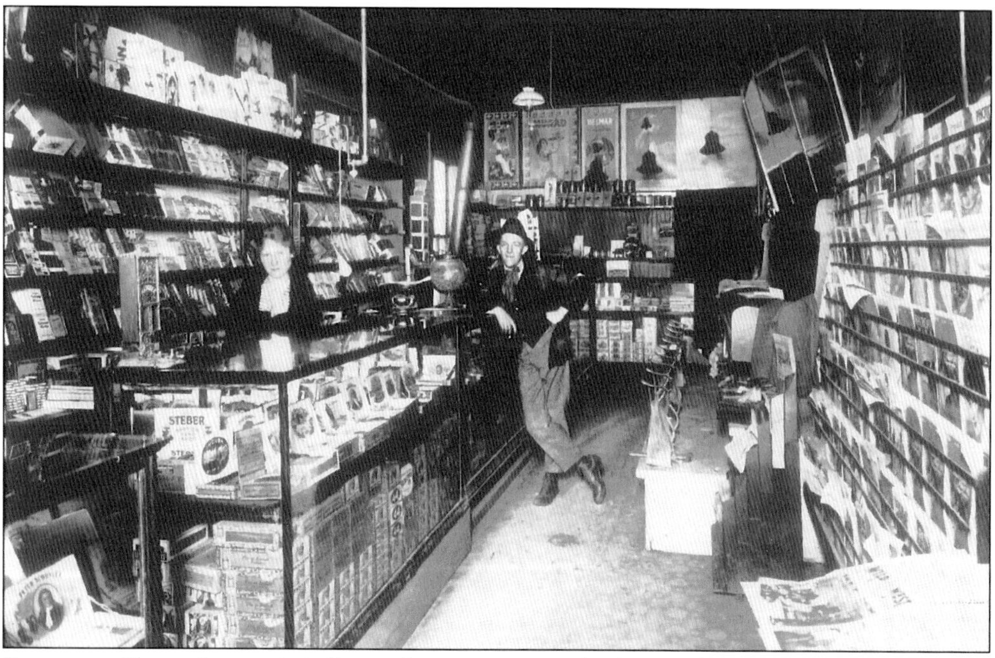

Schaeffer Cigar Store, 113 State Street, 1916. Charles F. Schaeffer ran a confectionery, tobacco, and newsstand on State Street.

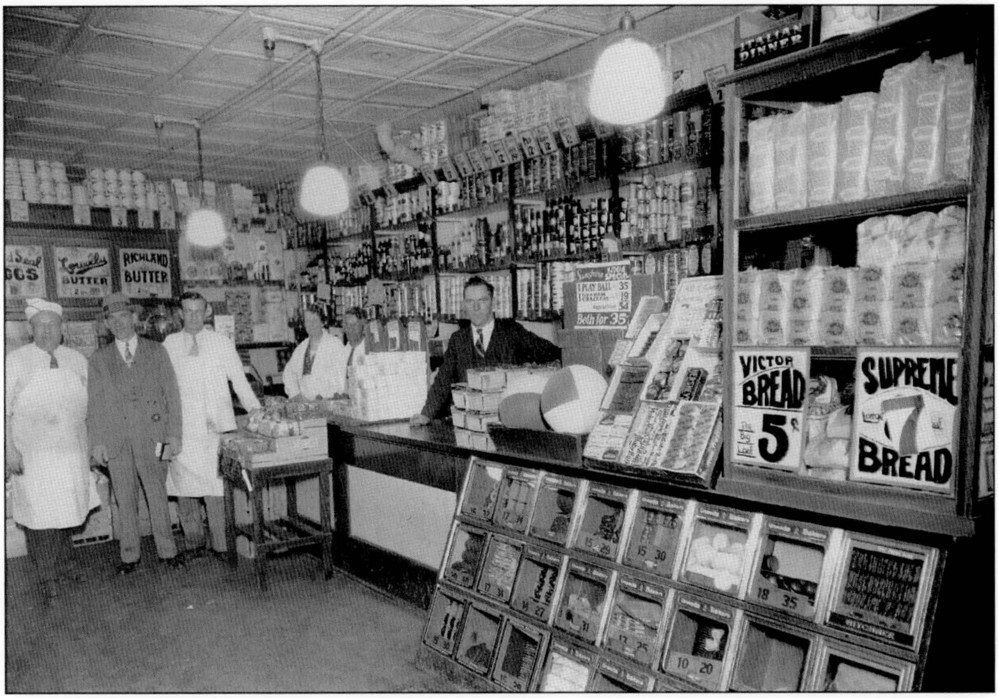

Froitzheim's Market, 193 State Street, c. 1910. Martin J. Froitzheim operated this meat market and grocery store on State Street, which opened in the early 1900s and closed in 1918.

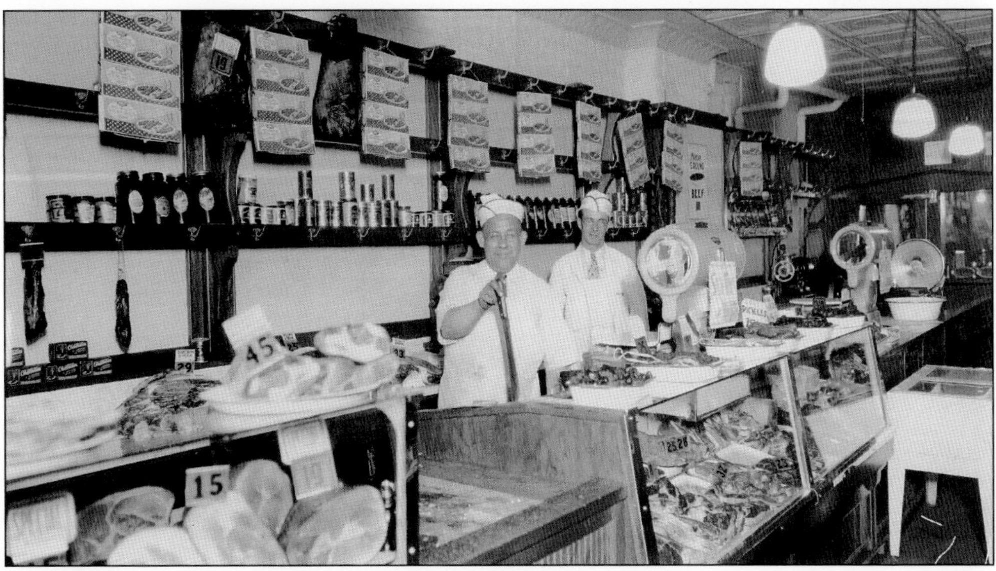

Meat Counter, Froitzheim's Market, c. 1910.

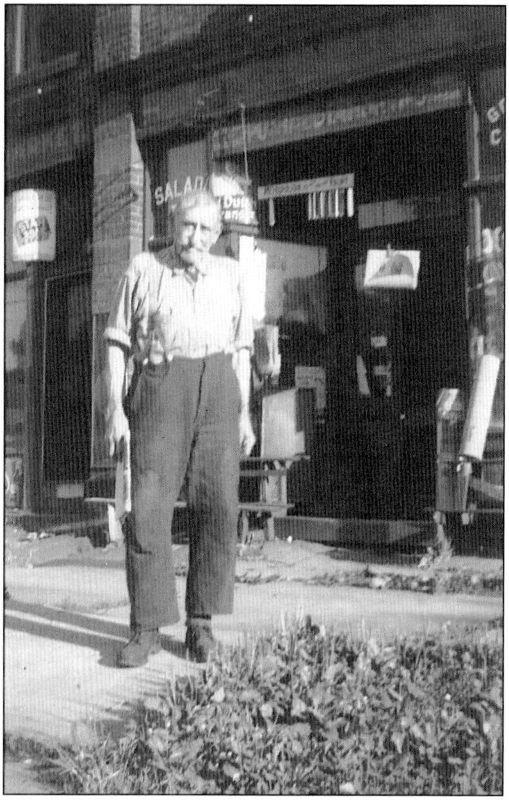

OLD ED PARKER, WALL STREET, c. 1920. F. Edwin Parker posed for posterity in front of his business and residence. He ran a popular grocery store on Wall Street from 1888 until 1925.

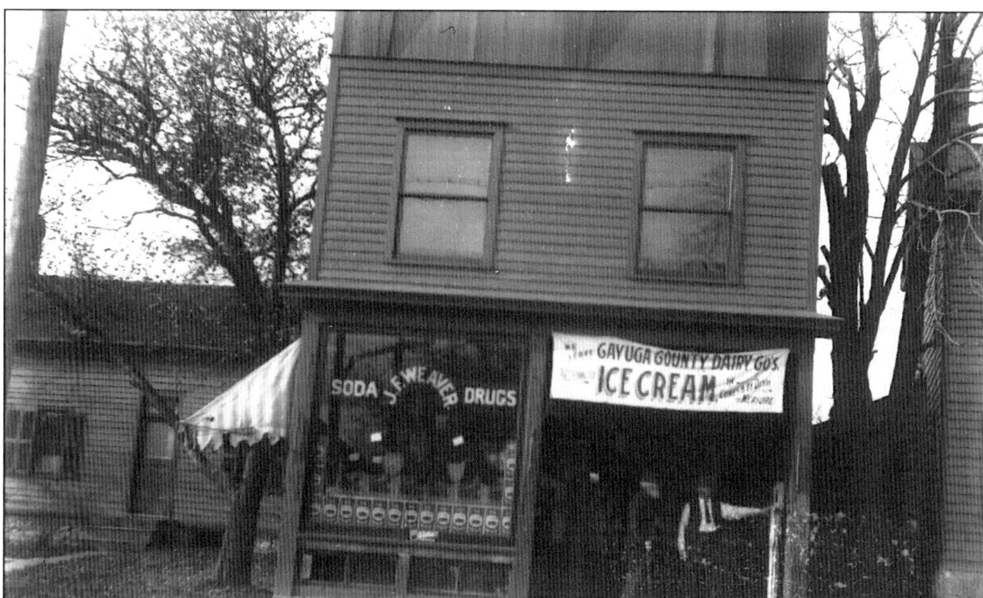

J.F. WEAVER DRUGSTORE, 17 AURELIUS AVENUE, c. 1911. Weaver, a druggist, operated this pharmacy and soda shop in the West End. Like old Ed Parker, Weaver lived above his store.

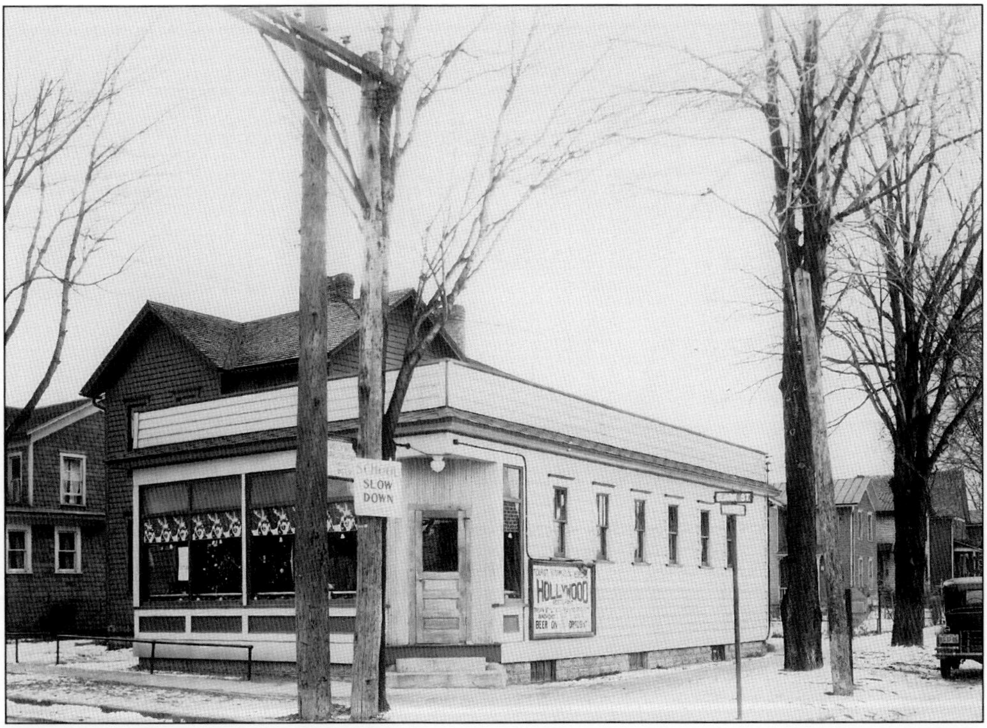

Hollywood Restaurant, c. 1932. This local landmark on Clark Street has changed greatly in appearance over the years, but still serves plenty of meals to hungry patrons.

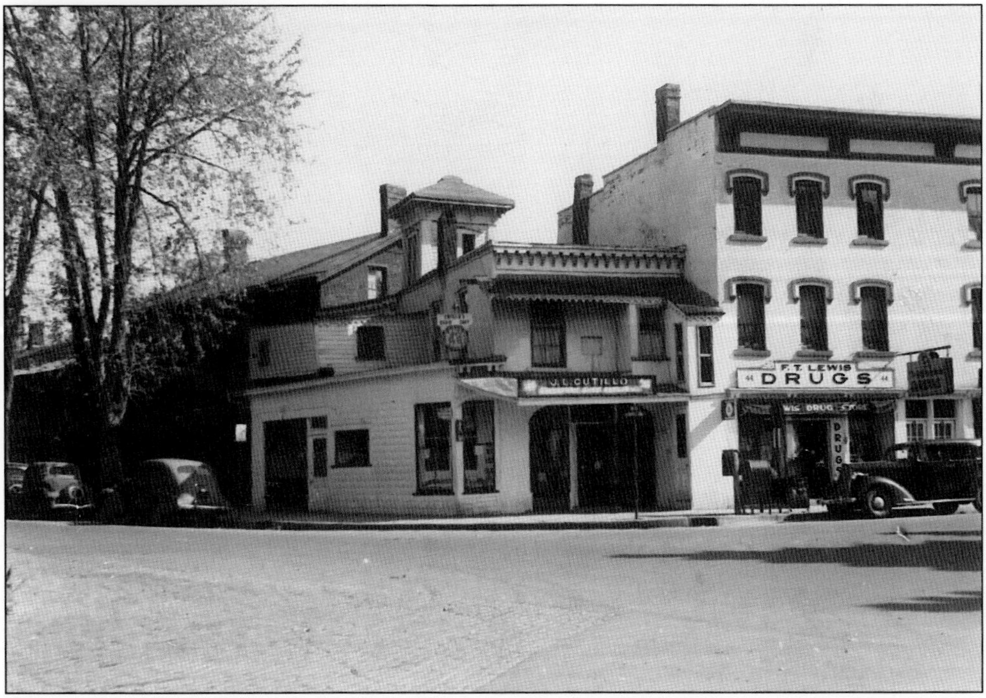

J.L. Cutillo Shoe Repair and F.T. Lewis Drugstore, Five Points, 1939–1942. These businesses operated at the corner of Lewis and Franklin Streets.

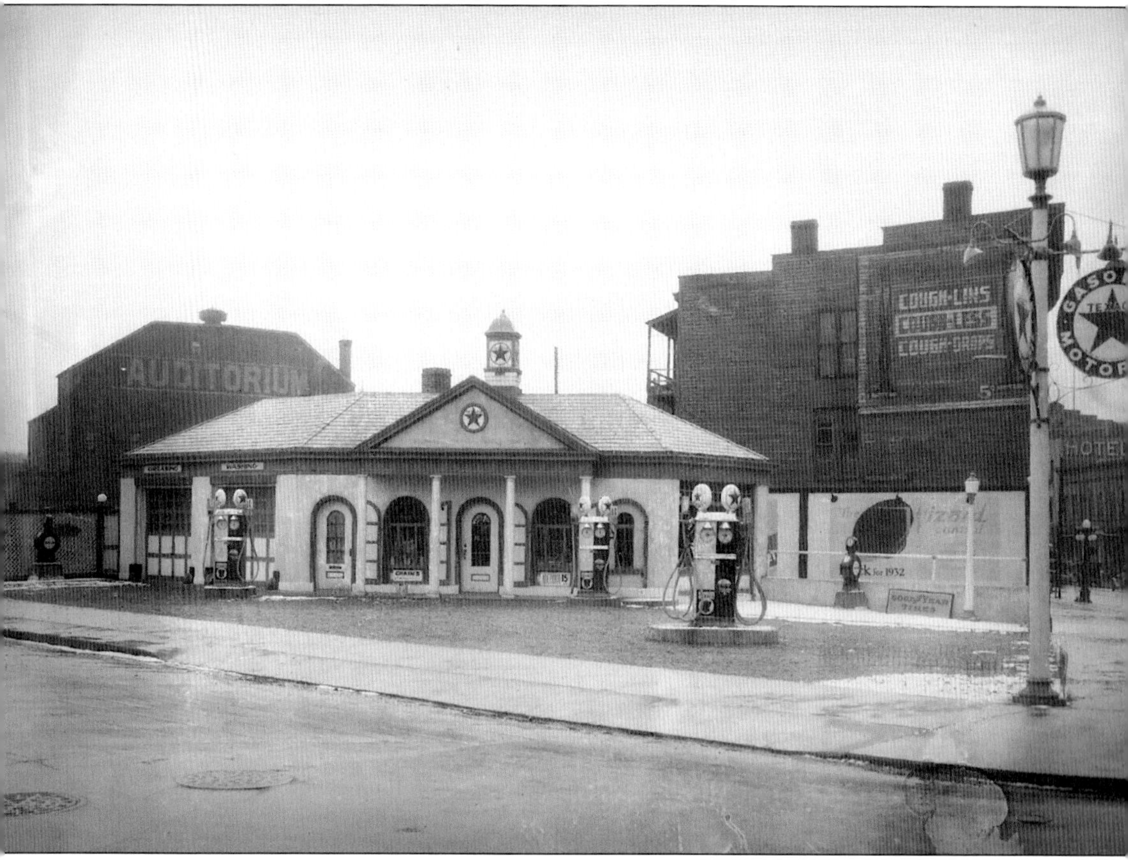

Texaco Station, Garden Street, c. 1932. This building still stands, but is almost unrecognizable. In the distance is the back of the Auditorium Theater on Market Street which, by the time this image was taken, had been renamed the Grand.

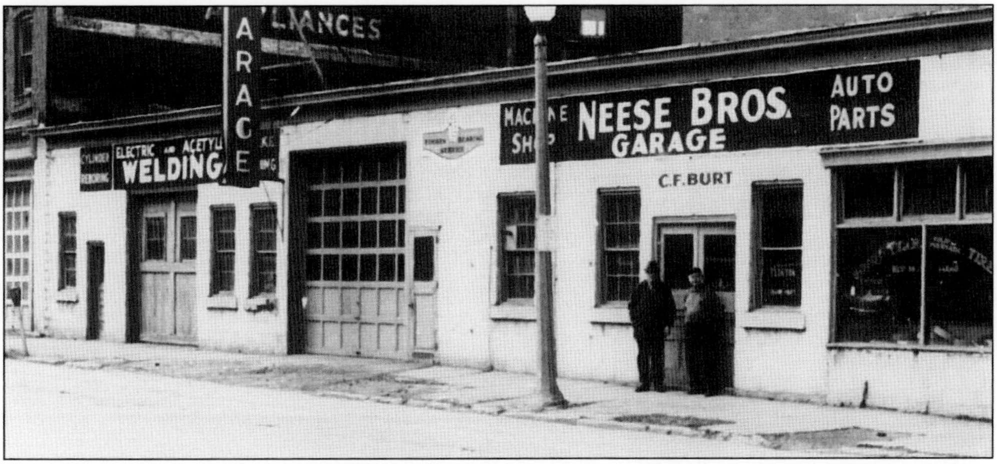

Neese Brothers Garage, Dill Street, 1940s. This structure on Dill Street housed an undertaker before shifting to automobile servicing.

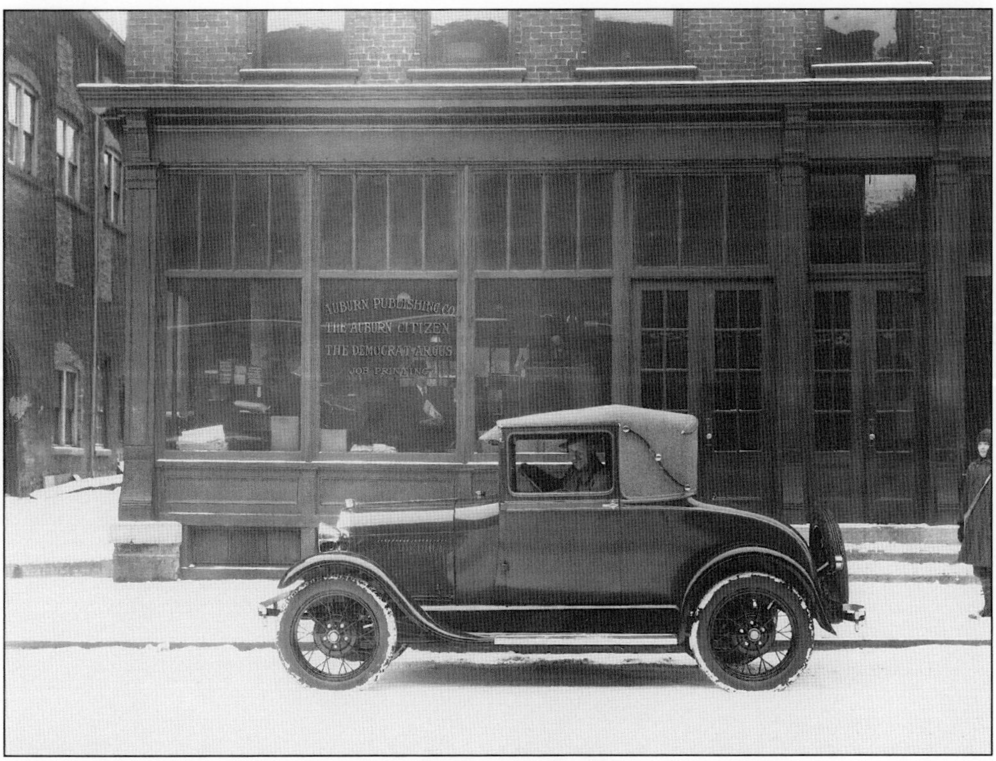

Auburn Publishing Company, Dill Street, 1930s. (Image from collection of Community Preservation Committee.)

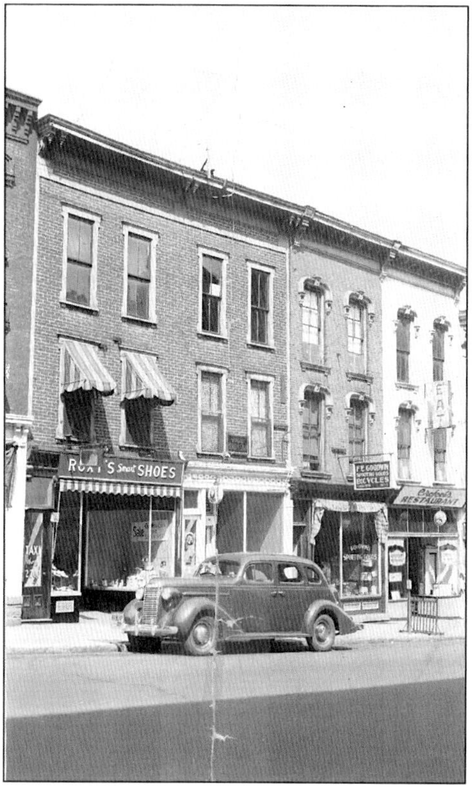

NORTH STREET BUSINESSES, AUGUST 1939. (Image from collection of Community Preservation Committee.)

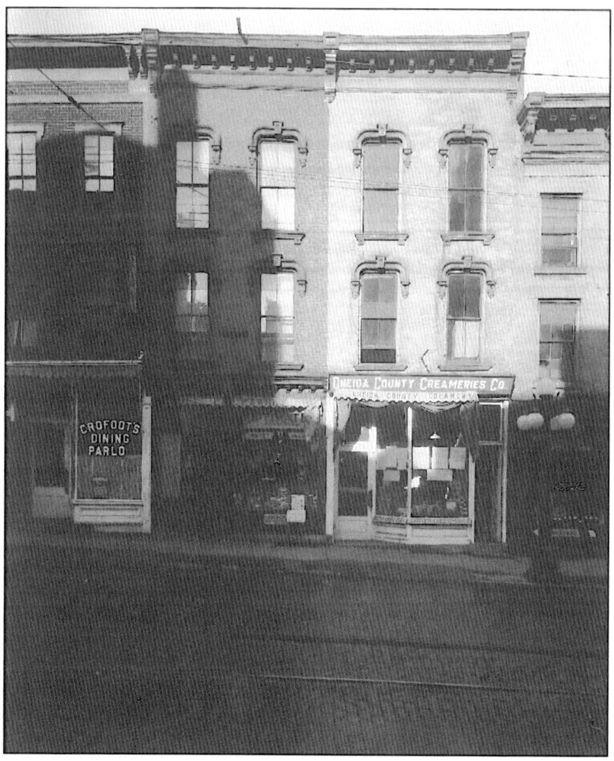

NORTH STREET BUSINESSES, 1939. This view includes Crofoot Dining Parlor, Feeley Smoke Shop and Billiards, and Oneida County Creamery. (Image from collection of Community Preservation Committee.)

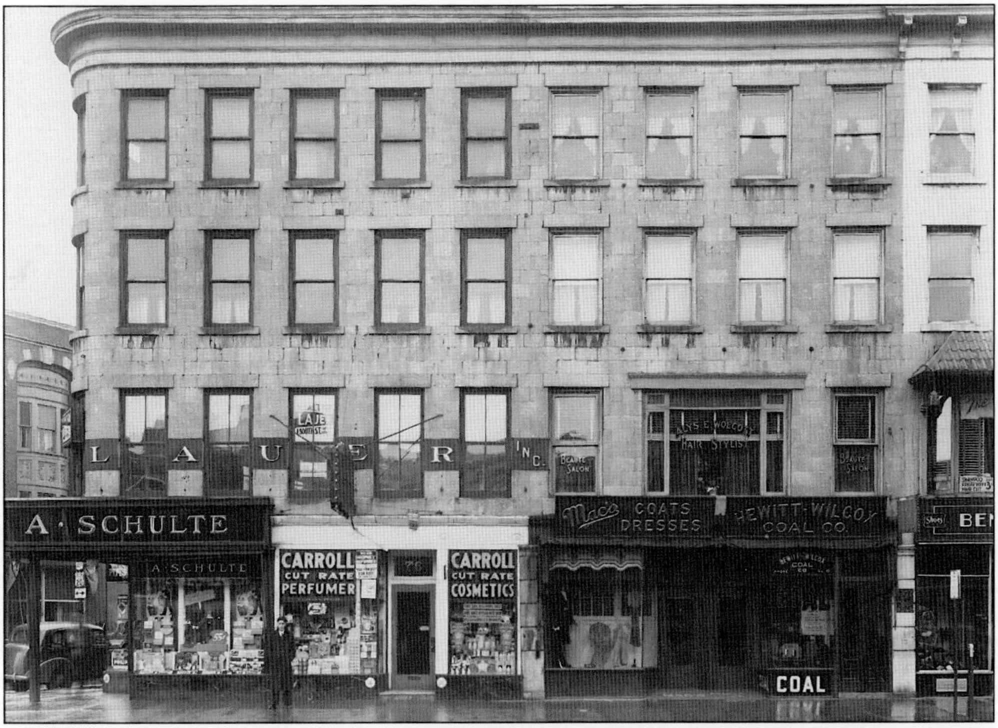

SHOPPER'S PARADISE, 1940S. This structure at the corner of Genesee and South Streets stood on the present location of the Genesee Street Mall.

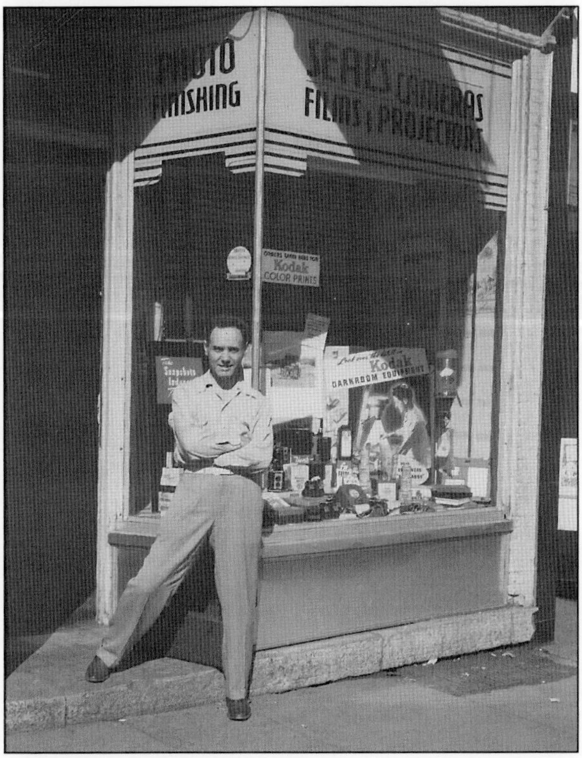

SEAL'S CAMERA, NORTH STREET, C. 1947. Selio DePasquale posed in front of his shop. This camera store has long been an Auburn fixture. (Image from collection of Community Preservation Committee.)

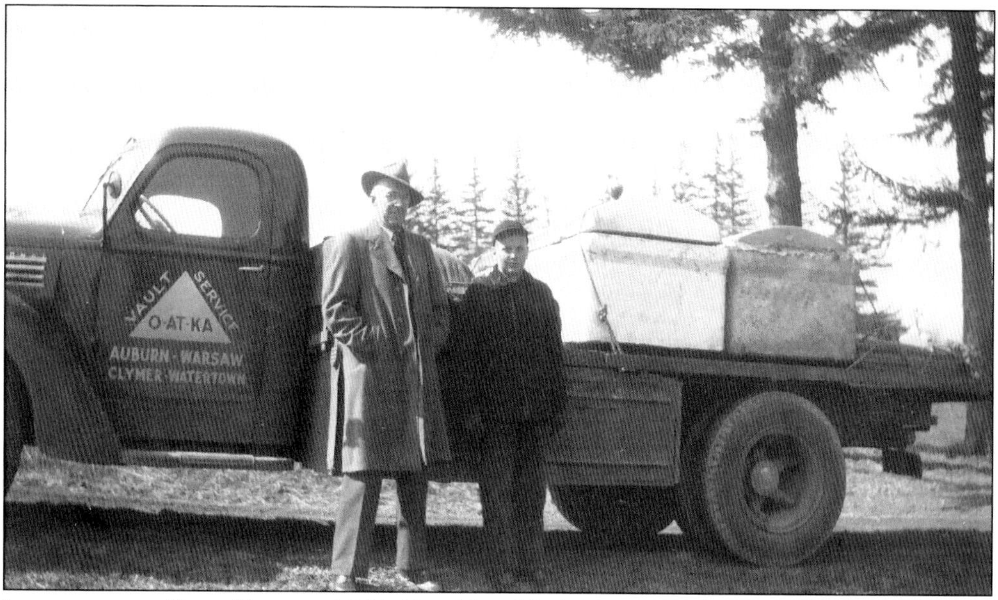

LOOKING FOR A FINAL REST, C. 1944. Harold and Jack String posed in front of a delivery truck for O-At-Ka Vault Service, which later became Sunnycrest.

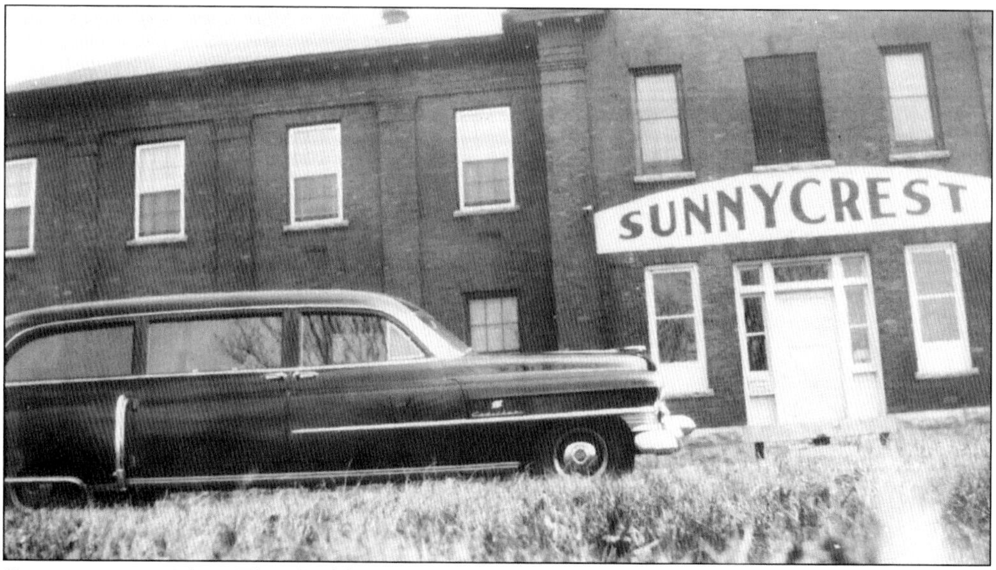

SUNNYCREST, 1950S. This building was constructed as an isolation hospital for infectious diseases in the early twentieth century. It now houses Sunnycrest, a burial vault company.

Five

Changing Neighborhoods

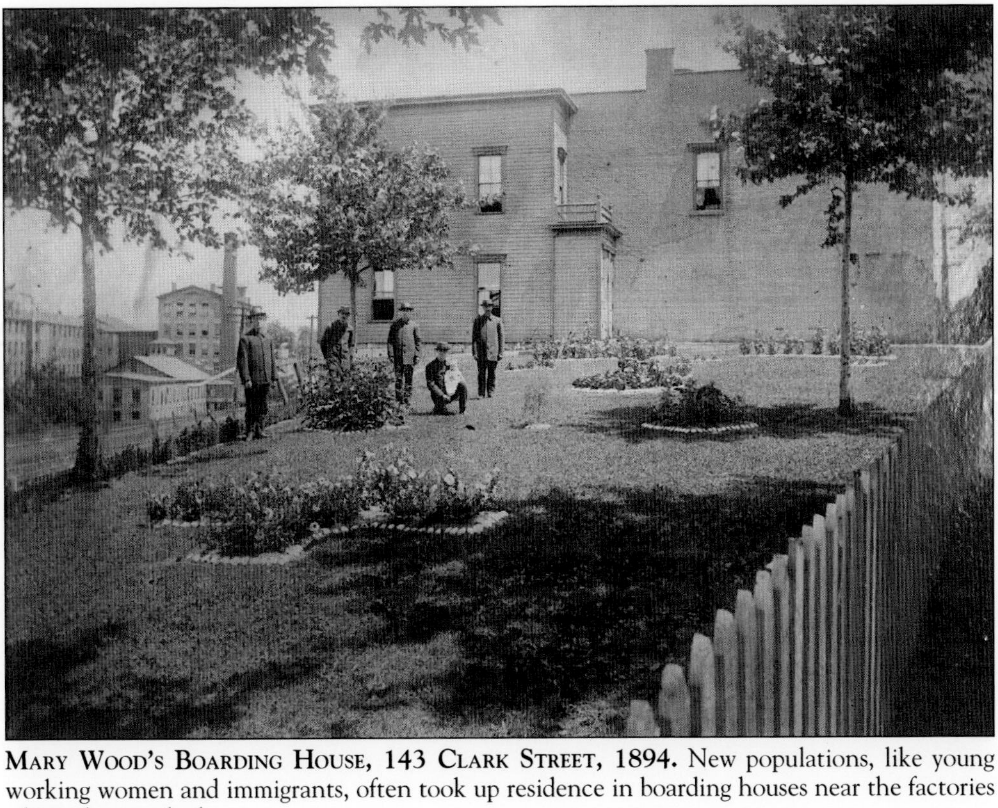

Mary Wood's Boarding House, 143 Clark Street, 1894. New populations, like young working women and immigrants, often took up residence in boarding houses near the factories where they worked.

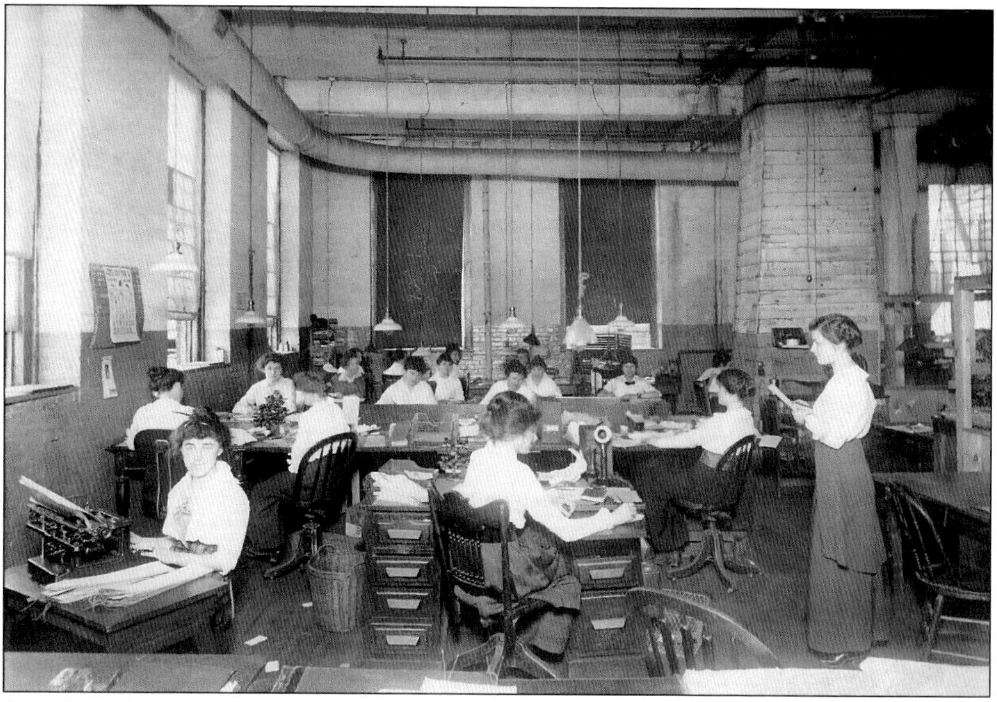

SHOE SHOP OFFICE, DUNN AND MCCARTHY. Women were often the favored workers in industries that required dexterity rather than strength. One of these women is 19-year-old Alice Adams, who entered the work force on April 20th, 1915.

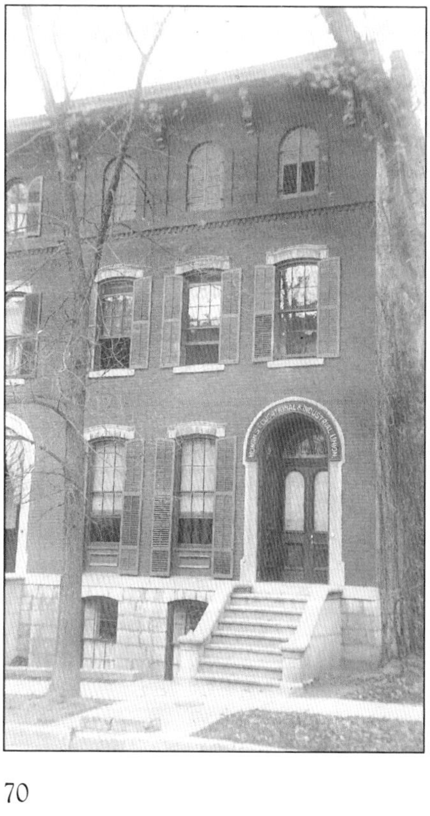

WOMAN'S EDUCATIONAL AND INDUSTRIAL UNION, 16 WILLIAM STREET, 1890s. The WEIU was founded in 1882 to benefit Auburn's working women.

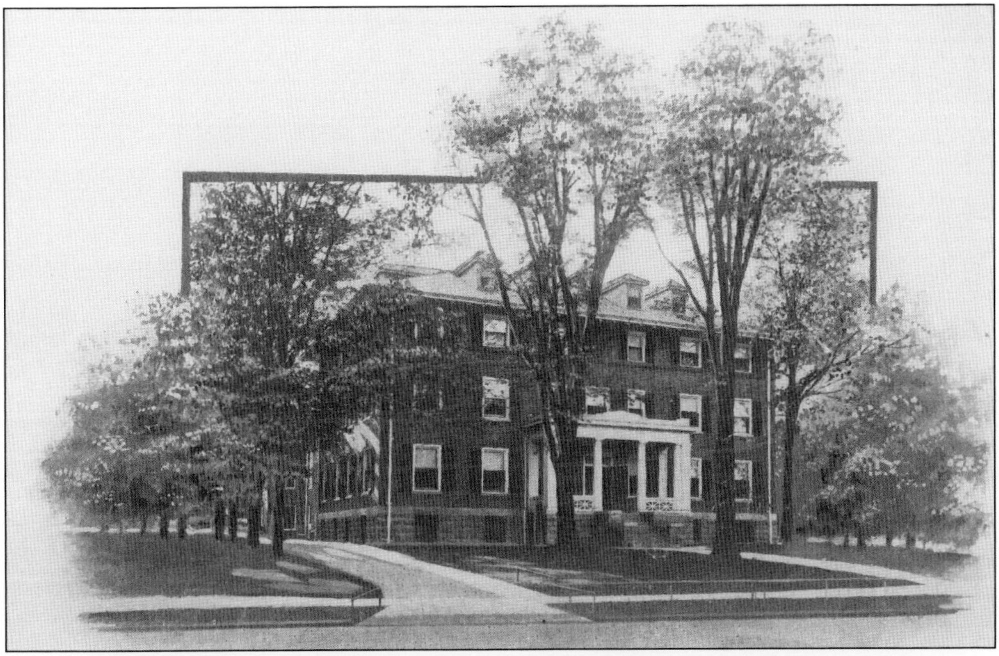

Woman's Educational and Industrial Union, South Street, c. 1907. This grand structure, built with funds from Eliza W. Osborne, featured electricity and other modern conveniences when it opened in 1907.

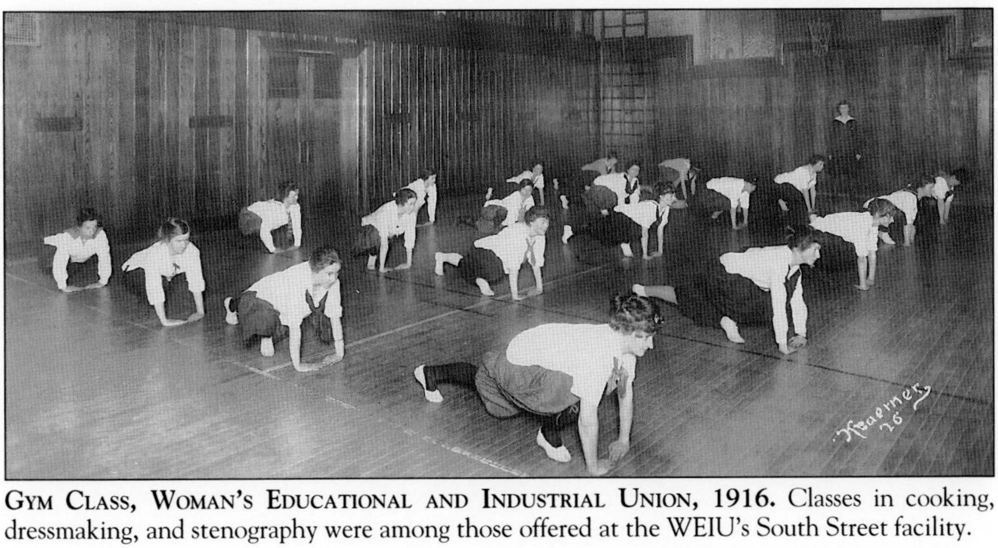

Gym Class, Woman's Educational and Industrial Union, 1916. Classes in cooking, dressmaking, and stenography were among those offered at the WEIU's South Street facility.

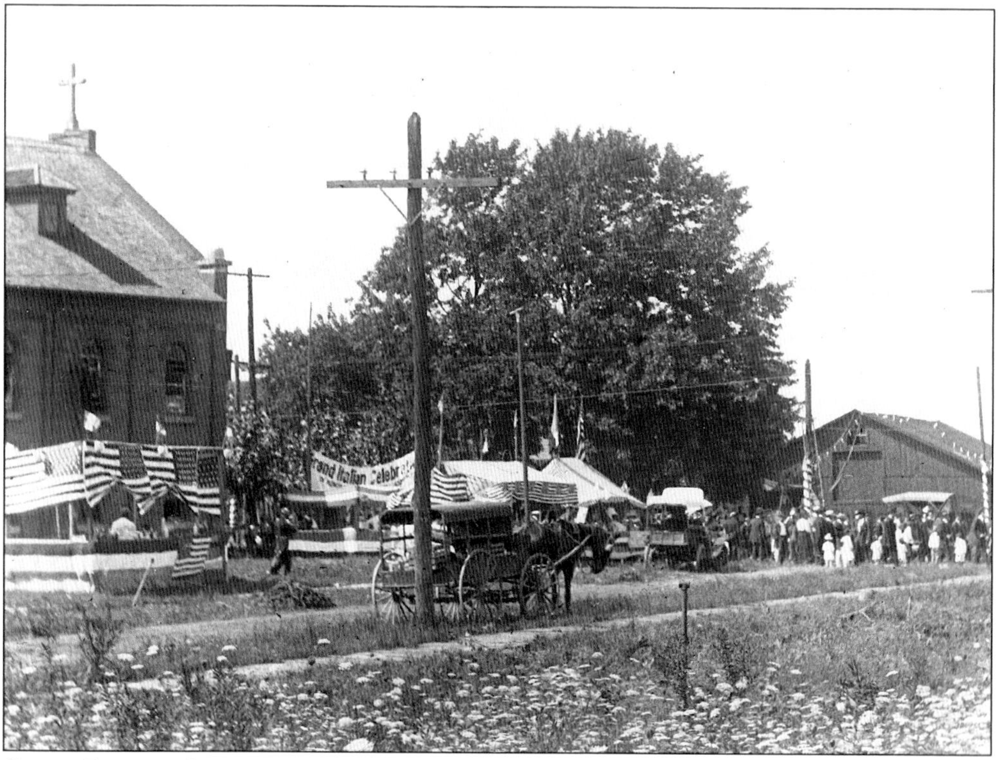

GRAND ITALIAN CELEBRATION, GROUNDS OF ST. FRANCIS ROMAN CATHOLIC CHURCH, 1910. Immigrants arriving in Auburn found plentiful employment opportunities in a sometimes-strange land. The contrast between maintaining cultural connections and assimilating into a new society is evident in flags, banners, and the nature of this celebration.

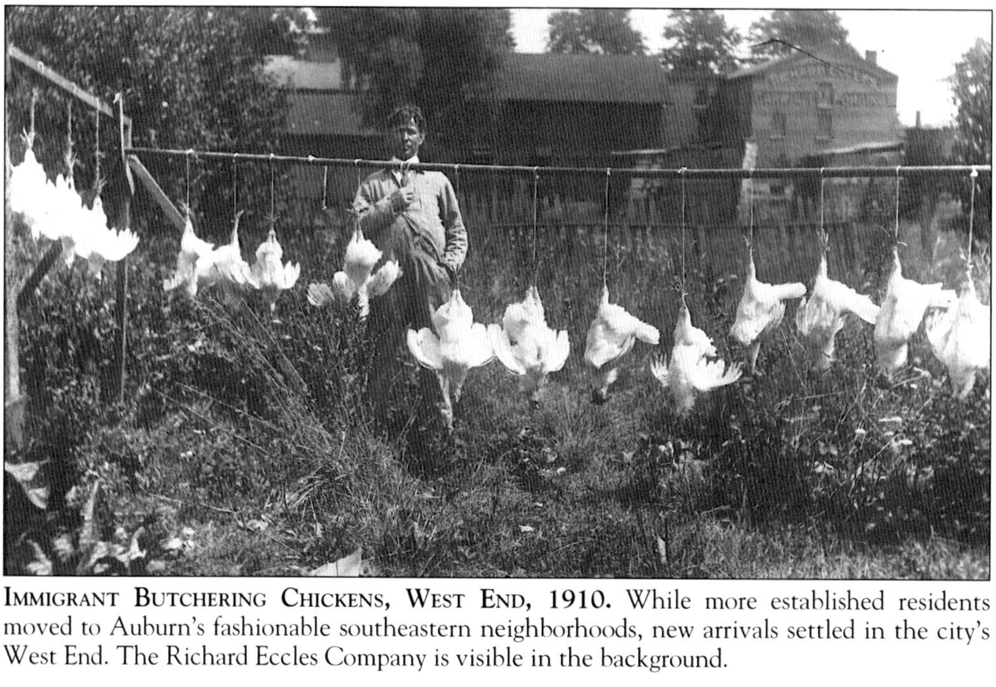

IMMIGRANT BUTCHERING CHICKENS, WEST END, 1910. While more established residents moved to Auburn's fashionable southeastern neighborhoods, new arrivals settled in the city's West End. The Richard Eccles Company is visible in the background.

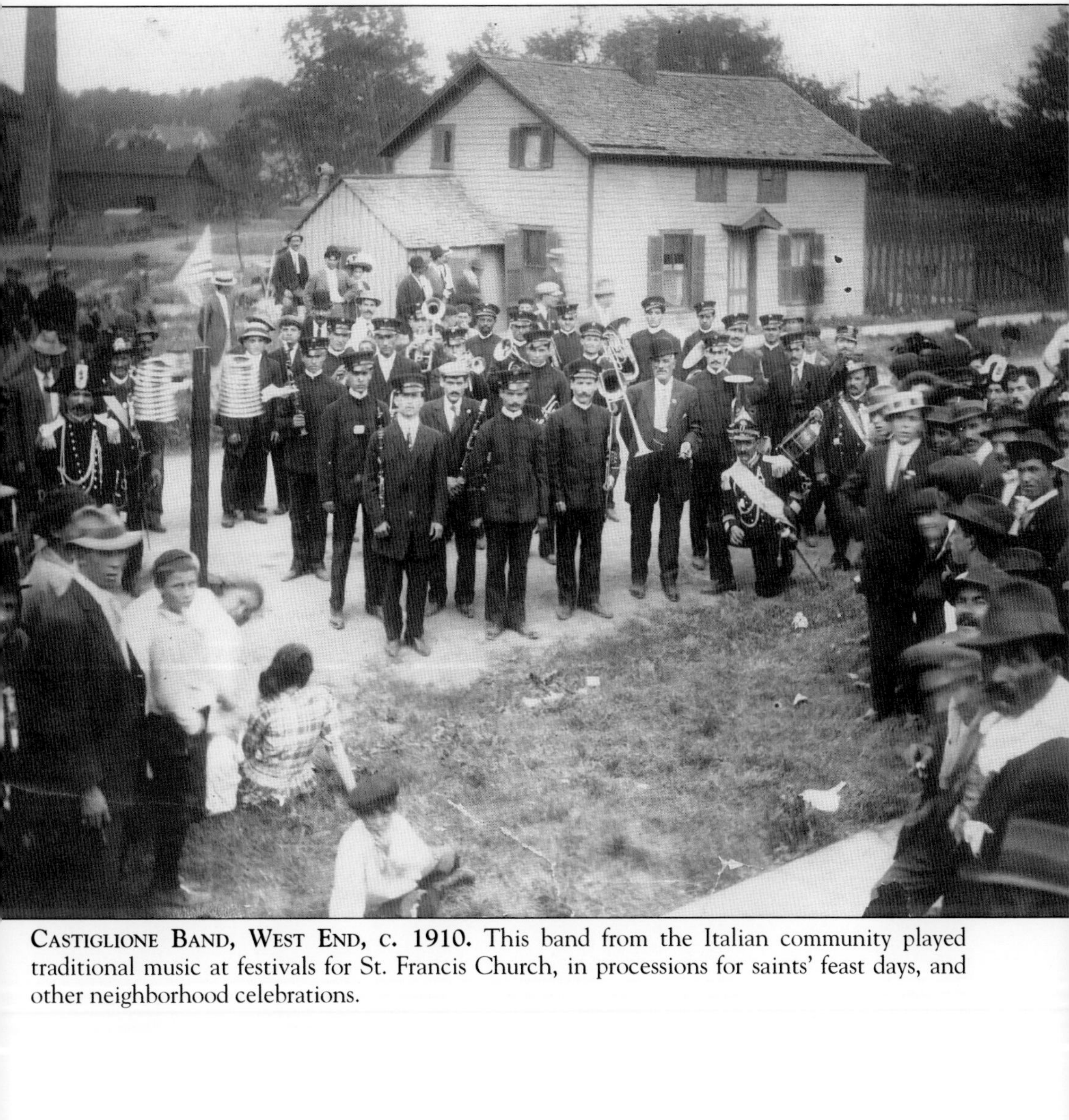

Castiglione Band, West End, c. 1910. This band from the Italian community played traditional music at festivals for St. Francis Church, in processions for saints' feast days, and other neighborhood celebrations.

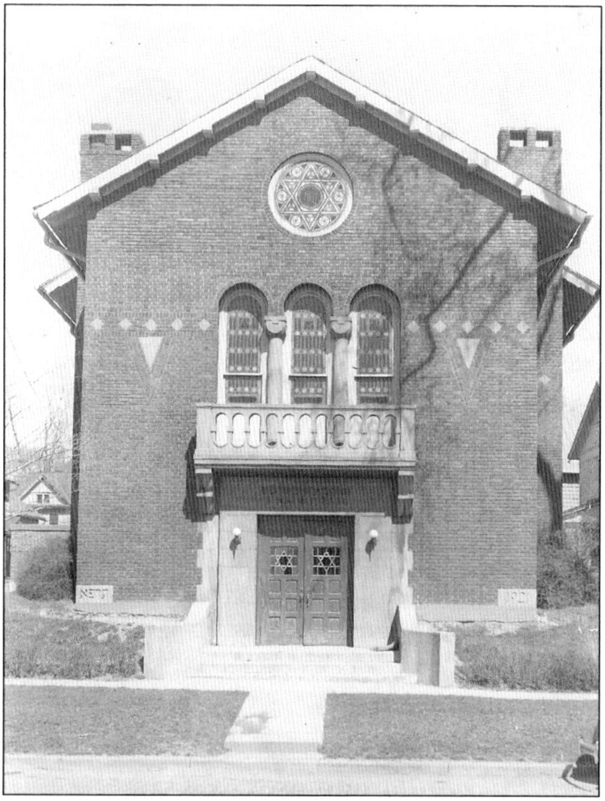

B'Nai Israel Synagogue, 18 Seminary Avenue. Jewish immigrants began settling in Auburn by the 1870s, and Congregation B'Nai Israel was formed in 1903. Built in 1921, this synagogue was used by the congregation until a new structure opened in 1975 on John Smith Avenue.

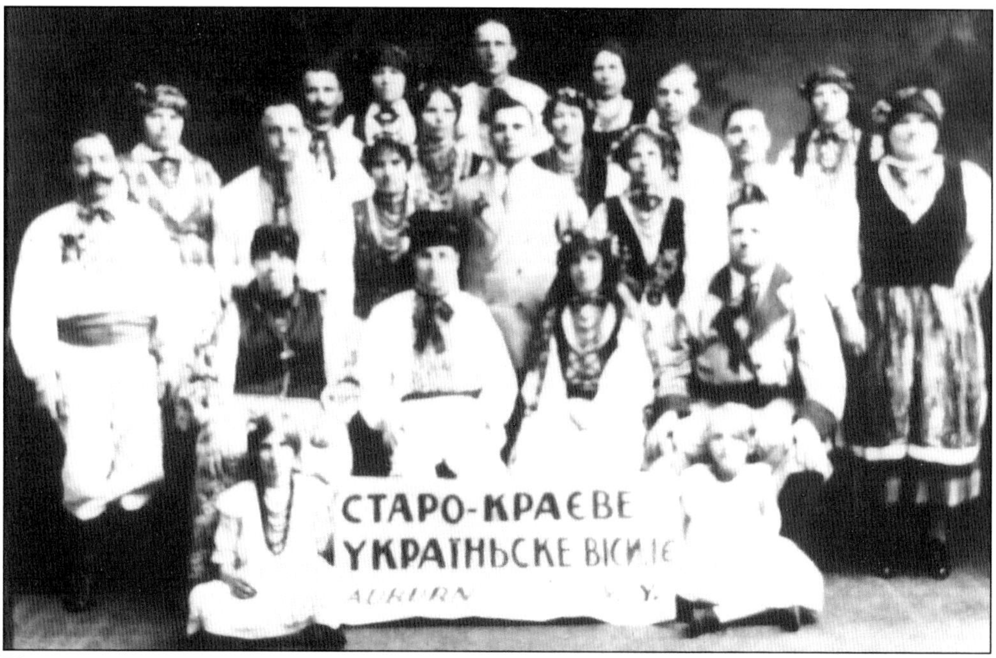

Ukrainian Wedding Portrait, Traditional Dress, Early Twentieth Century. Pride in ethnic origins, and determination to maintain connections to those origins, is evident in this group portrait.

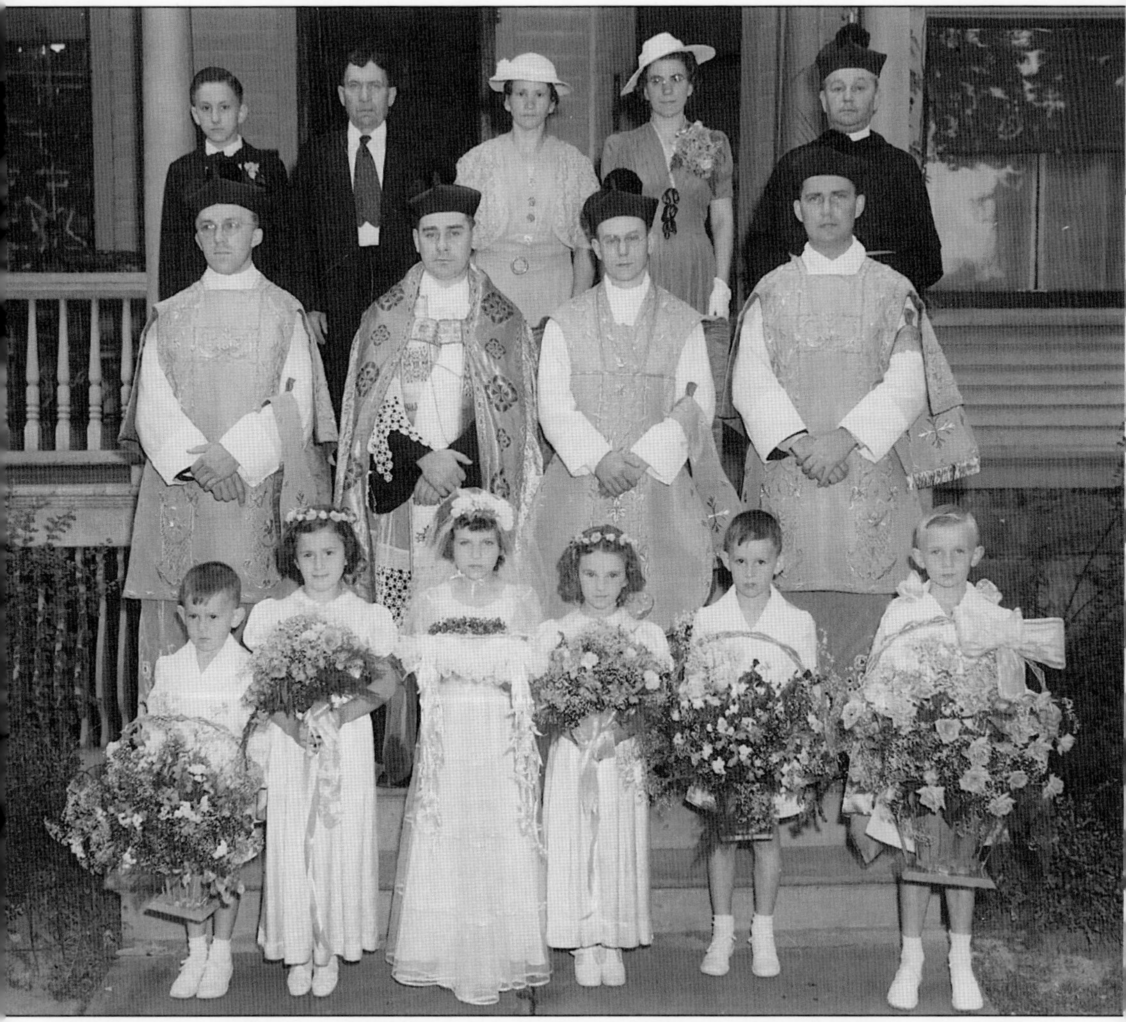

Celebration of Father Sixtus Wawrzaszek's First Mass at St. Hyacinth's Roman Catholic Church, July 23, 1939. Religious ceremonies and events played an integral role in the lives of many local residents. The character and strength of the ethnic communities remain vibrant to this day. Auburn native Father Wawrzaszek is second from right, second row.

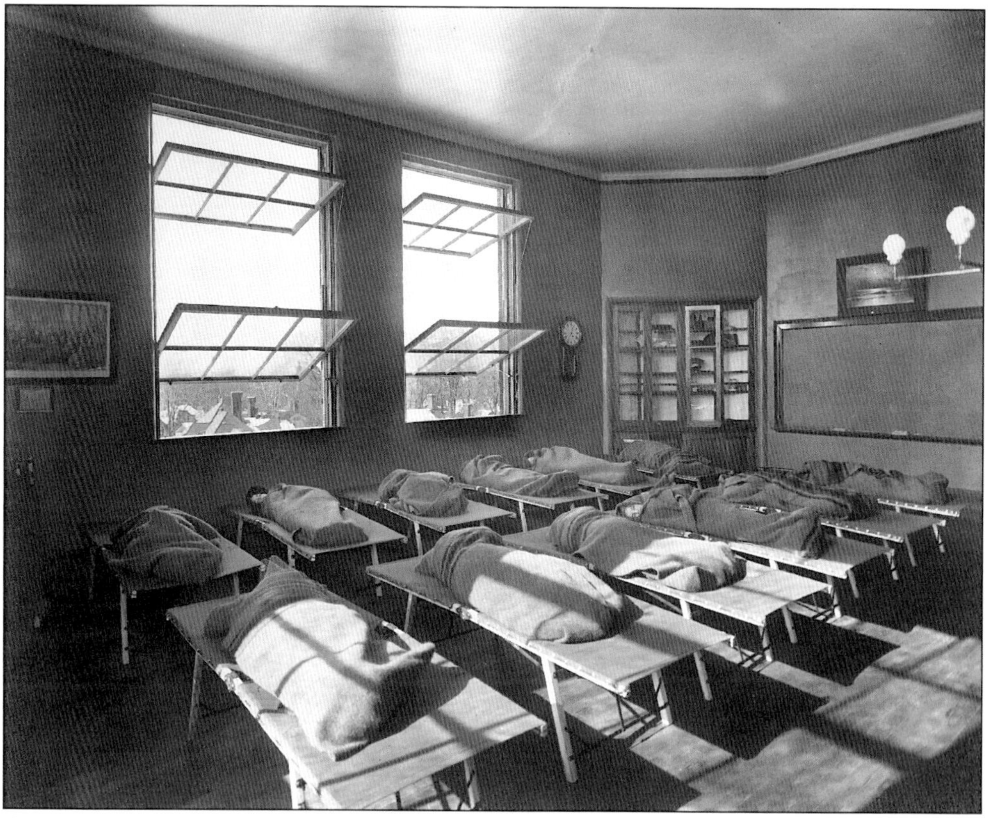

OPEN AIR CLASSROOM, SLEEPING QUARTERS, FULTON STREET SCHOOL, 1914. Red Cross Seals and the WEIU sponsored this experimental program. Breathing cold, fresh air was believed beneficial in the age of tuberculosis.

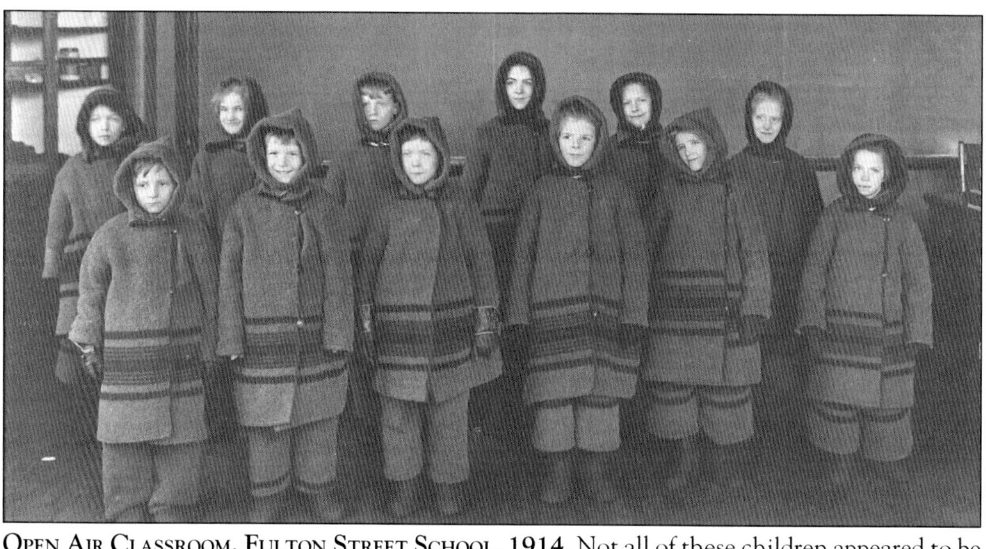

OPEN AIR CLASSROOM, FULTON STREET SCHOOL, 1914. Not all of these children appeared to be enjoying the experience. Their wool coats were made from blankets manufactured at Auburn Prison.

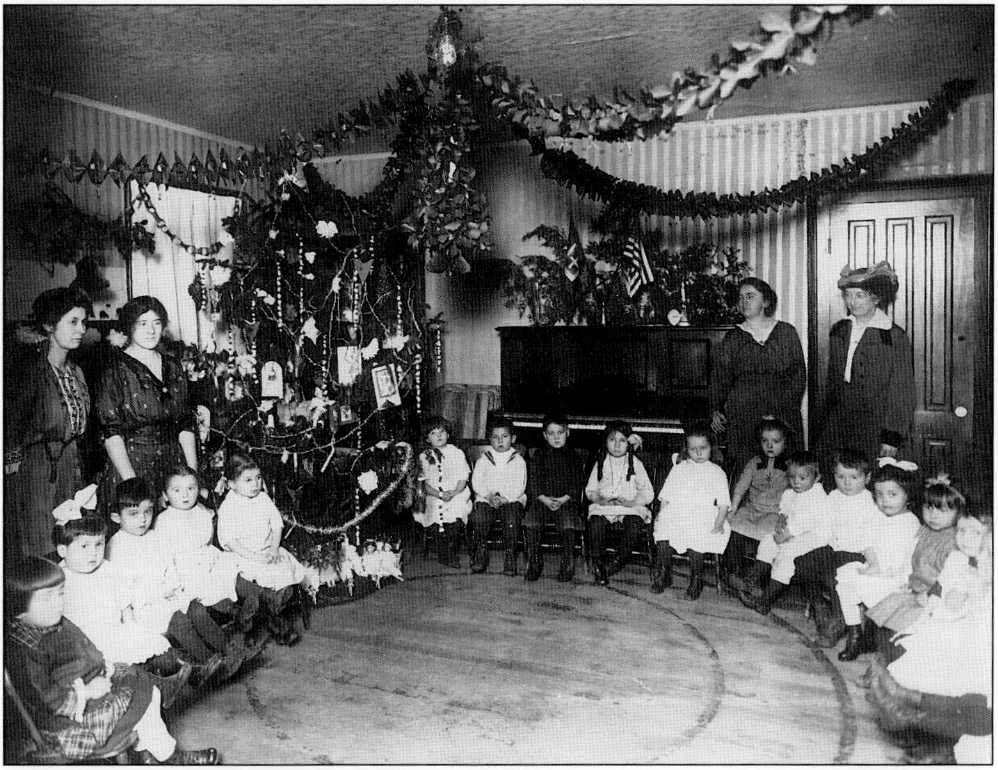

Day Nursery, Woman's Educational and Industrial Union, c. 1915. For many women working outside the home, whether they were native Auburnians or new immigrants, caring for their children was a pressing concern.

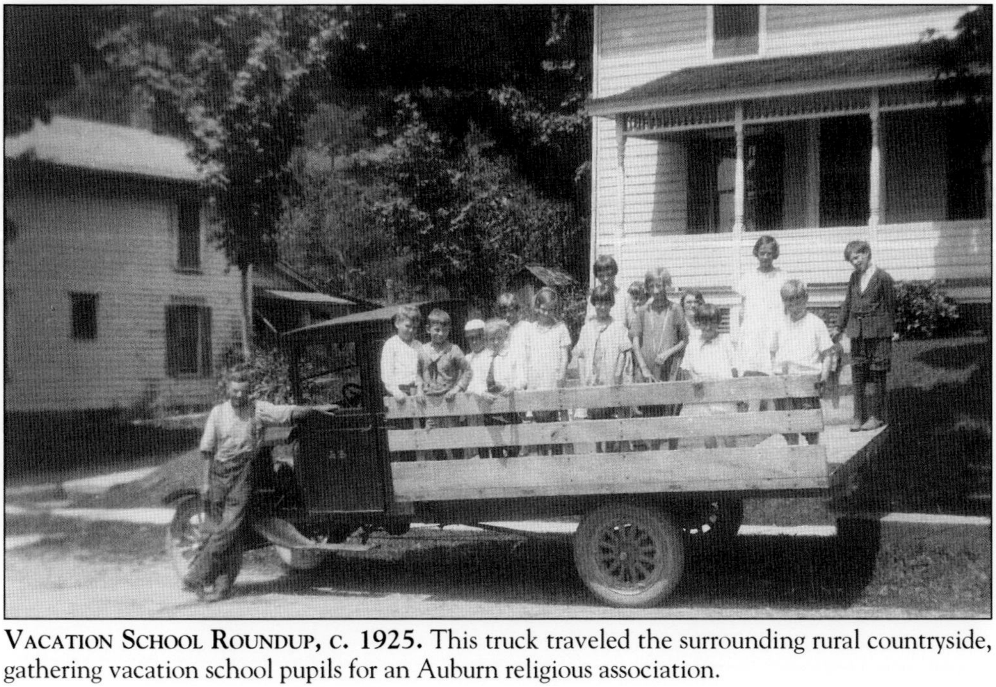

Vacation School Roundup, c. 1925. This truck traveled the surrounding rural countryside, gathering vacation school pupils for an Auburn religious association.

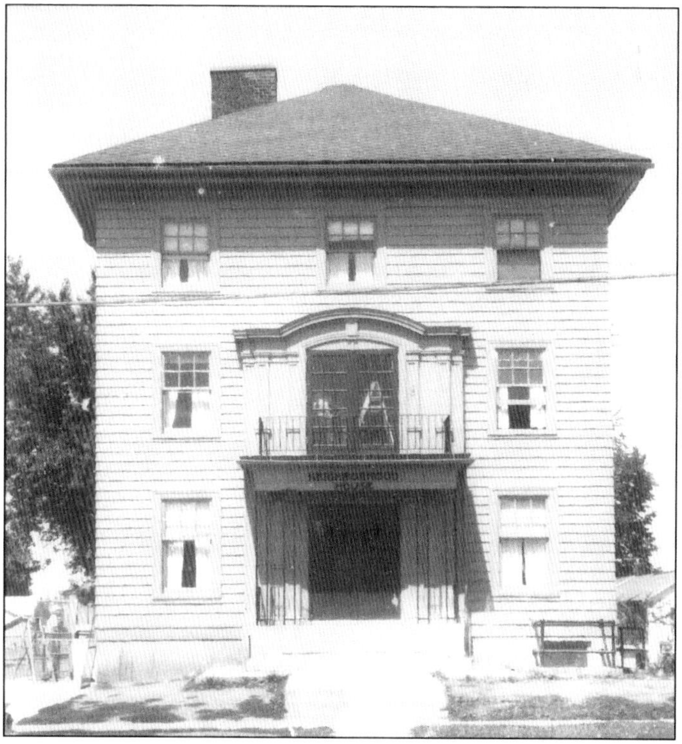

NEIGHBORHOOD HOUSE, 77 WALL STREET, 1960S. Neighborhood House began as a settlement facility for immigrant populations in the West End. It later became a popular community center, and a new facility still serves in that role today.

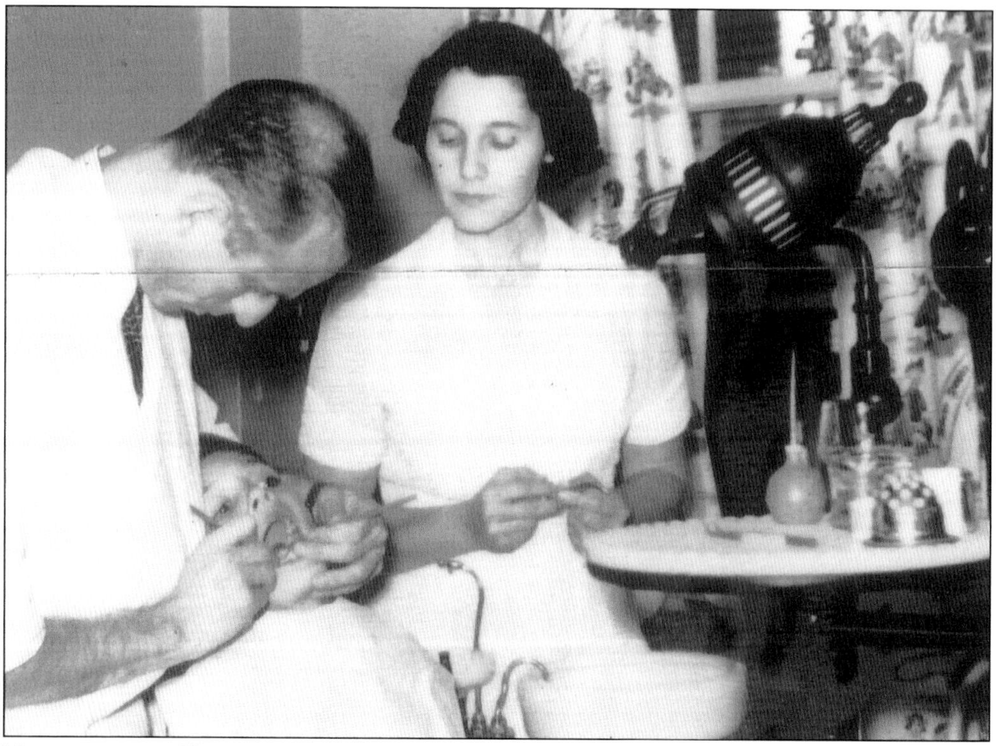

NEIGHBORHOOD HOUSE DENTAL CLINIC, C. 1940. One of the most common memories of Neighborhood House was a trip to the dental clinic, where a tooth could be pulled for 50¢.

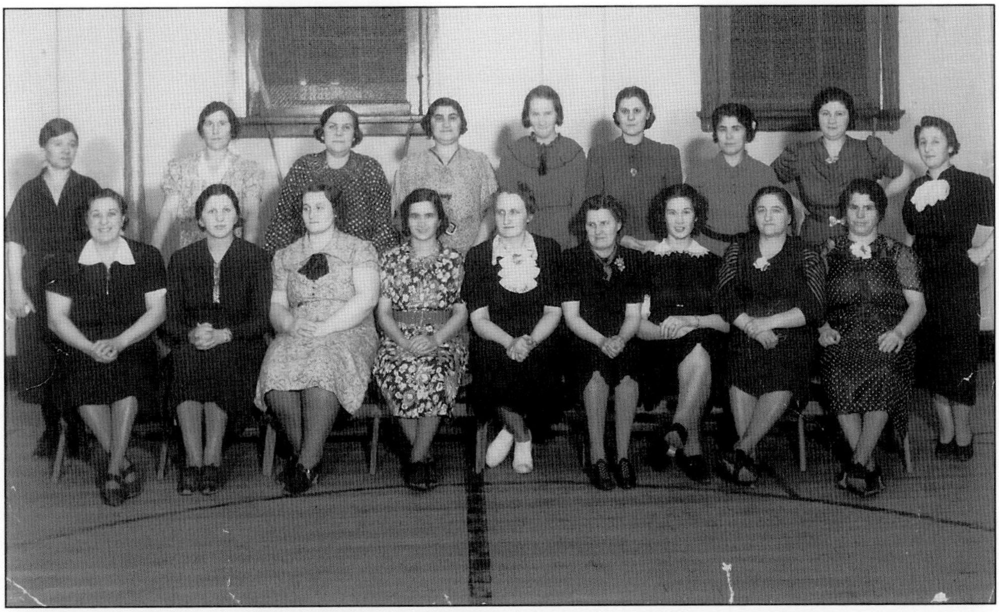

SEWING CLUB, NEIGHBORHOOD HOUSE, 1940.

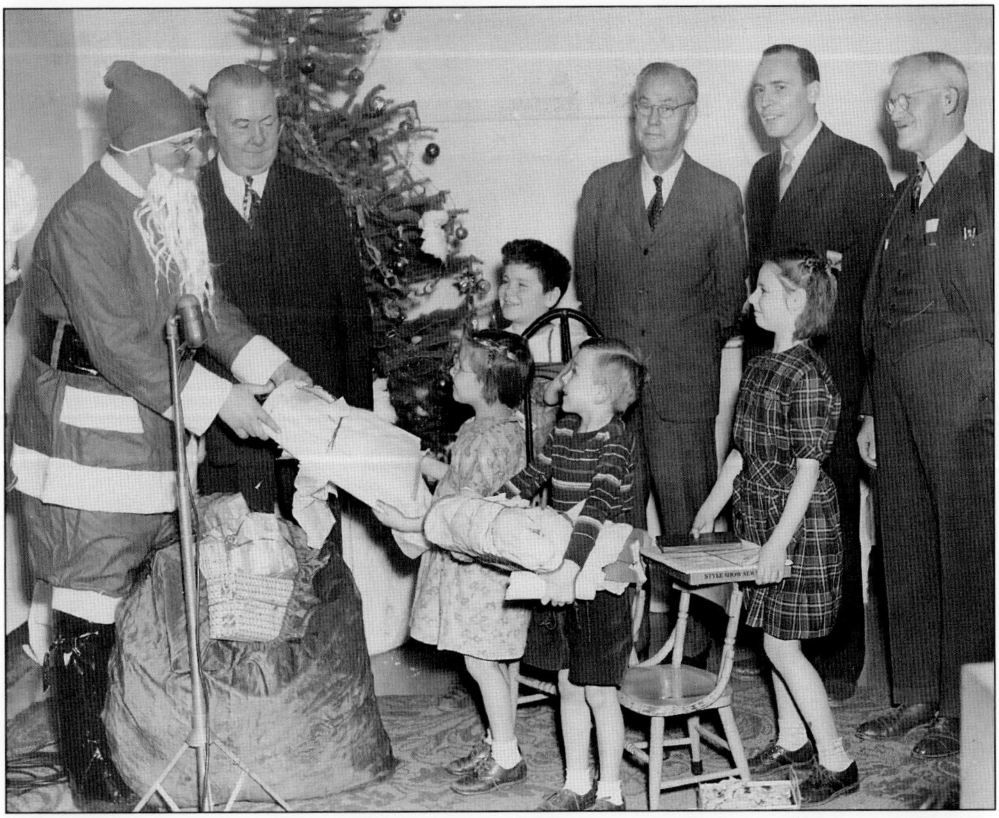

CHRISTMAS GIVING, C. 1940. Children looked to Santa in anticipation. The man at far right was Dr. George Sincerbeaux, who worked in the health clinic in Neighborhood House for many years.

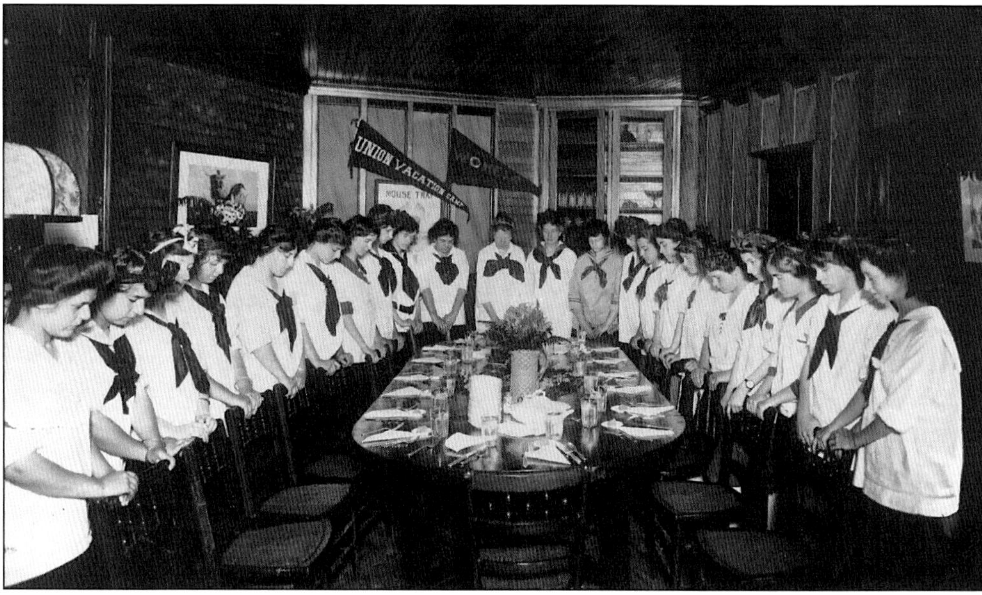

SAYING GRACE, UNION VACATION CAMP AT EDGEWATER, C. 1911. These young women said grace before a meal in the dining room at Edgewater, which was run by the WEIU. Edgewater began as a vacation camp for working women, and later served as a Girl Scout camp and a health camp for undernourished children.

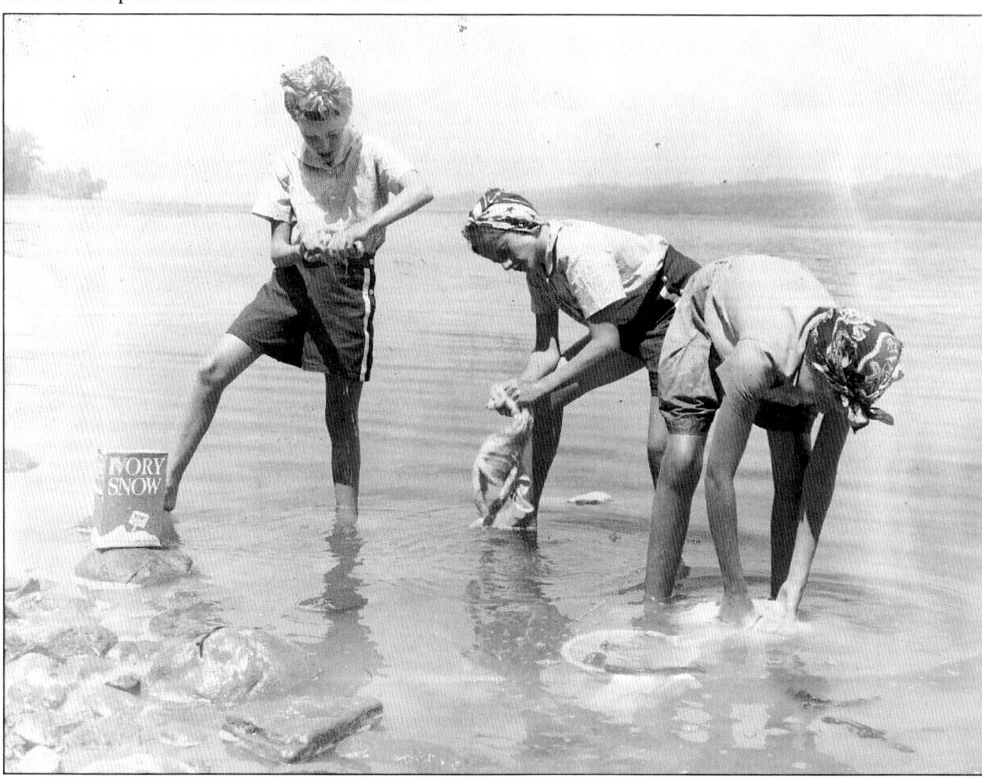

WASH DAY, CAYUGA COUNTY GIRL SCOUTS AT CAMP EDGEWATER, 1941. A trip to Edgewater each August was a tradition for many local Girl Scouts.

Six

Community, Culture, and Celebration

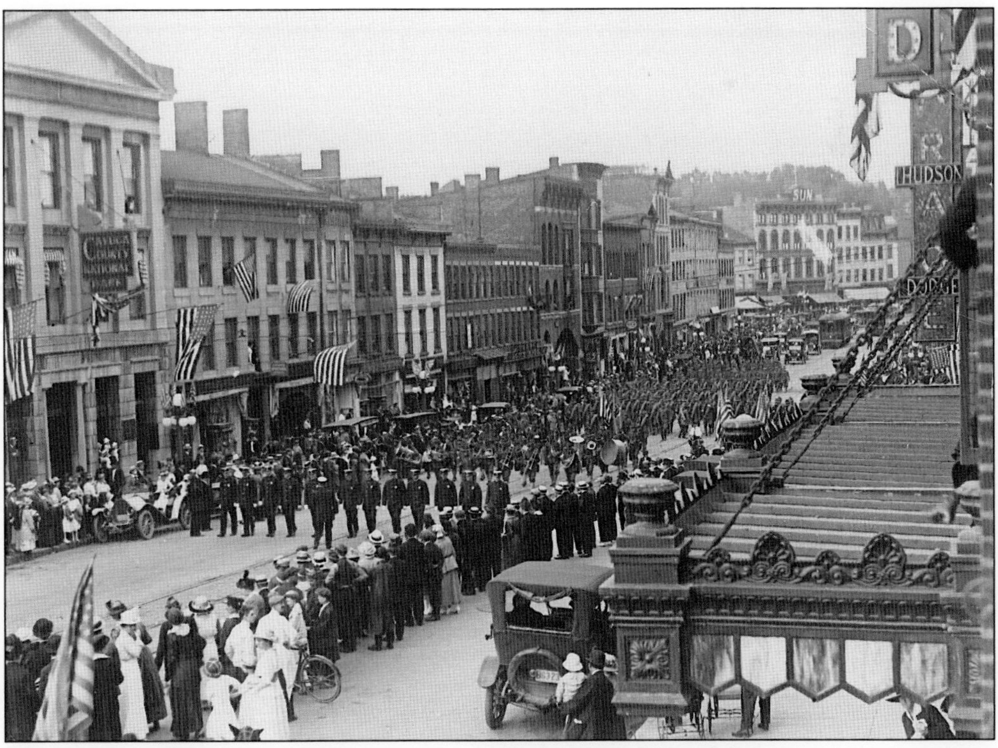

Parade, Genesee Street, 1920s. Crowds gathered to enjoy the celebration.

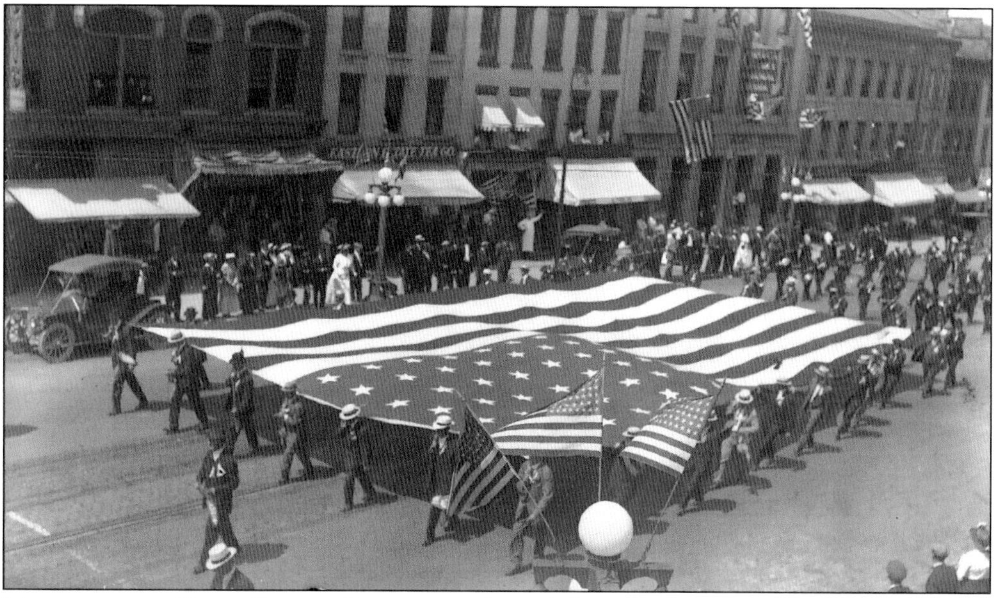

UNFURLING THE FLAG, GENESEE STREET, c. 1900. Auburnians have always displayed pride in their community and country.

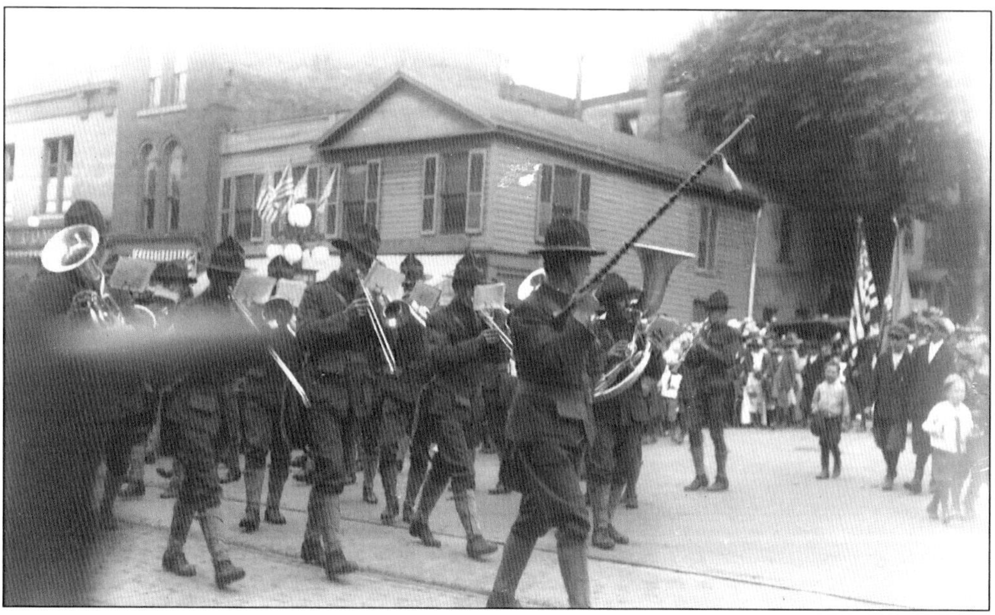

HORNS UP, 1915–1917. Music plays a prominent role in celebration. The Company M band and Drum Major Hall led the way in this gathering. Many of the men also belonged to the Wheeler Rifles.

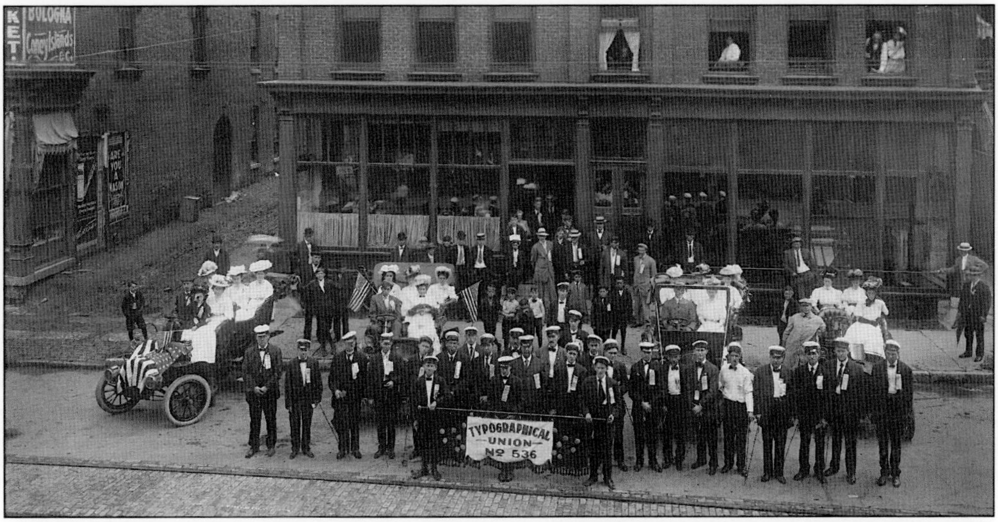

Typographical Union Number 536, 1909. Organized in 1902, the group met monthly in the Catholic Mutual Benefit Association Hall on Franklin Street.

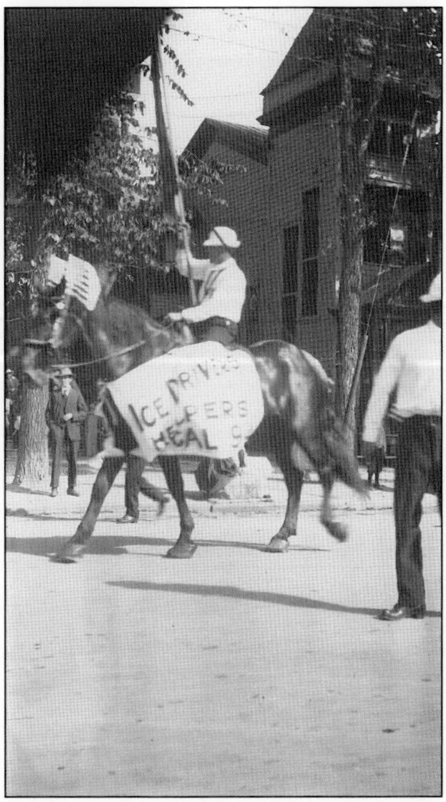

Ice Drivers Local Rider, Early Twentieth Century. Parade participants ran the gamut from large floats and displays to a single man on horseback.

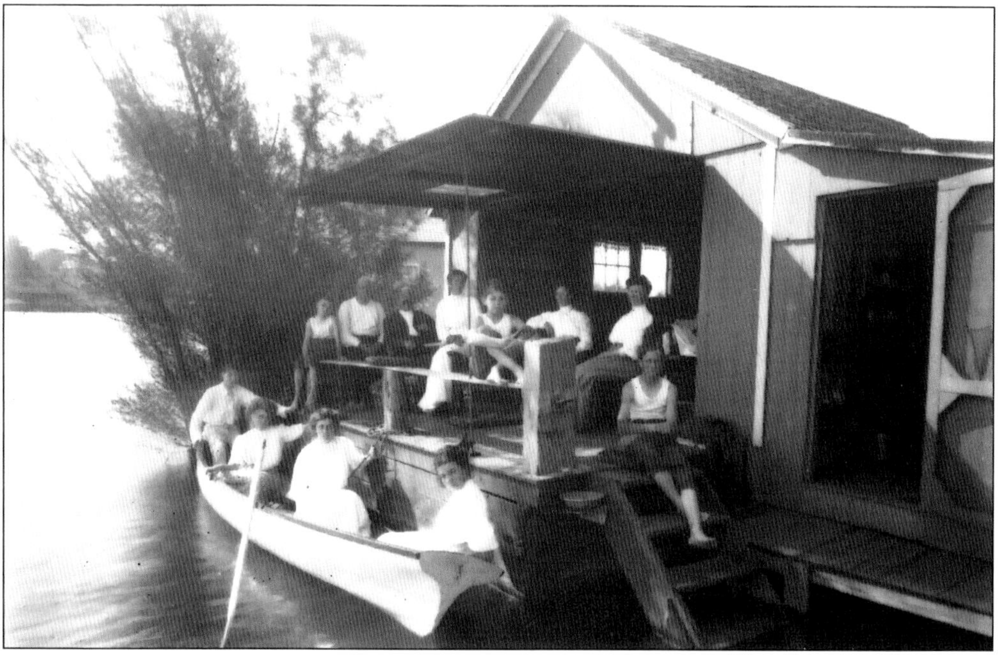

Boat House along Owasco Outlet, c. 1900.

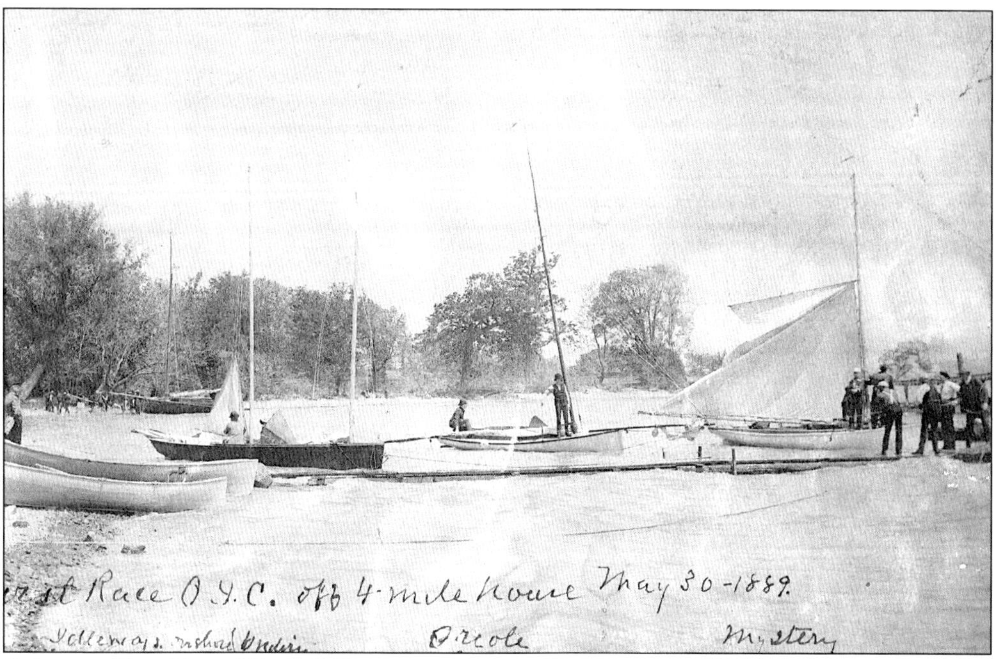

"May the Best Boat Win," Owasco Lake, 1889. Participants paused for a portrait before the first race of the Owasco Yacht Club off Four-Mile House on May 30, 1889.

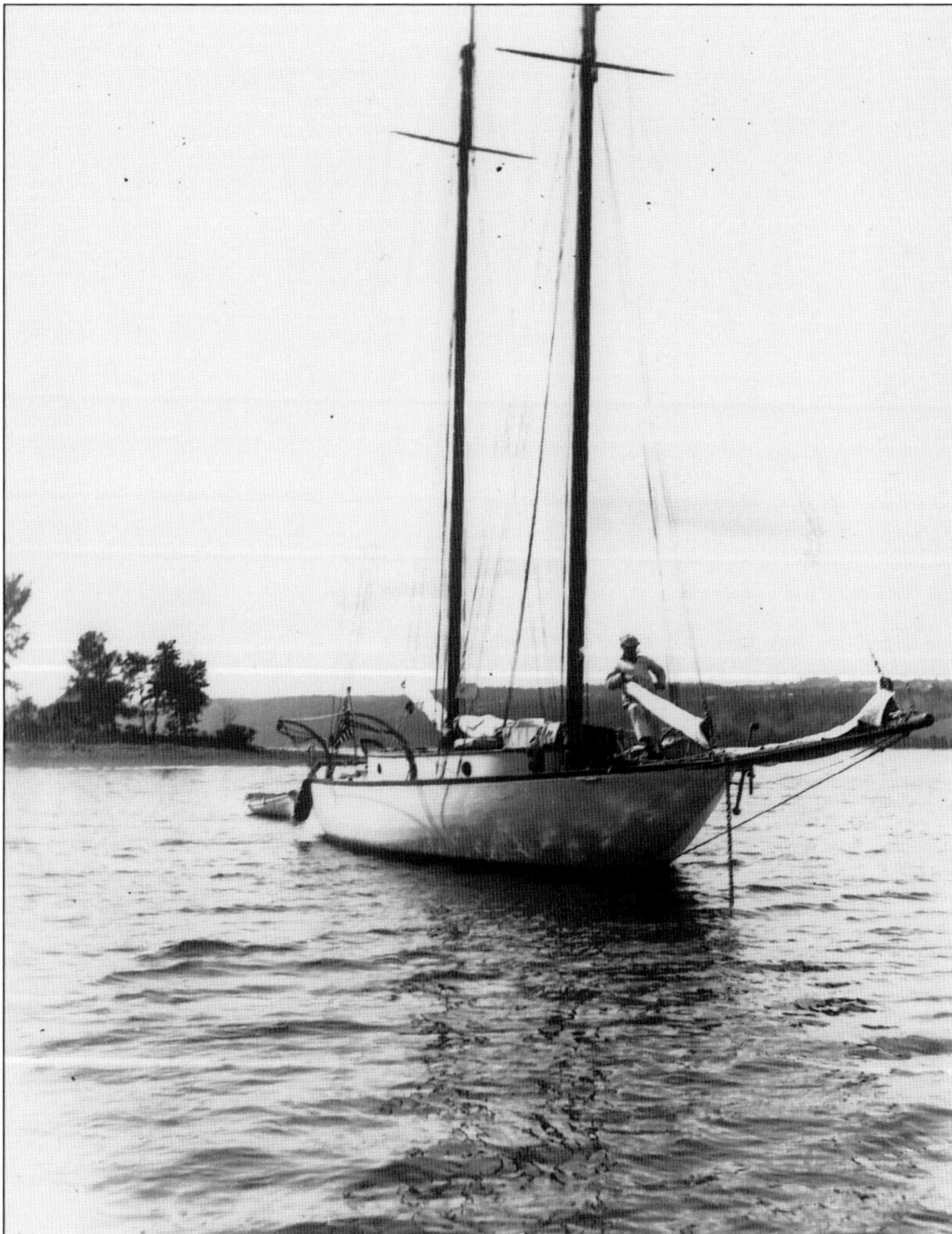

OUANANICHE UNDER ANCHOR, C. 1890. F.T. Peet, a member of the Dolphin Point Association, captained this double-masted schooner, with a name that meant "landlocked salmon." Peet later belonged to the Owasco Yacht Club. Equipment on this 50-foot-long boat included a saluting cannon.

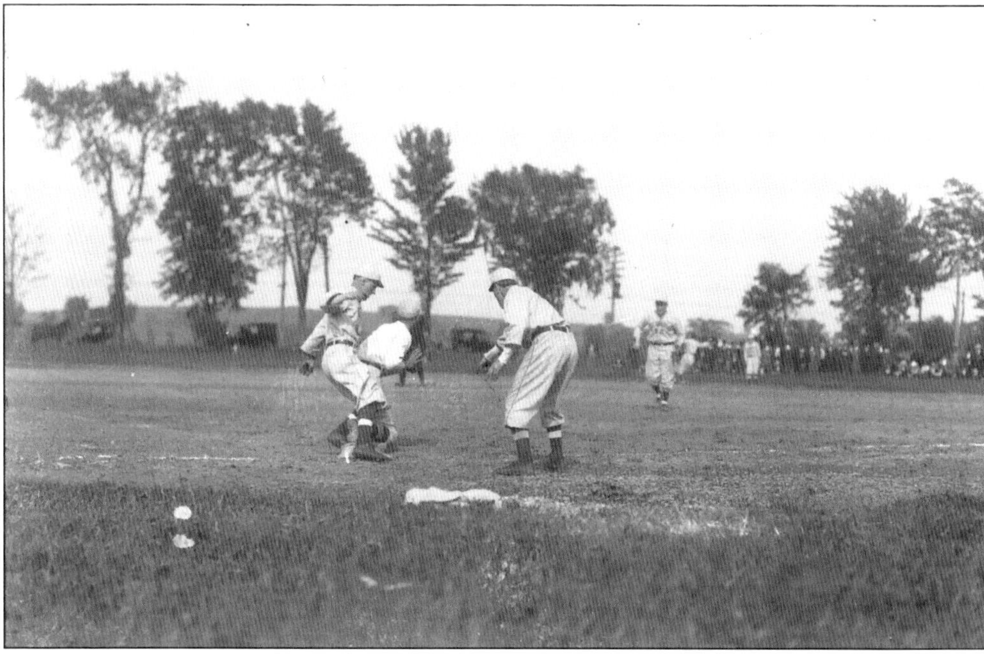

Quick Play at Third, 4 p.m., June 1916. Amateur photographer C.J. Heiser captured the action of a ballgame in progress at Norwood Park.

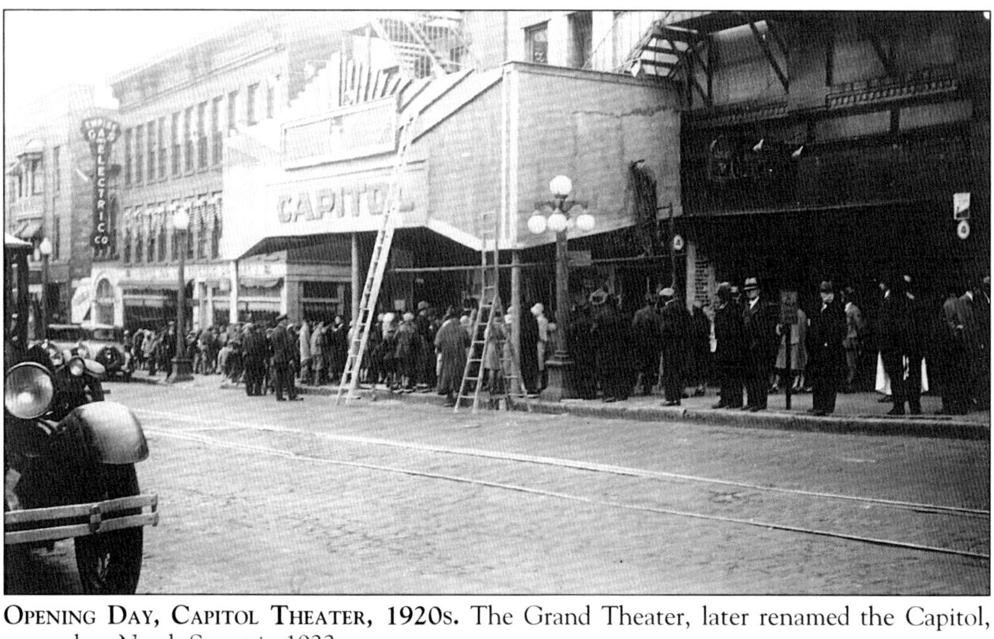

Opening Day, Capitol Theater, 1920s. The Grand Theater, later renamed the Capitol, opened on North Street in 1922.

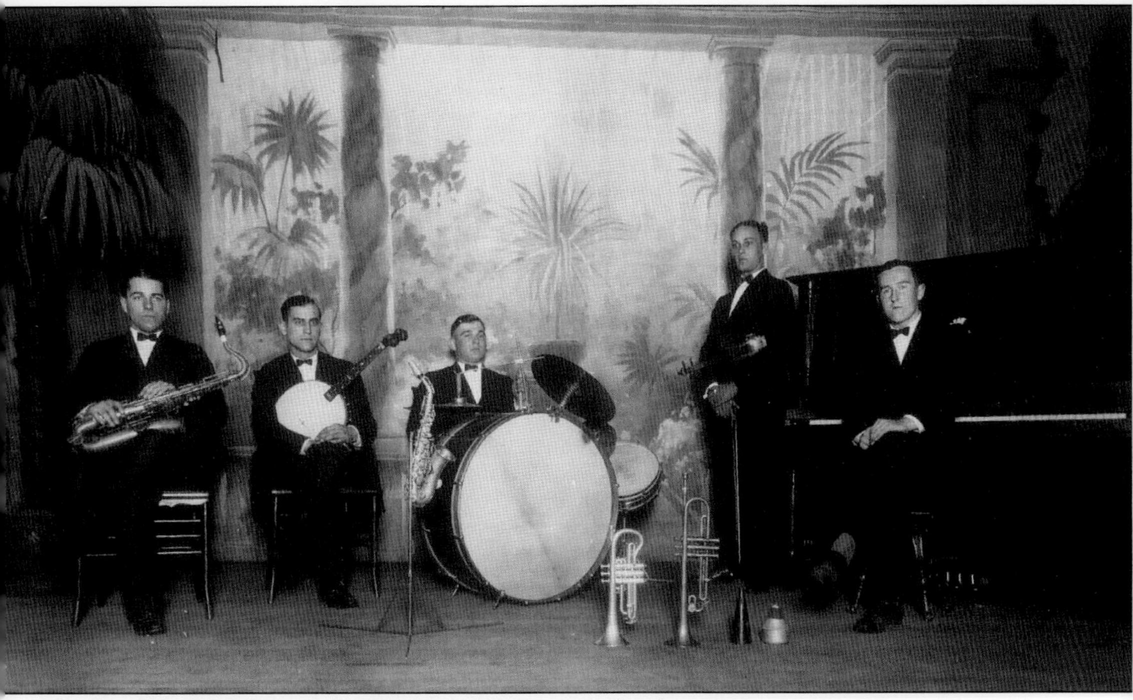

"And the Band Played On," 1926. Freddie Laxton's band is on stage in the carriage house of the Willard/Case estate at 203 Genesee Street. The band played for several of inventor Theodore Case's test films in the 1920s. Musicians included Bill Sullivan on piano, Hank Steigerwald on trumpet and violin, Carl Smith on drums, an unidentified banjo player, and Freddie Laxton on sax (Laxton also served as the vocalist).

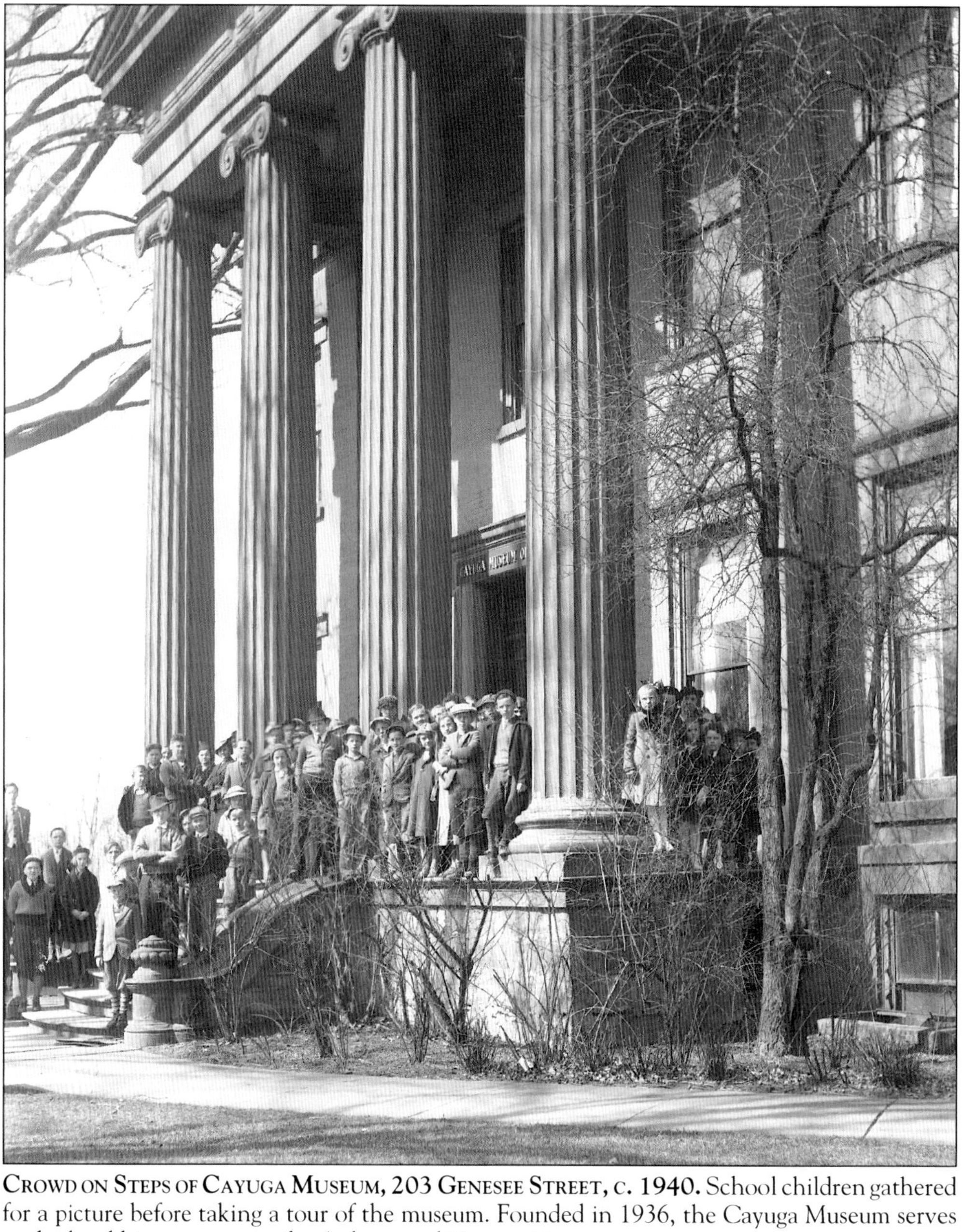

CROWD ON STEPS OF CAYUGA MUSEUM, 203 GENESEE STREET, C. 1940. School children gathered for a picture before taking a tour of the museum. Founded in 1936, the Cayuga Museum serves as the local history museum for Auburn and Cayuga County.

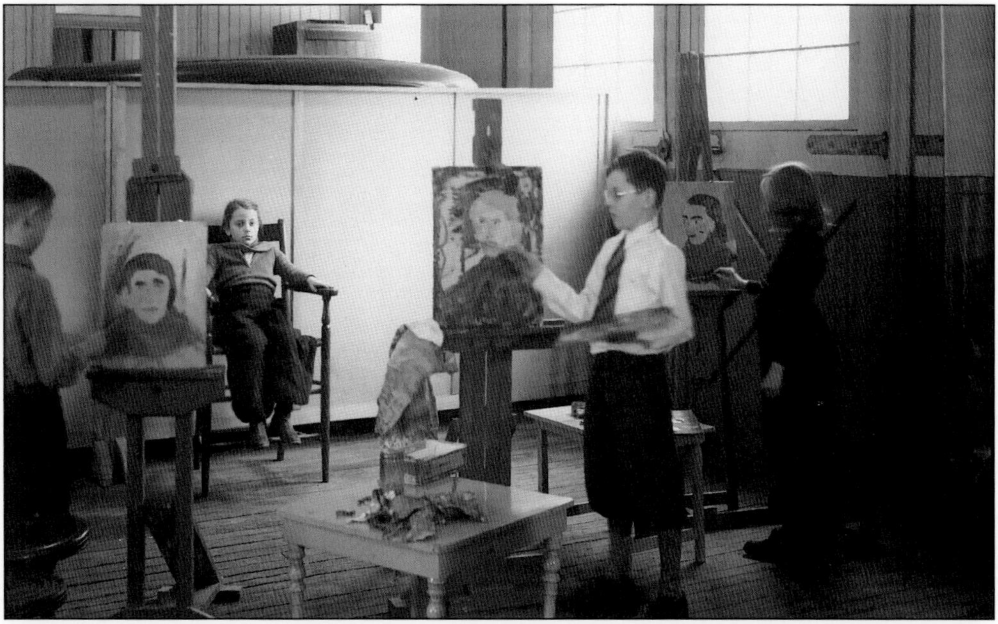

PAINTING CLASS, CAYUGA MUSEUM, C. 1940. Students tried their hand at portraiture. The model for this lesson did not seem particularly happy.

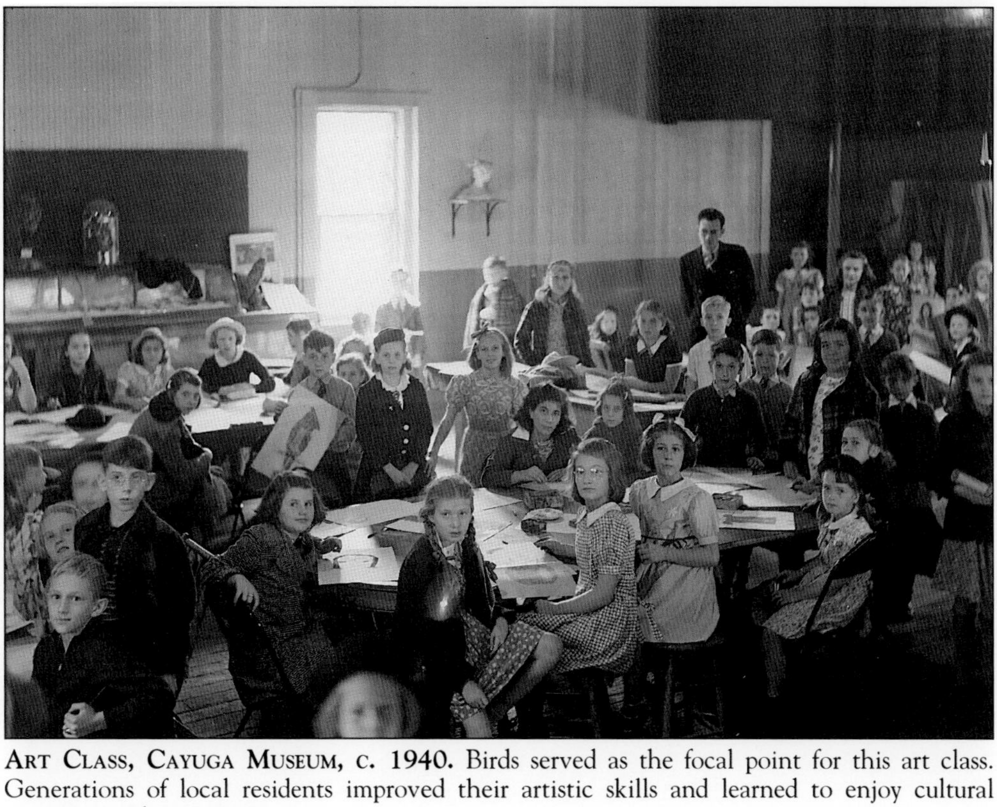

ART CLASS, CAYUGA MUSEUM, C. 1940. Birds served as the focal point for this art class. Generations of local residents improved their artistic skills and learned to enjoy cultural activities at the museum.

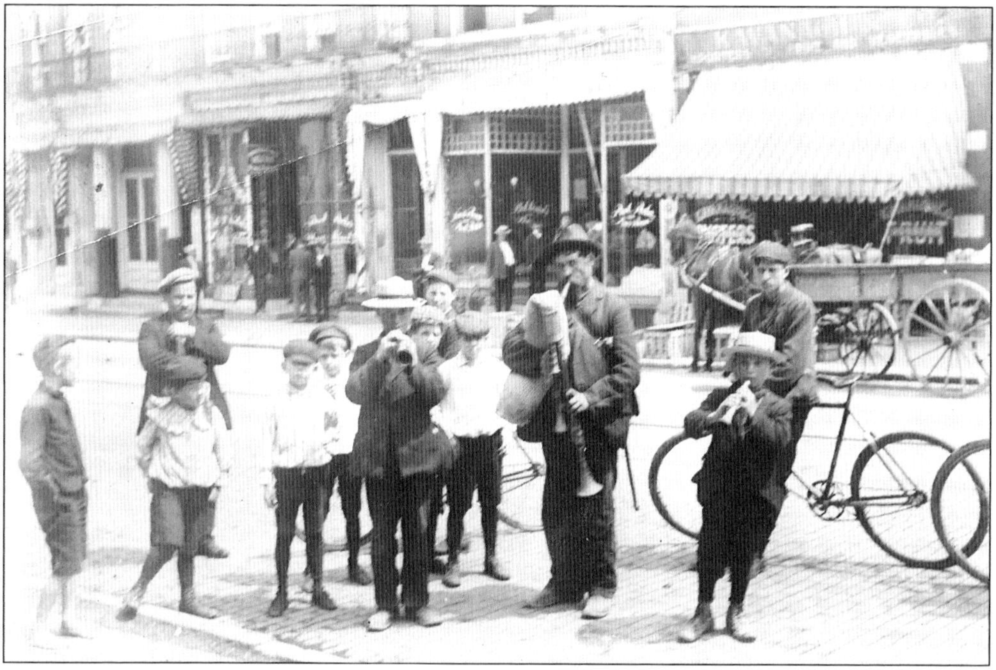

Impromptu Orchestra, Dill Street, Early Twentieth Century. These unidentified street musicians played in front of Kavanagh and Company, a fruit and vegetable dealer on Dill Street in the 1910s.

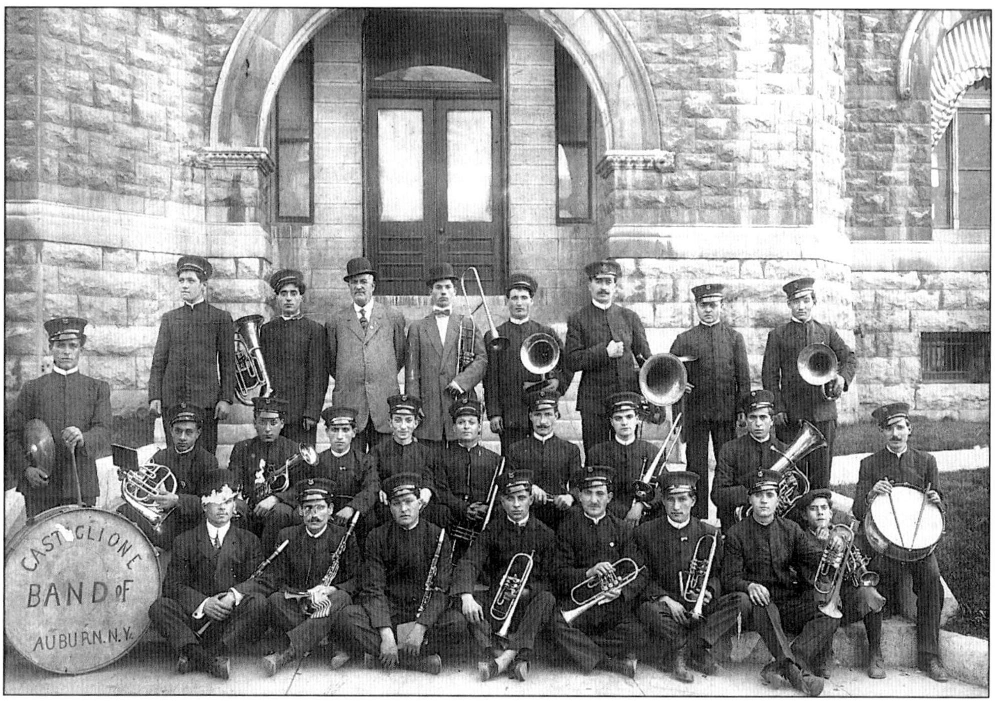

Castiglione Band, Steps of Post Office, 1910s. The Italian community band posed for a formal portrait. Players included Genaro (James) Gatto on tuba, third from right on top row; and Joseph Di Stefano on cornet, second from right in front row.

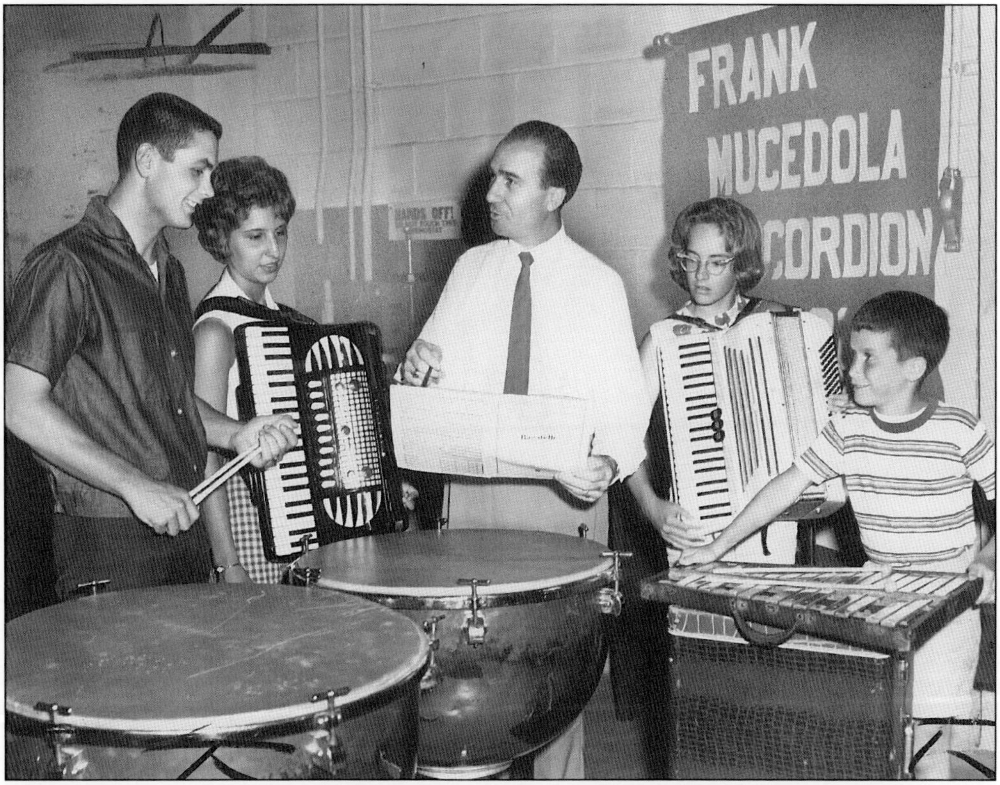

FRANK MUCEDOLA ACCORDION SCHOOL, 1950S. Mucedola, a noted accordion artist and member of the Mantovani Orchestra, has entertained and educated generations of Auburn residents.

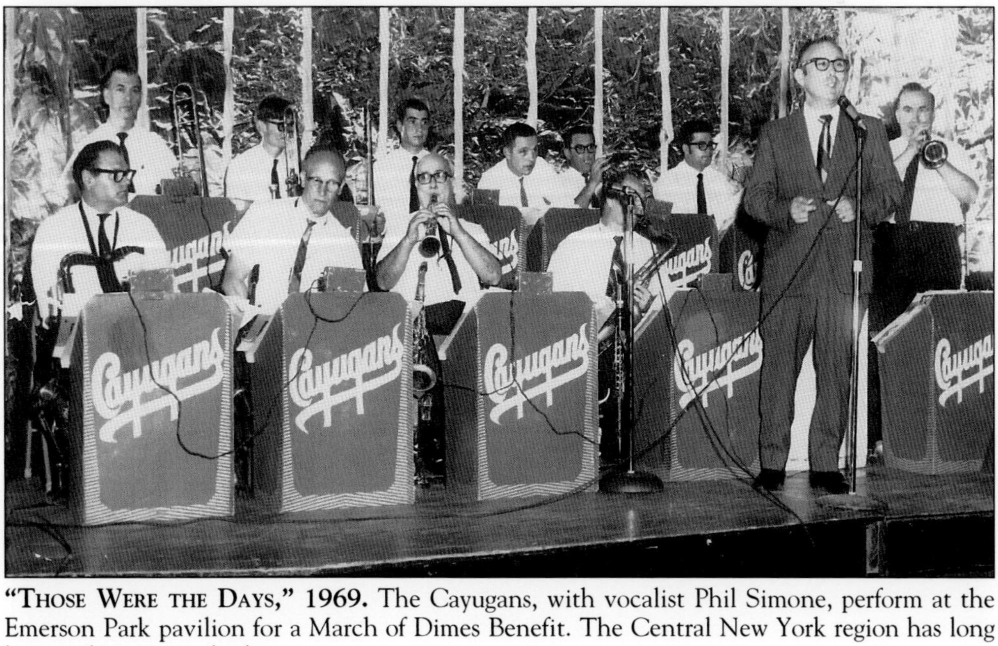

"THOSE WERE THE DAYS," 1969. The Cayugans, with vocalist Phil Simone, perform at the Emerson Park pavilion for a March of Dimes Benefit. The Central New York region has long been rich in musical talent.

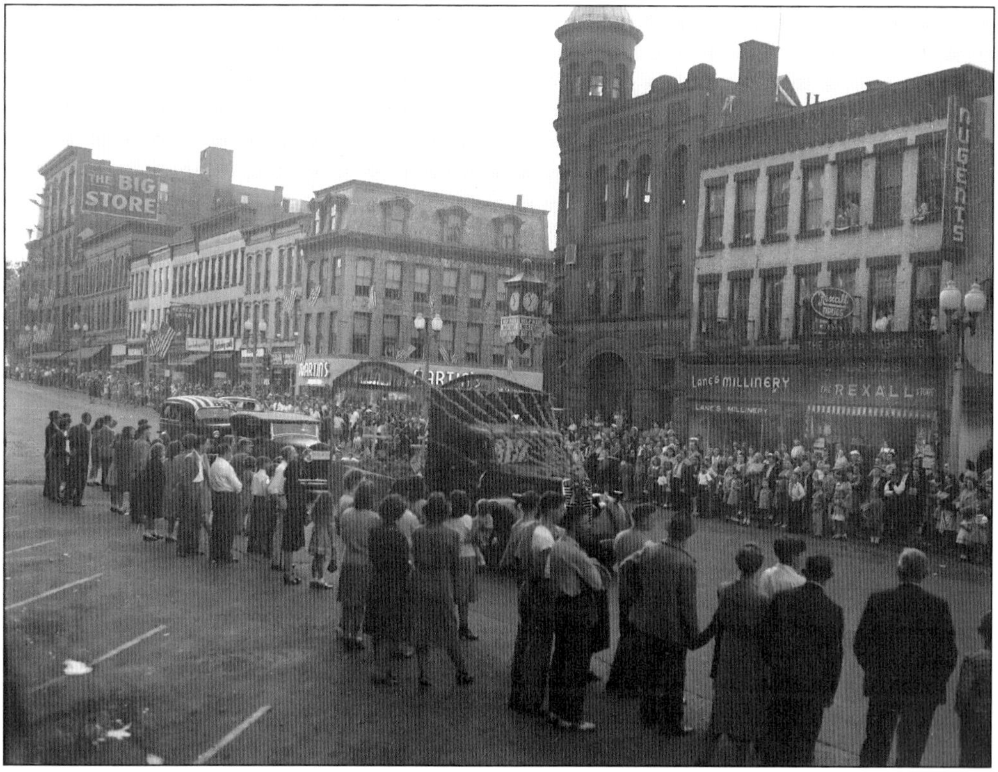

ARMISTICE DAY VICTORY PARADE, GENESEE STREET, 1945. All facets of the community came together to celebrate local dedication to the war effort and the end of WW II.

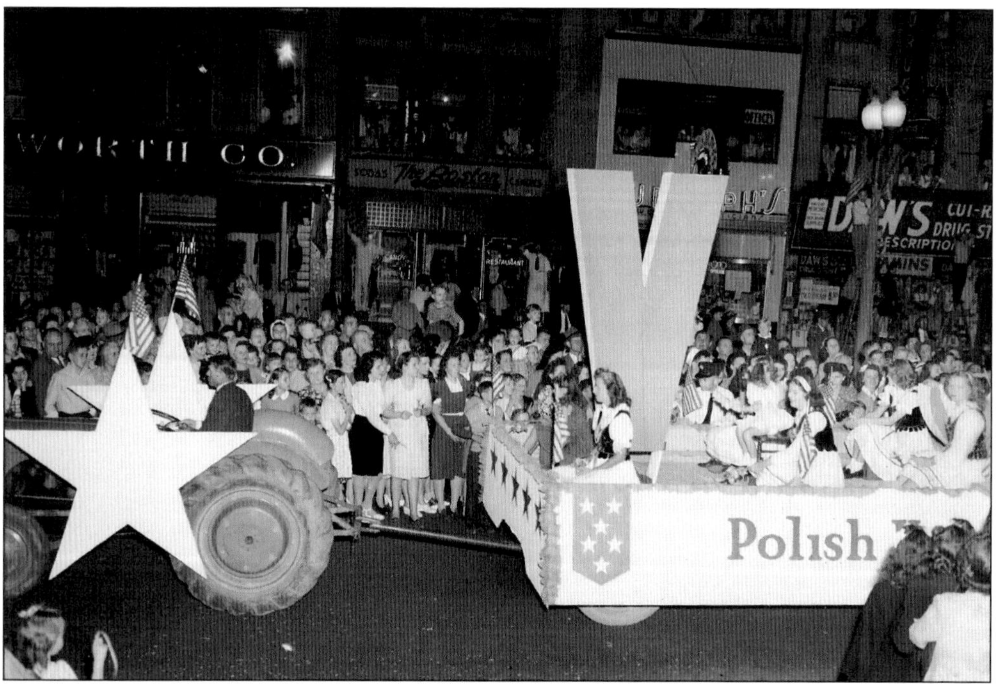

POLISH FALCONS FLOAT, ARMISTICE DAY VICTORY PARADE, 1945.

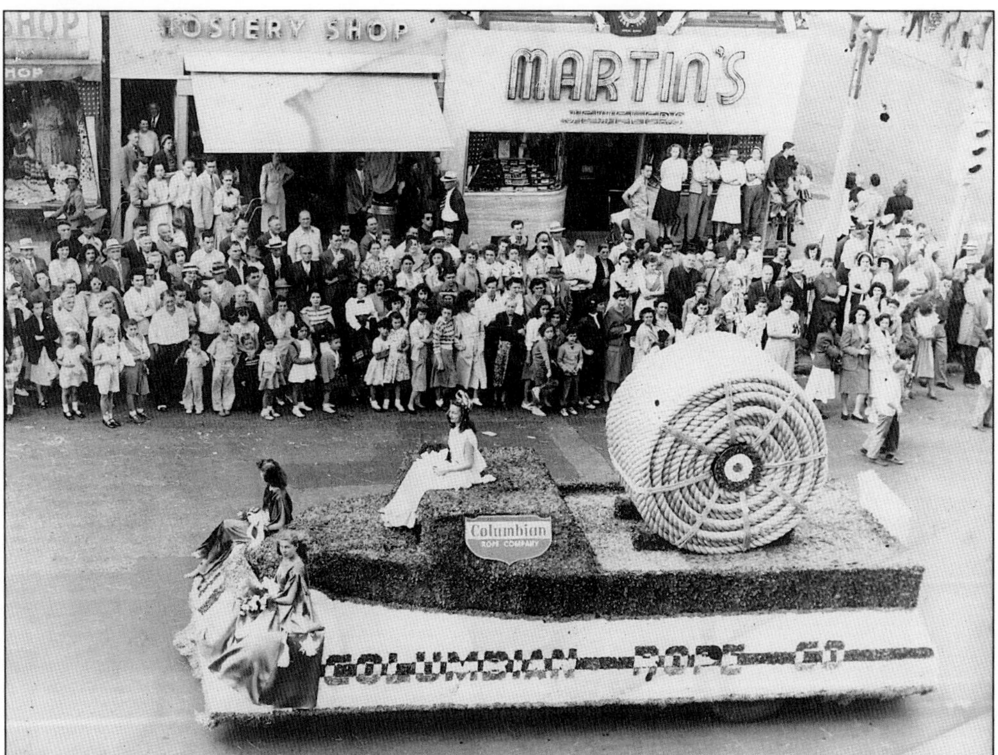

COLUMBIAN ROPE FLOAT, ARMISTICE DAY VICTORY PARADE, 1945.

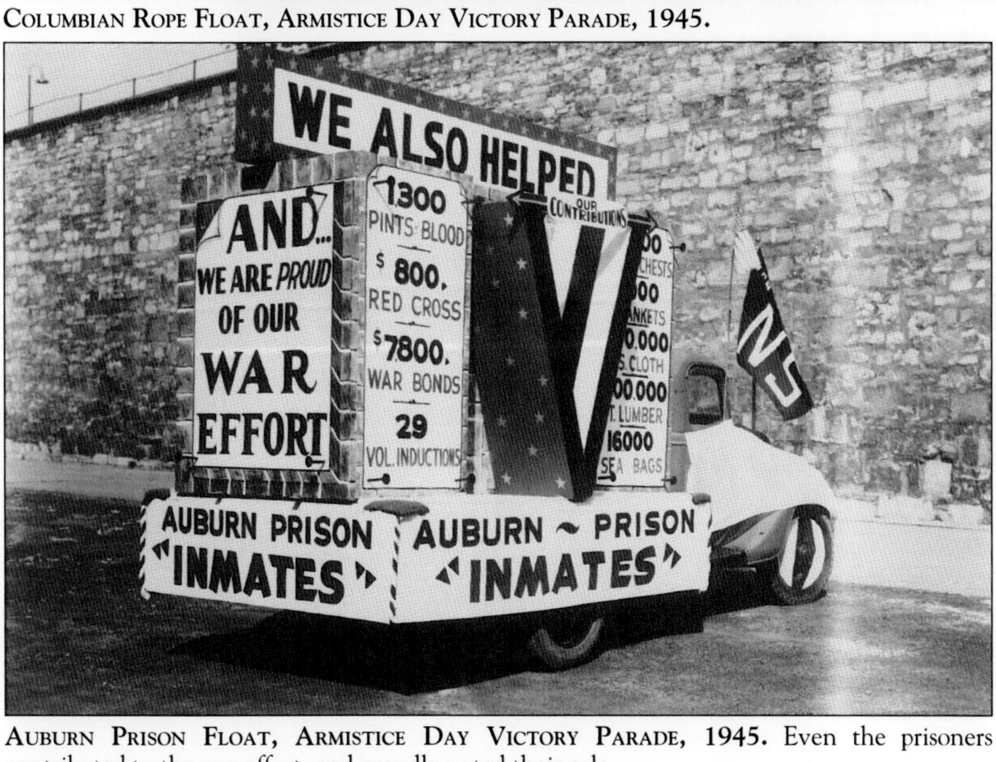

AUBURN PRISON FLOAT, ARMISTICE DAY VICTORY PARADE, 1945. Even the prisoners contributed to the war effort, and proudly noted their role.

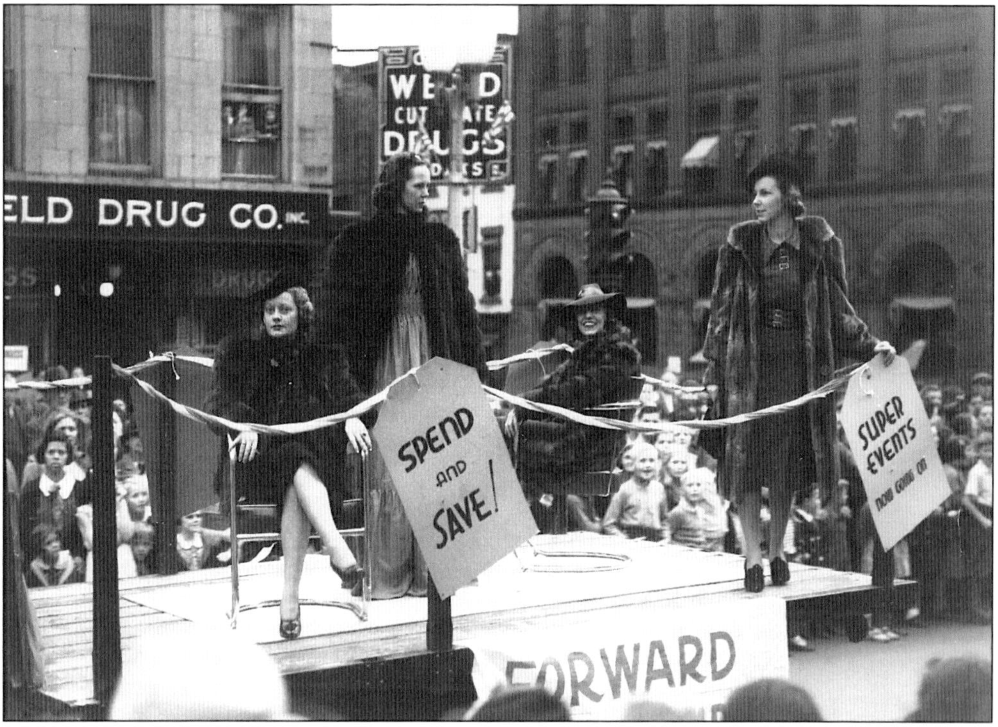

FASHION SHOW IN FRONT OF WELD DRUG COMPANY, CORNER OF GENESEE AND STATE STREETS, c. 1940. The stores along busy Genesee Street constantly vied for patrons' attention.

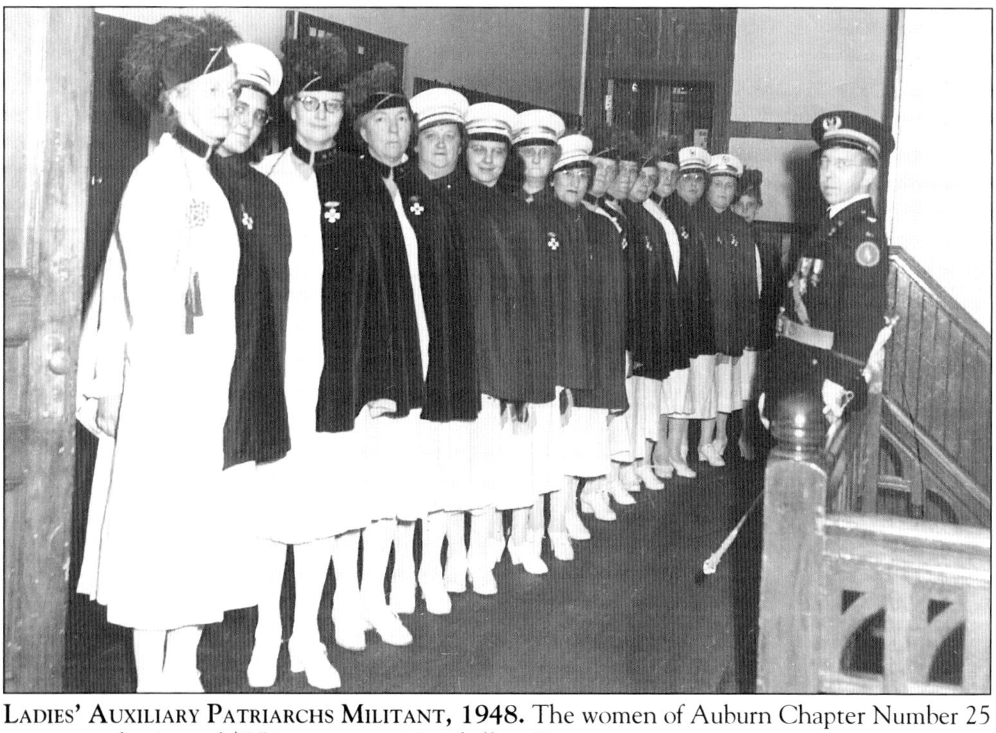

LADIES' AUXILIARY PATRIARCHS MILITANT, 1948. The women of Auburn Chapter Number 25 won second prize and $25 in a competitive drill in Geneva.

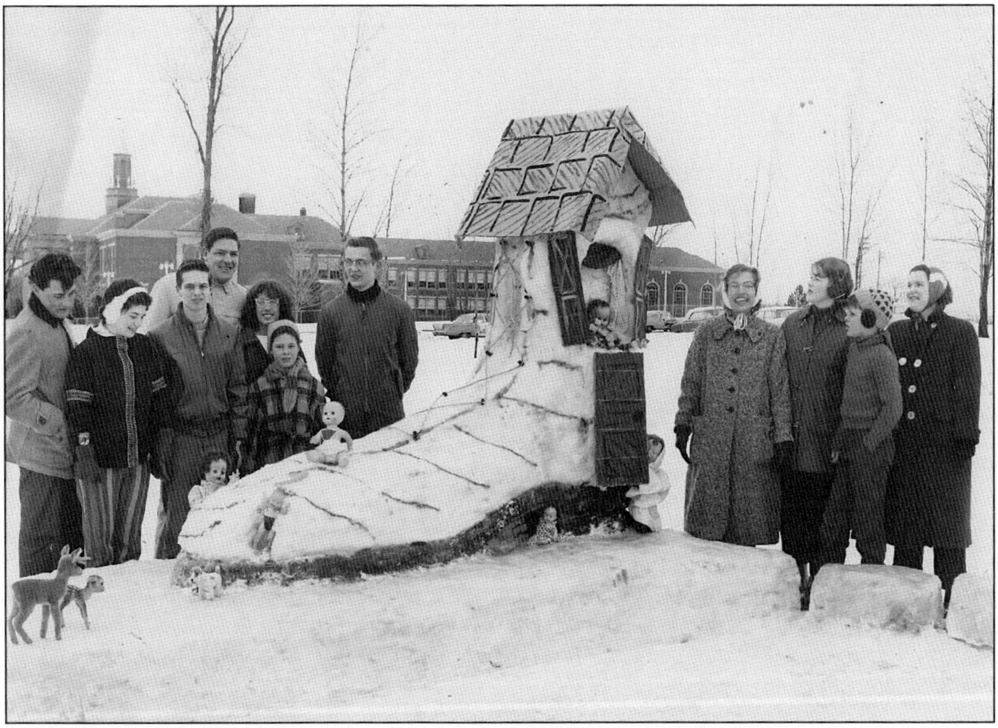

SNOW SCULPTURE, EAST HIGH SCHOOL, FRANKLIN STREET, 1960S. Bambi looks at the big shoe with trepidation. Enjoying Central New York winters takes a creative mindset.

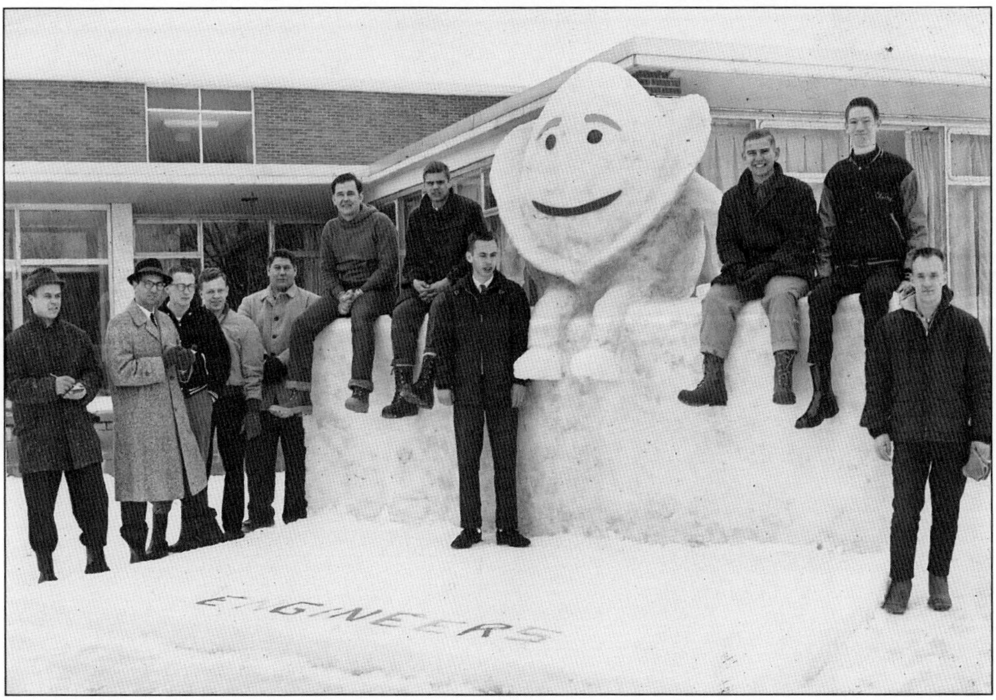

FUN WITH SNOW. If Humpty Dumpty falls, can they put him back together again? Engineering students from Auburn Community College built this snow sculpture in the 1960s.

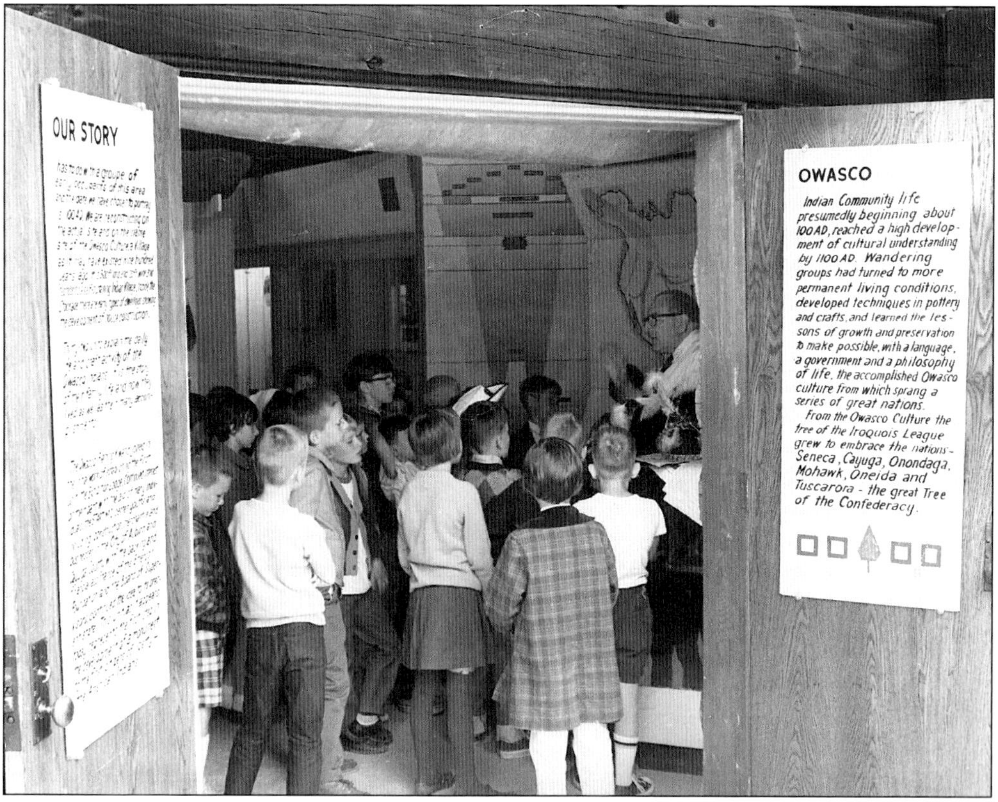

OWASCO STOCKADED INDIAN VILLAGE, LATE 1960s. Cayuga Museum Director Walter Long led a tour of school children. The village was a popular attraction near Owasco Lake, until most of the structures came down in the late 1980s. One building still exists, and functions as the Cayuga Museum's Iroquois Center at Emerson Park.

Seven

EMERSON PARK
OWASCO LAKE'S CONEY ISLAND

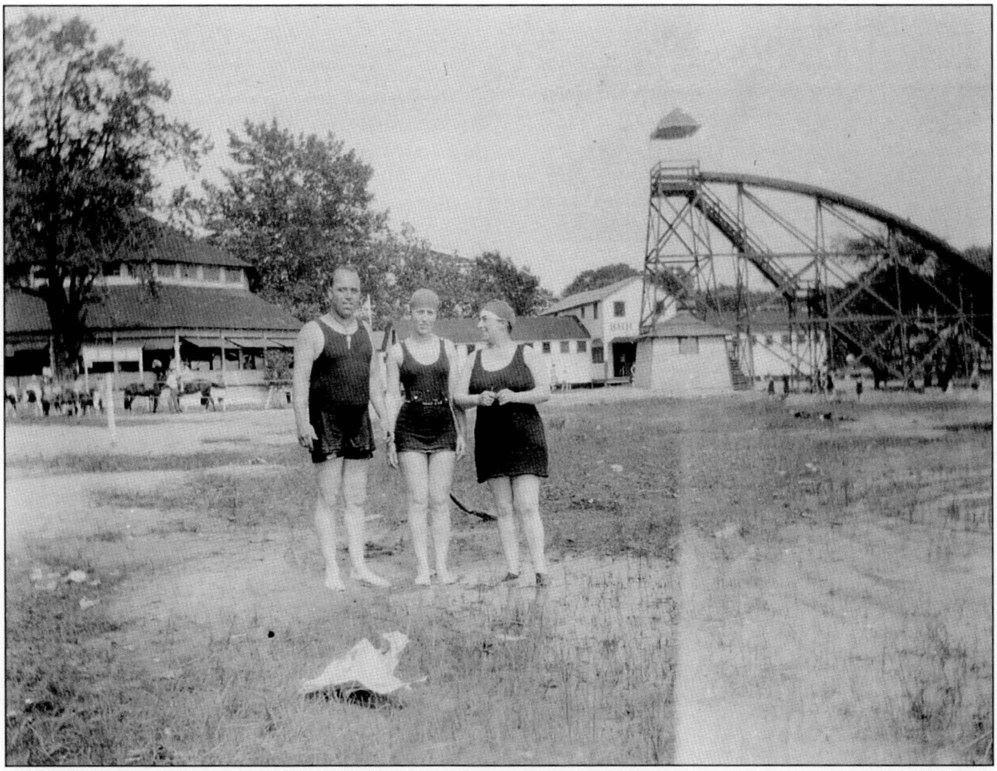

BATHERS AT ISLAND PARK, C. 1921. Emerson Park, under many different names, has served as Auburn and Cayuga County's summer playground since the late nineteenth century.

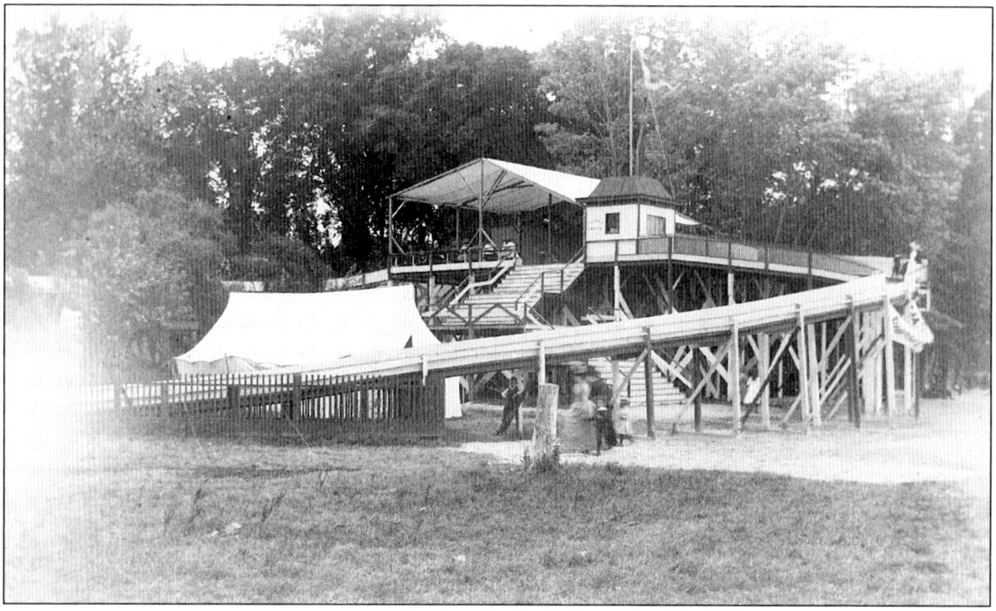

UNIDENTIFIED RIDE, OWASCO LAKE PARK, C. 1889. This odd machine, an early park ride, was built by the "notorious" Charles Haines. The unscrupulous park promoter skipped town with the profits following a single season of operation.

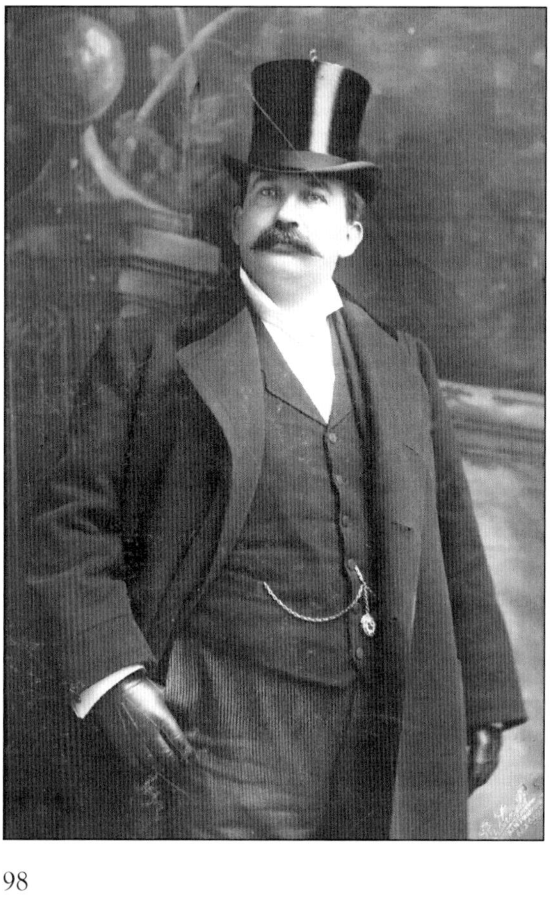

JACK WEST, C. 1890. Jack and brother Billy, both Auburn natives, owned and operated a successful traveling vaudeville show. Following his retirement, Jack returned to Auburn and ran the train at Island Park.

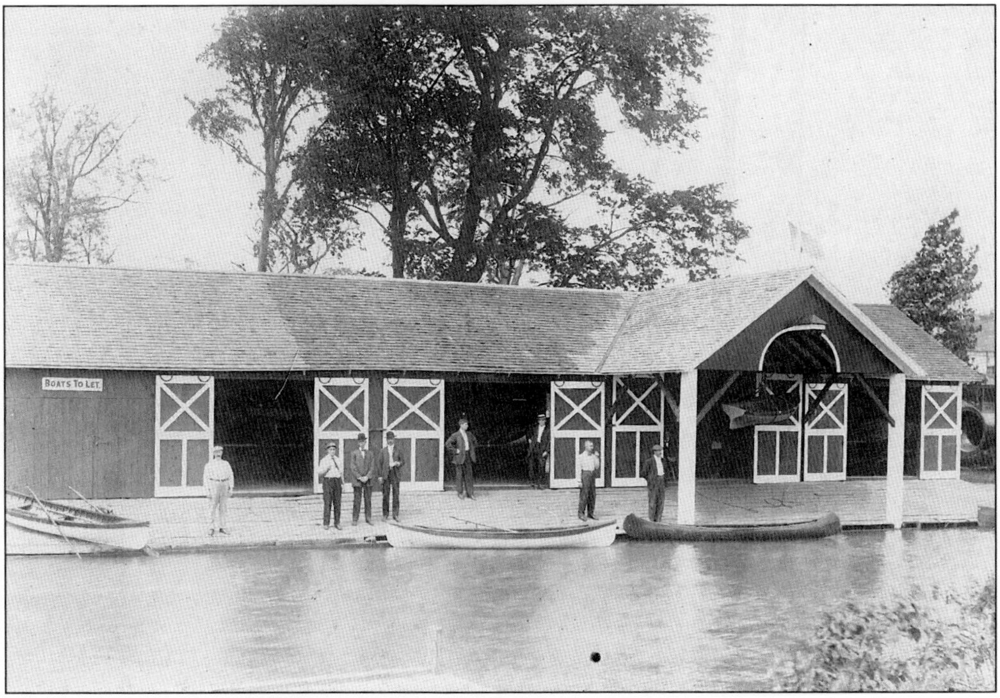

Boathouse at Island Park, c. 1900. Rental boats gave visitors plenty of opportunity to enjoy the relaxing waters of the Owasco Outlet.

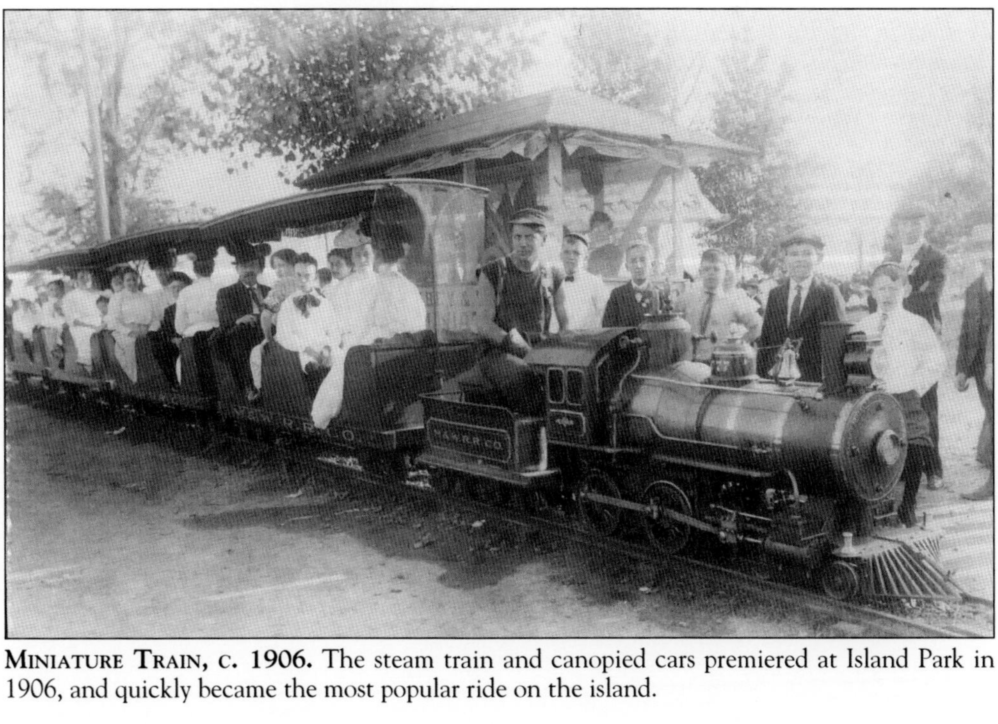

Miniature Train, c. 1906. The steam train and canopied cars premiered at Island Park in 1906, and quickly became the most popular ride on the island.

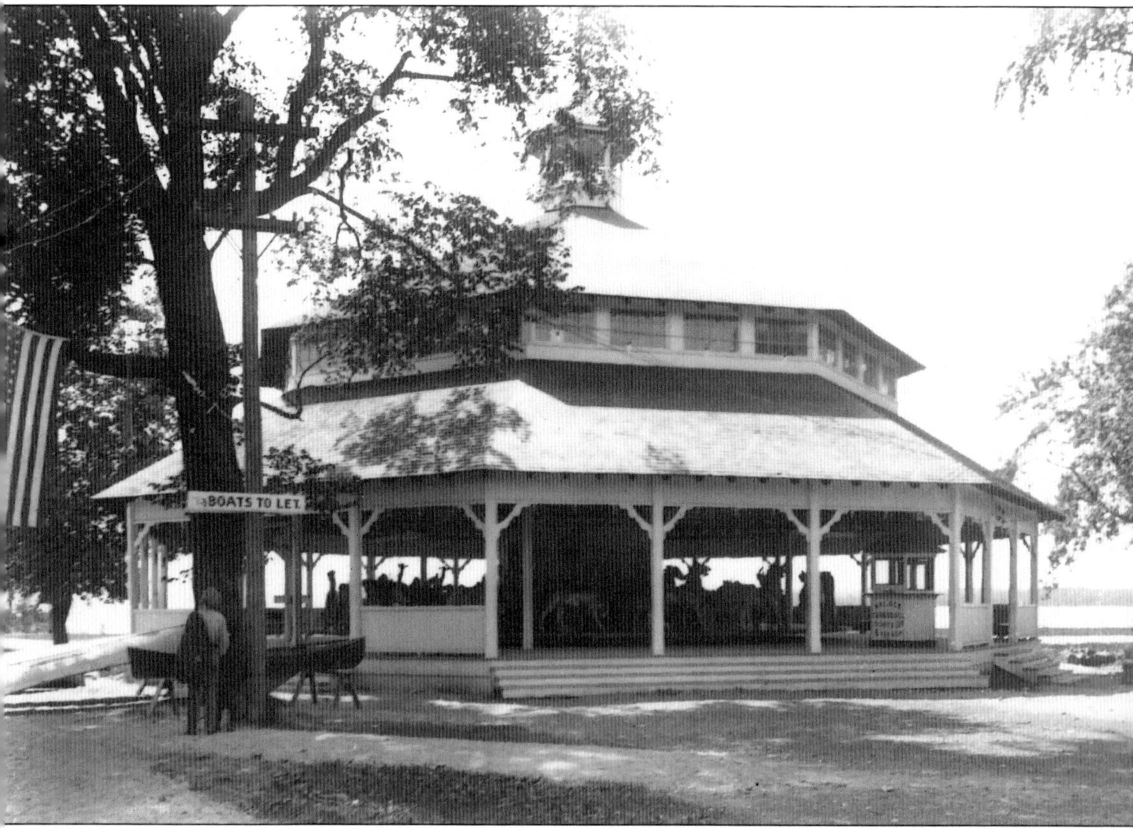

CAROUSEL, ISLAND PARK, C. 1906. This machine, with figures carved by Daniel Muller, was an attraction on the island until the 1920s. The building was later used as a roller skating rink, boxing ring, and penny arcade before it was razed in 1968.

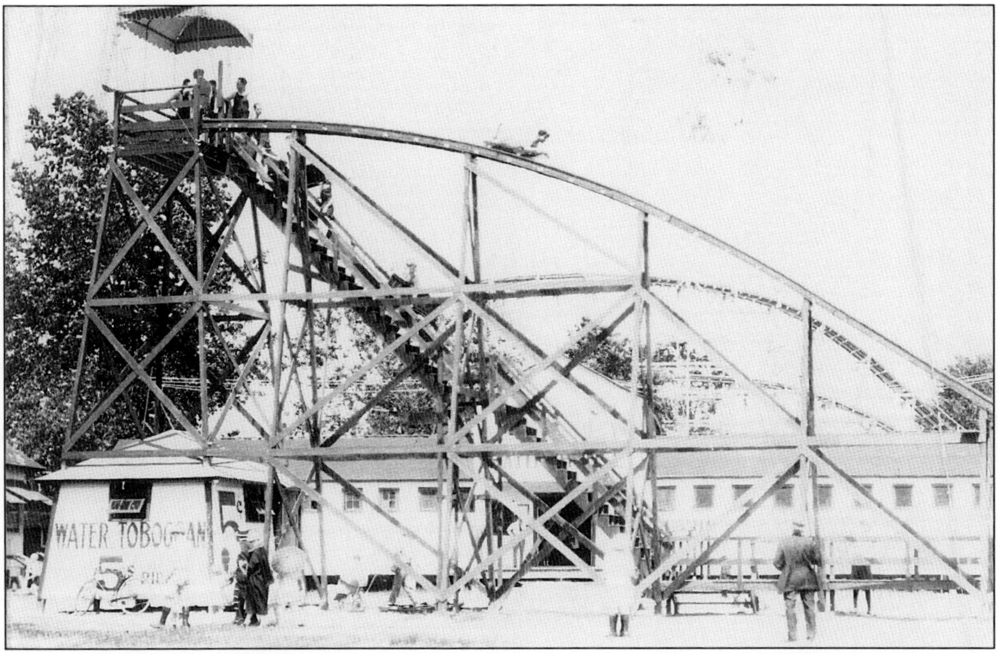

Water Toboggan, Island Park, c. 1921. With water everywhere, this ride naturally figured as one of the park's prime attractions.

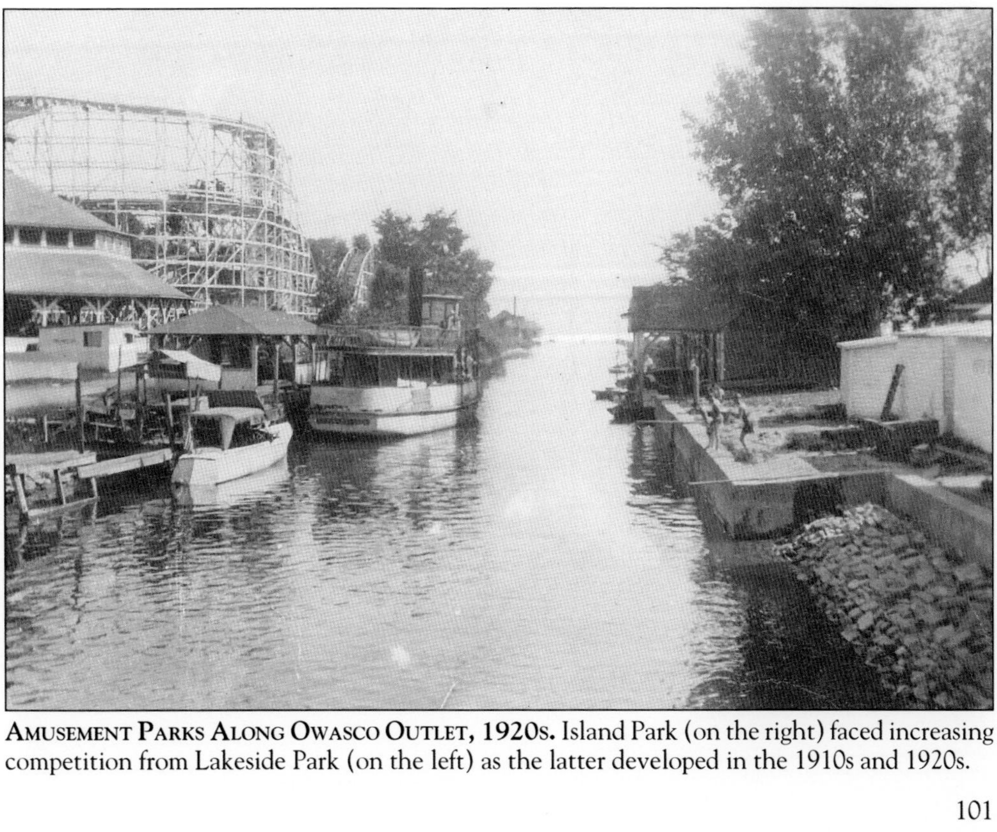

Amusement Parks Along Owasco Outlet, 1920s. Island Park (on the right) faced increasing competition from Lakeside Park (on the left) as the latter developed in the 1910s and 1920s.

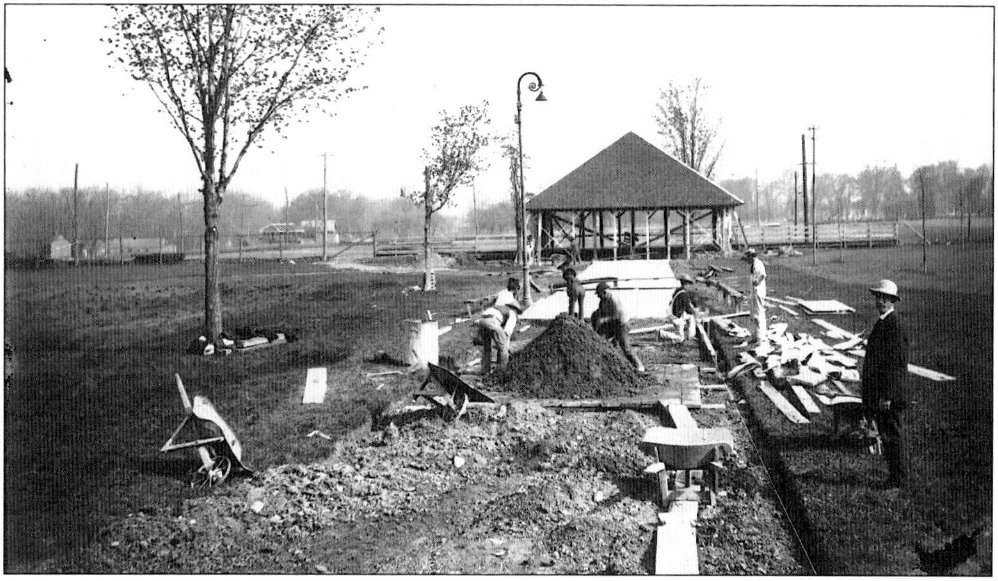

Construction of Loading Platform and Boardwalk, Lakeside Park, 1900–1910. Auburn City Railway purchased the mainland property along the Owasco Outlet in 1891 to develop it into a resort area.

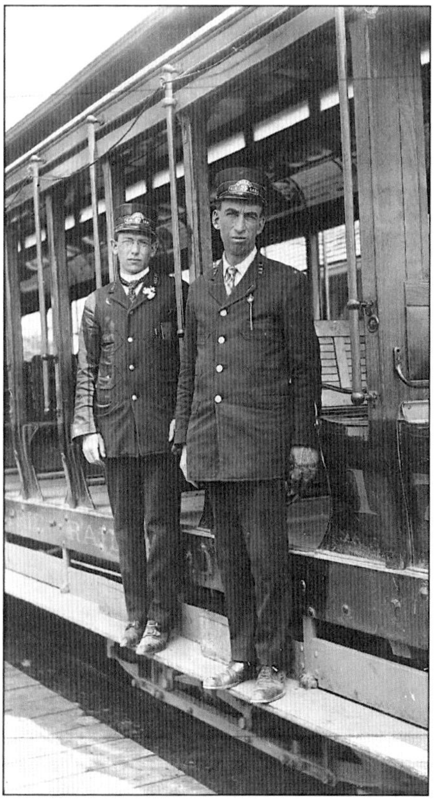

Conductors, Auburn and Syracuse Electric Railway, Early 1900s. All lines led to Lakeside Park! The rail company actively advertised its pleasures for patrons as far away as Rochester and Syracuse.

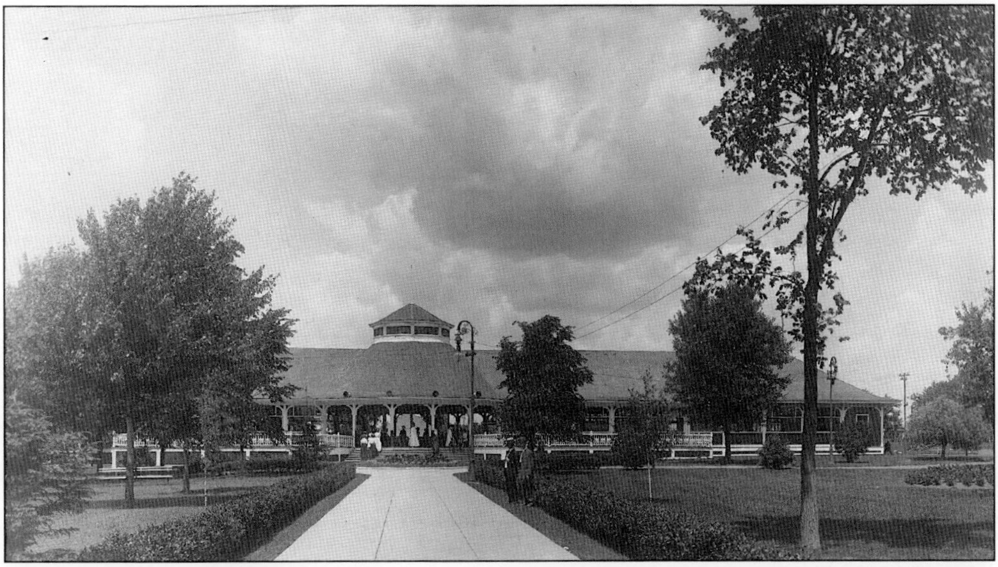

PAVILION, LAKESIDE PARK, C. 1900. This open-air structure with arched entrances featured music and dancing until it burned in 1913. Another pavilion, built on the same location, became a huge park draw, and came alive with the sounds of the big bands in the 1930s.

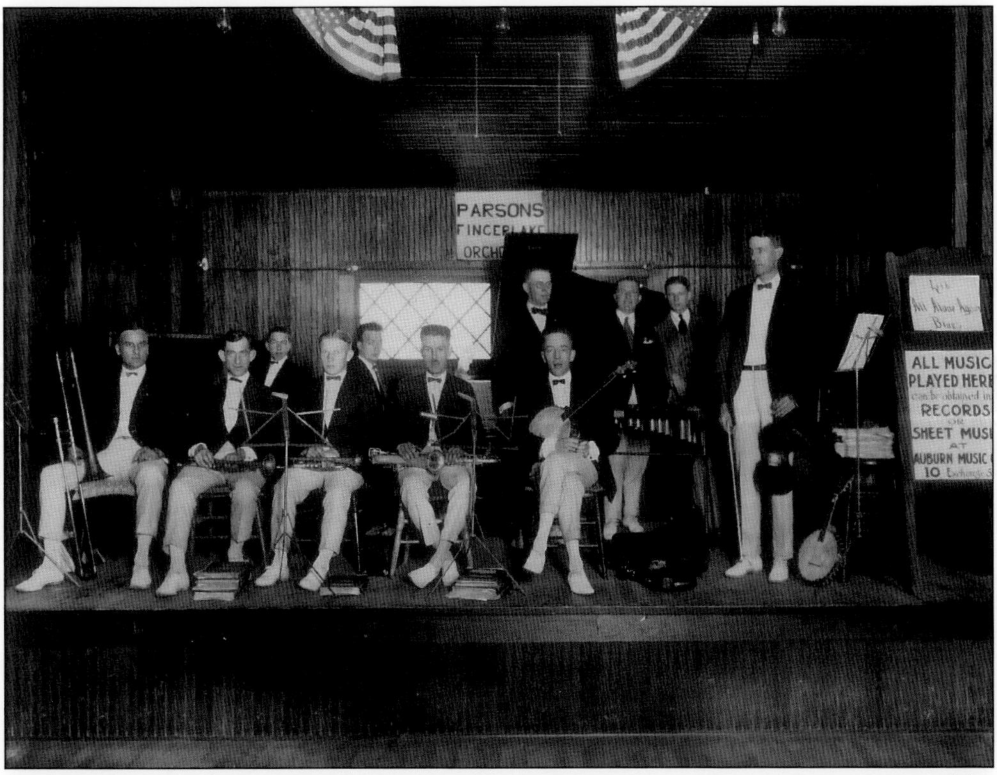

PARSONS FINGERLAKE ORCHESTRA, LAKESIDE PARK PAVILION, C. 1910. Parsons was one of the lesser-known groups to play at the park. Later headlining musical names included Les Brown, Tommy Dorsey, and Count Basie.

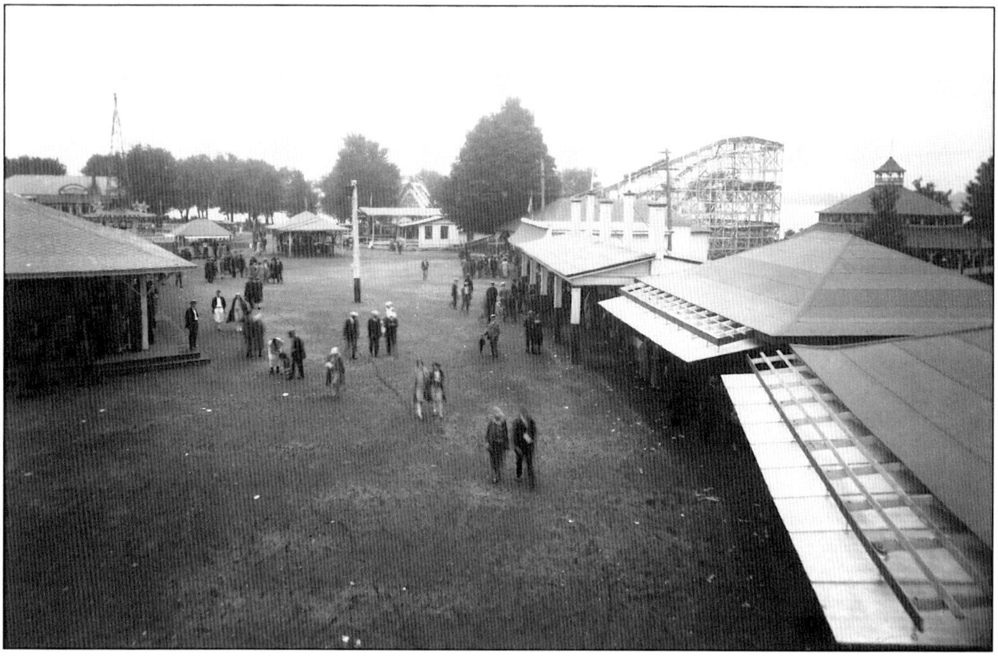

Midway, Lakeside Park, 1920s. By the 1920s, Lakeside Park eclipsed Island Park in prominence and popularity, and featured games and amusements of all kinds.

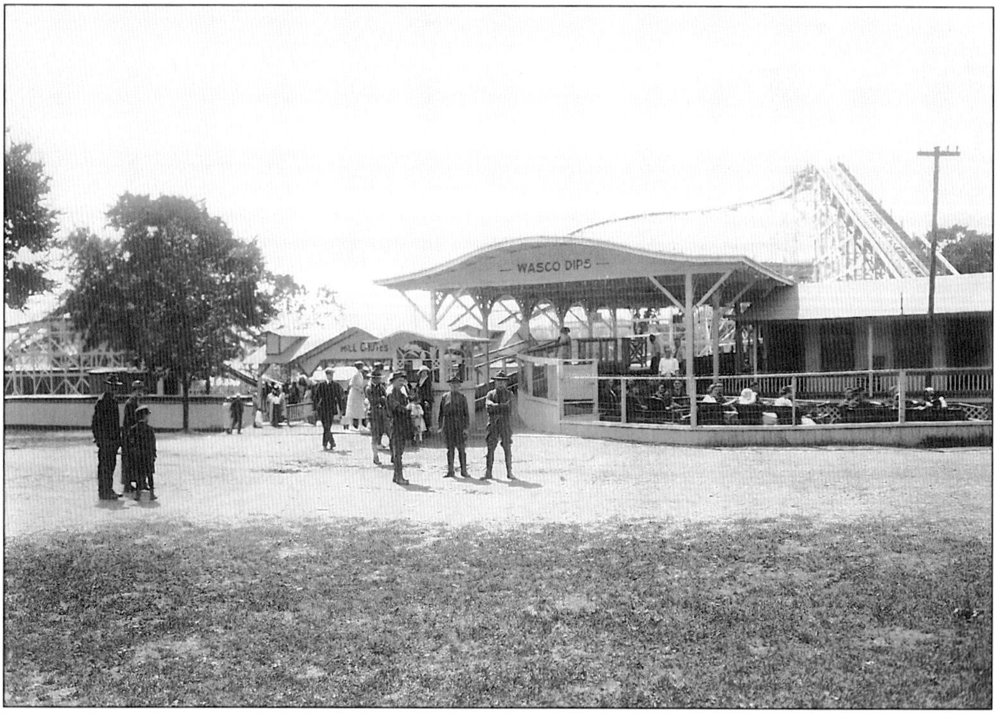

Wasco Dips Coaster and Mill Chute, Lakeside Park, 1920s. Traditional rites of summer at Owasco Lake included a ride on the Wasco Dips and a trip through the Mill Chute, better known to many locals as the Tunnel of Love. (Image courtesy of Philadelphia Toboggan Coasters, Inc.)

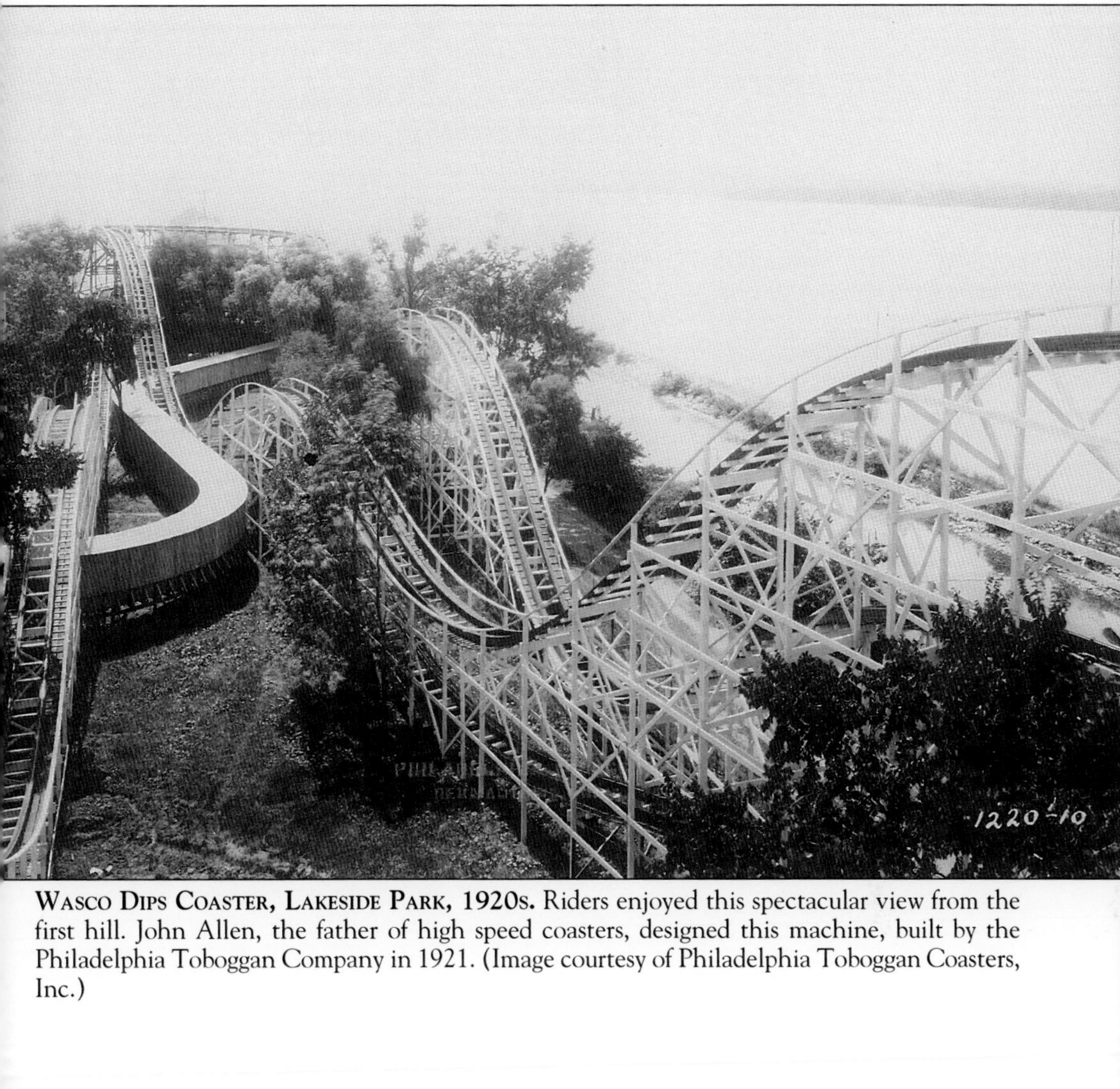

WASCO DIPS COASTER, LAKESIDE PARK, 1920s. Riders enjoyed this spectacular view from the first hill. John Allen, the father of high speed coasters, designed this machine, built by the Philadelphia Toboggan Company in 1921. (Image courtesy of Philadelphia Toboggan Coasters, Inc.)

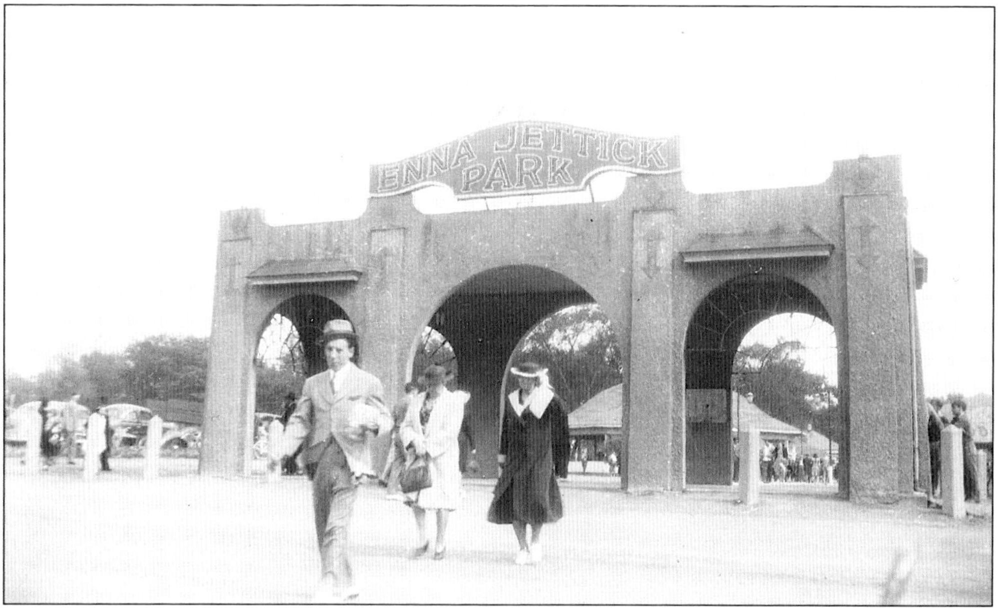

ENTRANCE ARCH, ENNA JETTICK PARK, 1930. Fred L. Emerson of Dunn and McCarthy Company purchased Lakeside Park in 1930 and renamed it for his famed brand of women's shoes.

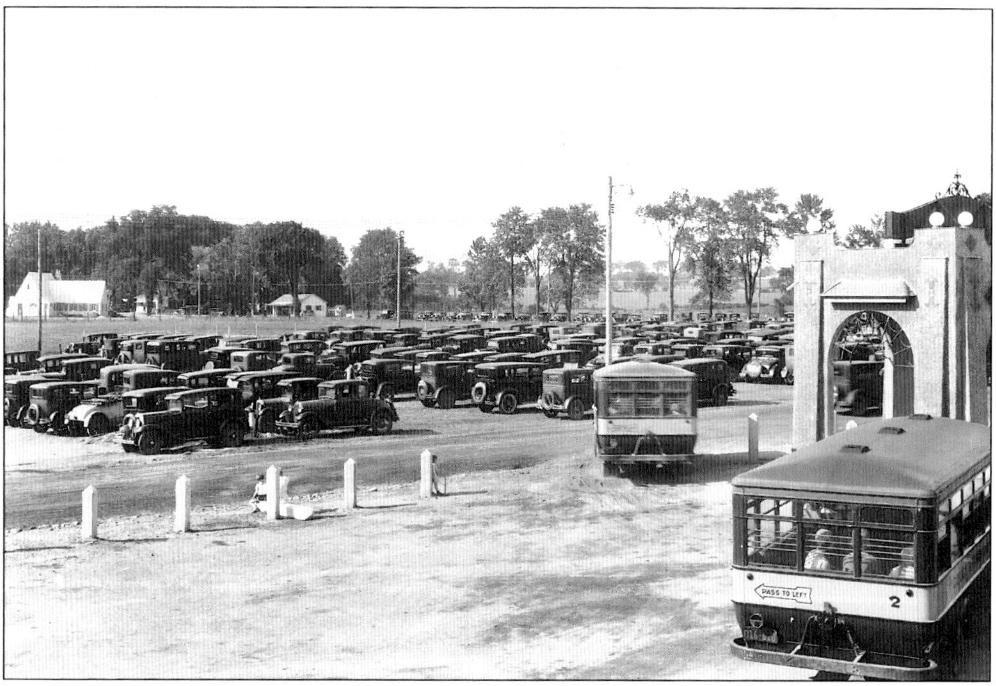

PARKING LOT, ENNA JETTICK PARK, 1930S. Parking lots filled to capacity meant successful summer seasons for the park, which drew visitors from throughout the Finger Lakes region.

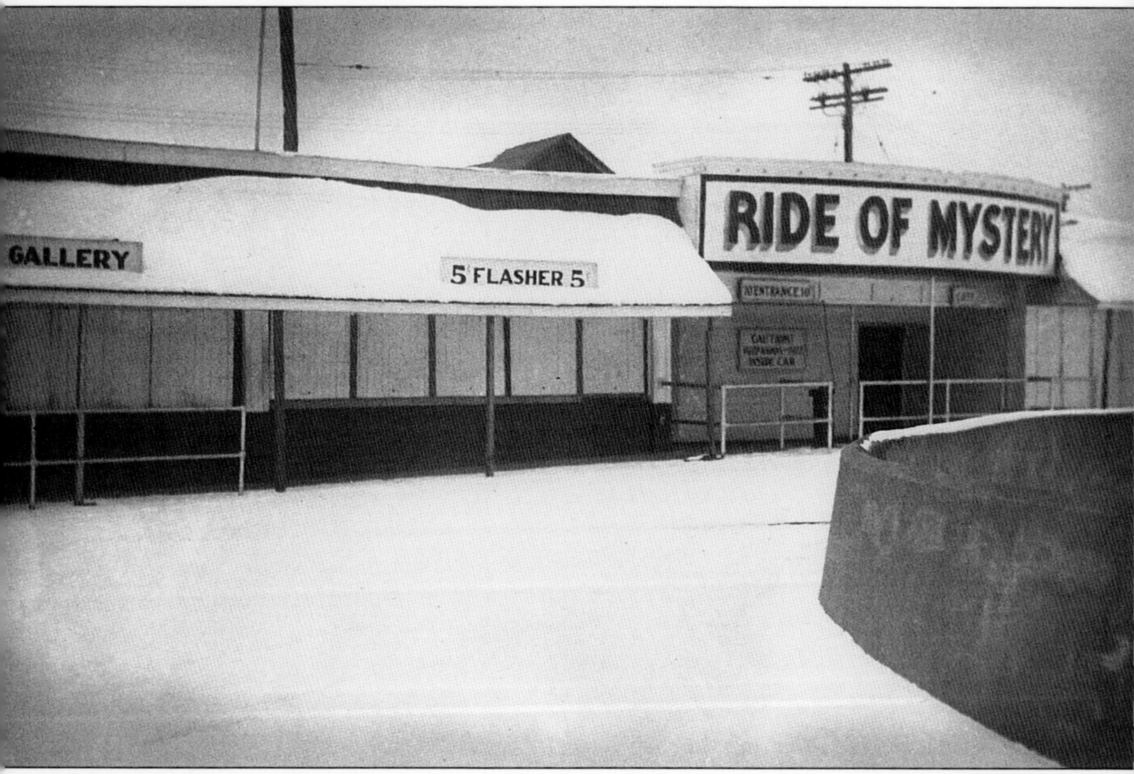

Ride of Mystery, c. 1935. Winter lent an air of mystery to this dark ride, which opened as the Pretzel in 1930. It was housed in one of the concession buildings on the midway. At right is the cement enclosure of Monkey Island, another park highlight for visitors. (Image courtesy of Philadelphia Toboggan Coasters, Inc.)

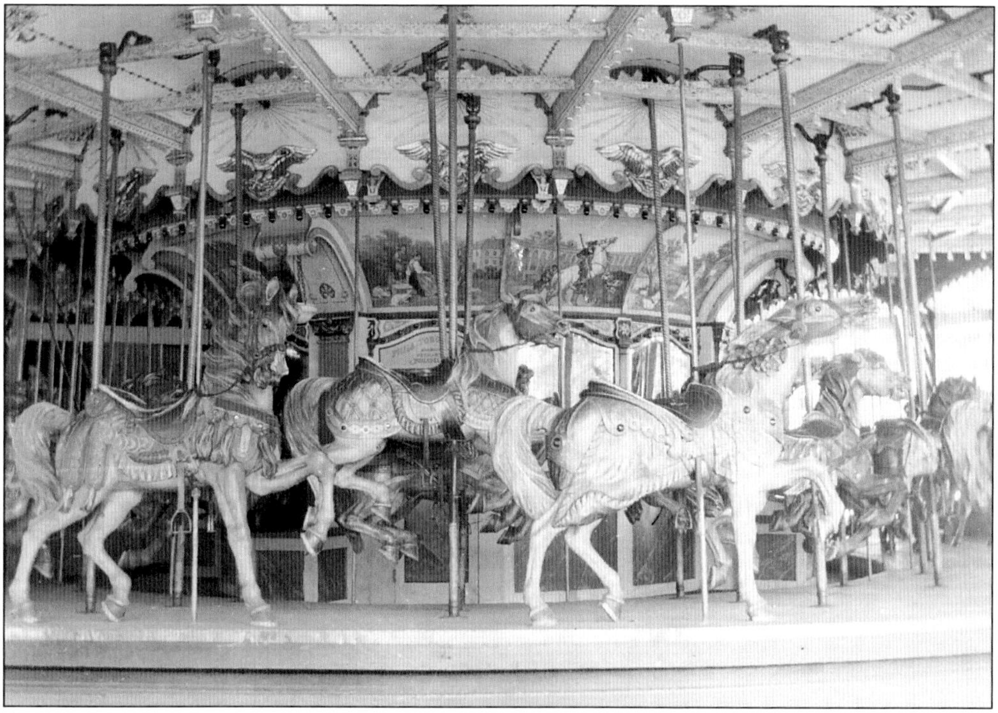

CAROUSEL, ENNA JETTICK PARK, C. 1930. Brought to the park in 1930, this carousel entertained patrons until Enna Jettick closed in 1942. Hersheypark purchased the machine in 1944, and moved it to Pennsylvania where it still delights riders. (Image courtesy of Philadelphia Toboggan Coasters, Inc.)

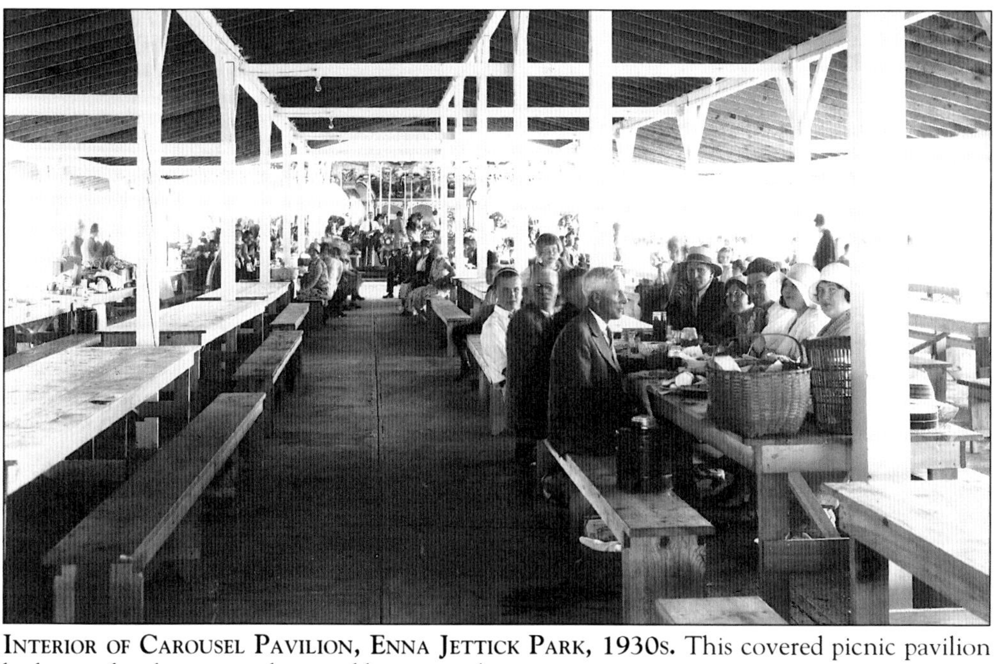

INTERIOR OF CAROUSEL PAVILION, ENNA JETTICK PARK, 1930S. This covered picnic pavilion had room for almost one thousand hungry park patrons.

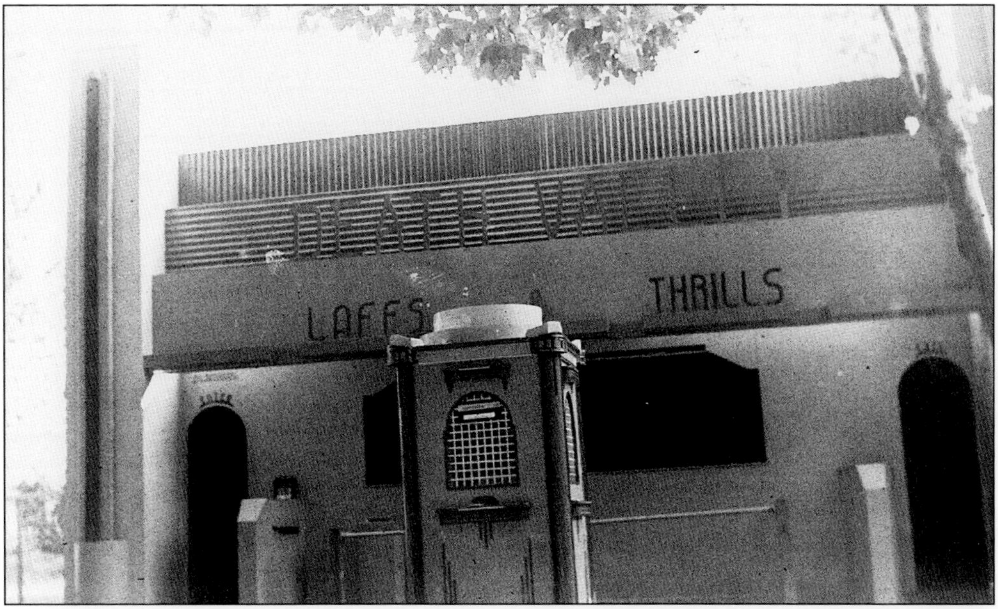

DEATH VALLEY FUNHOUSE, ENNA JETTICK PARK, 1930S. What park would be complete without one of these places? This curiously named funhouse featured rubber snakes, tilting lily pads, air jets, and the raucous voice of Laughing Sal. (Image courtesy of Philadelphia Toboggan Coasters, Inc.)

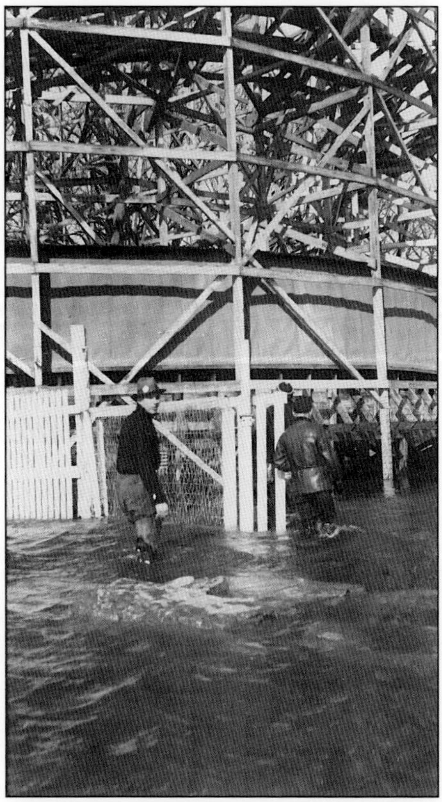

FLOOD, ENNA JETTICK PARK, MARCH 22, 1936. Workers braved the water to check if the roller coaster and Mill Chute had weathered the storm.

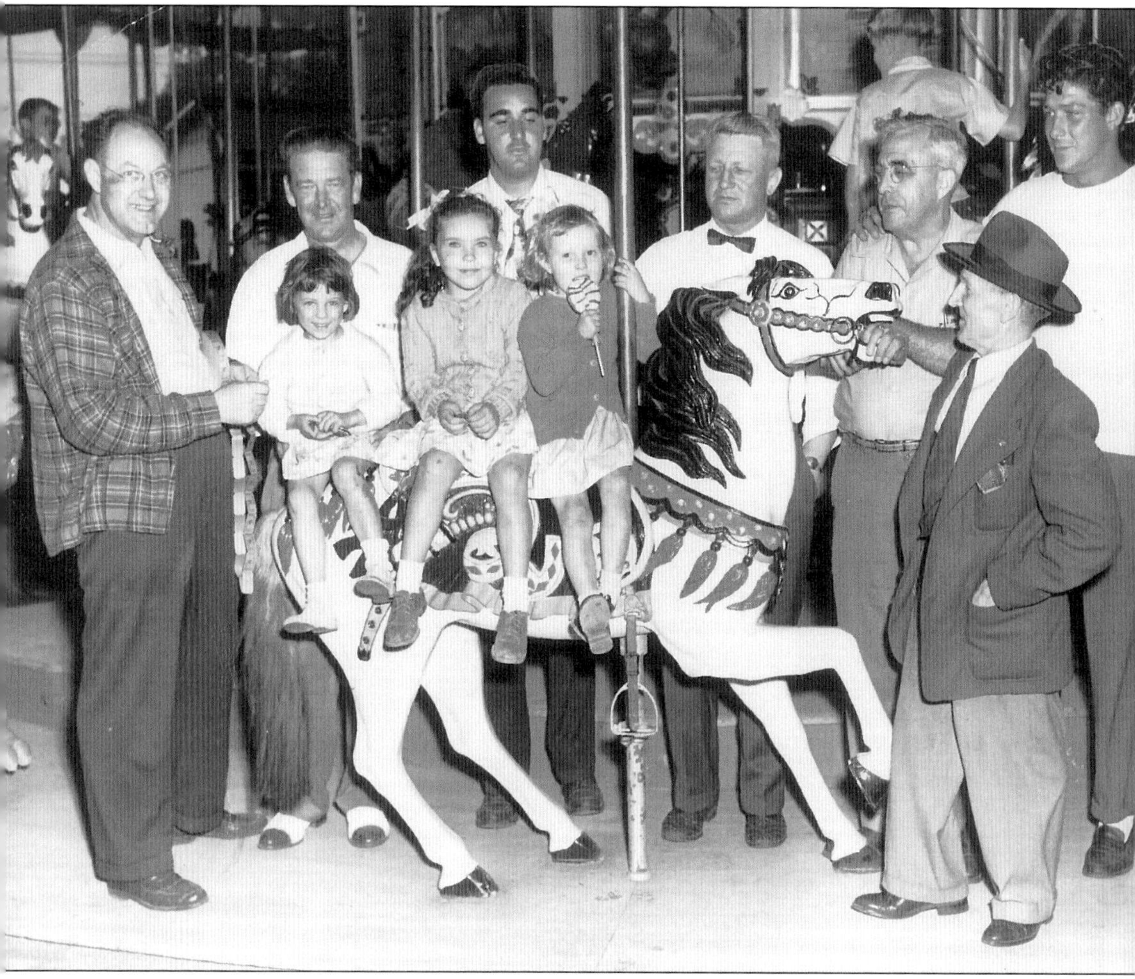

ANNUAL OUTING OF CAYUGA CHILDREN'S HOME, DEAUVILLE ISLAND, 1950S. Children rode the Herschell-Spillman Carousel, which featured zebras, ostriches, and other wild animals. Island Park, renamed Deauville Island, continued to entertain local residents until it closed in 1968. This carousel was moved to the mainland and remained a popular feature of Emerson Park until it was sold to a museum on Long Island in 1972.

Eight

Into the Present

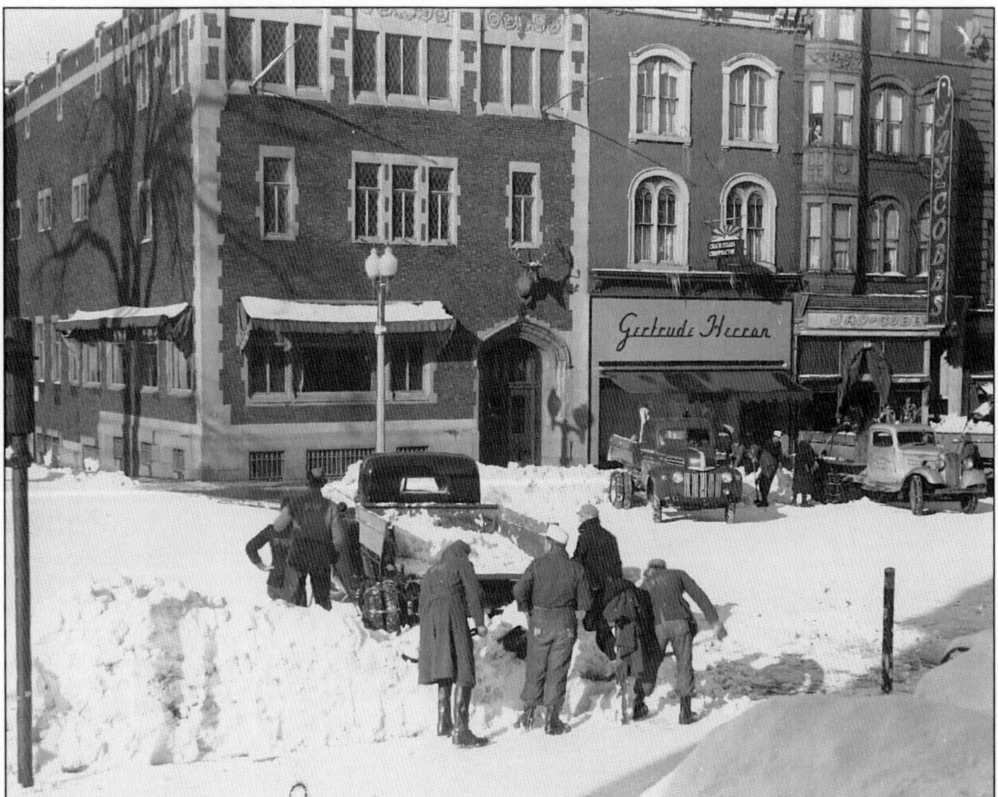

Wartime Service, c. 1944. German POWs, under charge of a United States Army officer, shoveled snow on Genesee Street during World War II. The prisoners were interred on Howland's Island, north of Auburn.

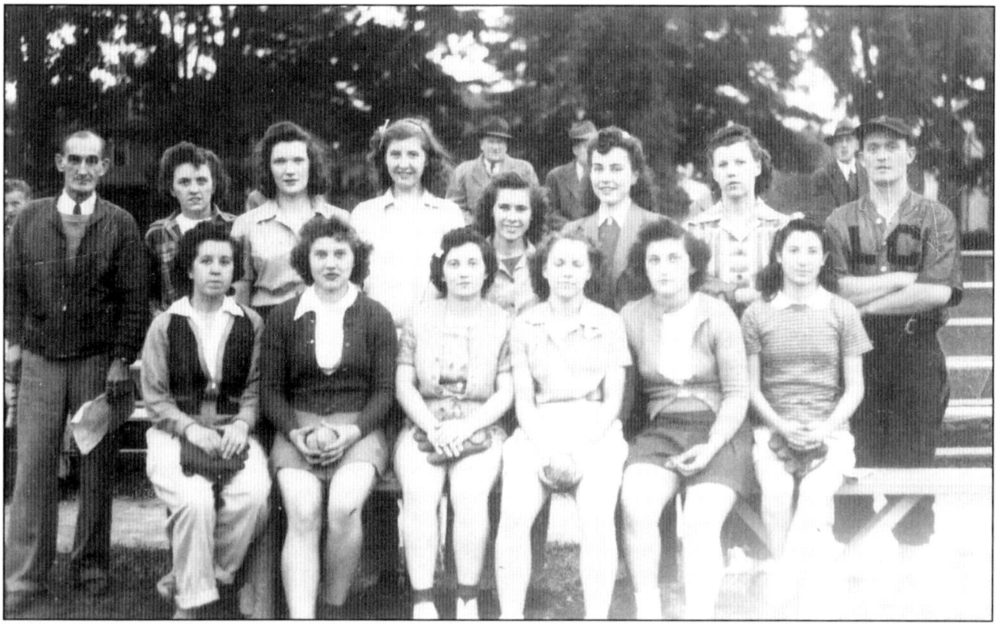

ALCO MAC'S, WOMEN'S SOFTBALL TEAM, 1943–1944. The Alco Mac's (short for McIntosh) were runners-up to the champs from Columbian Rope. During WW II, factories in Auburn sponsored a women's fast pitch softball league. Other participants included Firth Carpet Company and Beacon Milling Company.

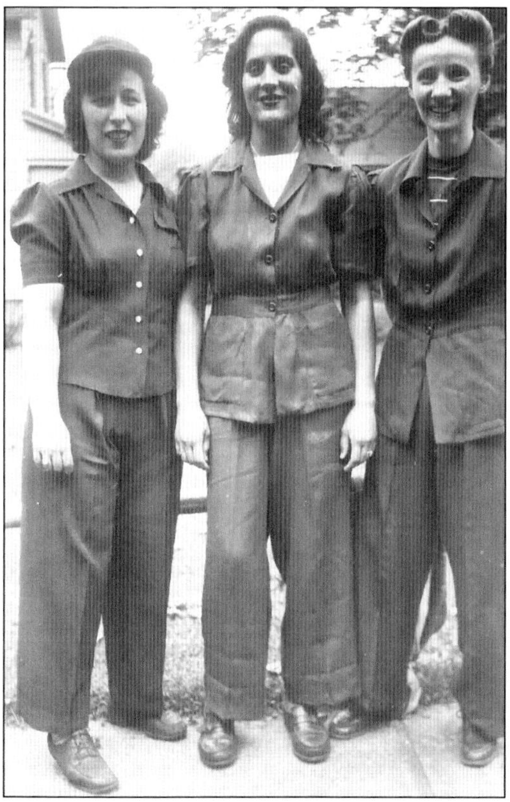

PLAYERS, WOMEN'S SOFTBALL LEAGUE, 1943–1944. From left to right, catcher Lucy Icolano, pitcher Bianco "Babe" Locastro, and shortstop Pearl Tarby O'Brien modeled the latest in sportswear.

No Left Turn, c. 1948. Police officers Paul Kilborn and Joseph Conboy paused after putting up this traffic sign. Much to Auburn residents' chagrin, these movable signs were placed in the middle of the road at several points along Genesee Street between 10 a.m. and 6 p.m. daily during the workweek.

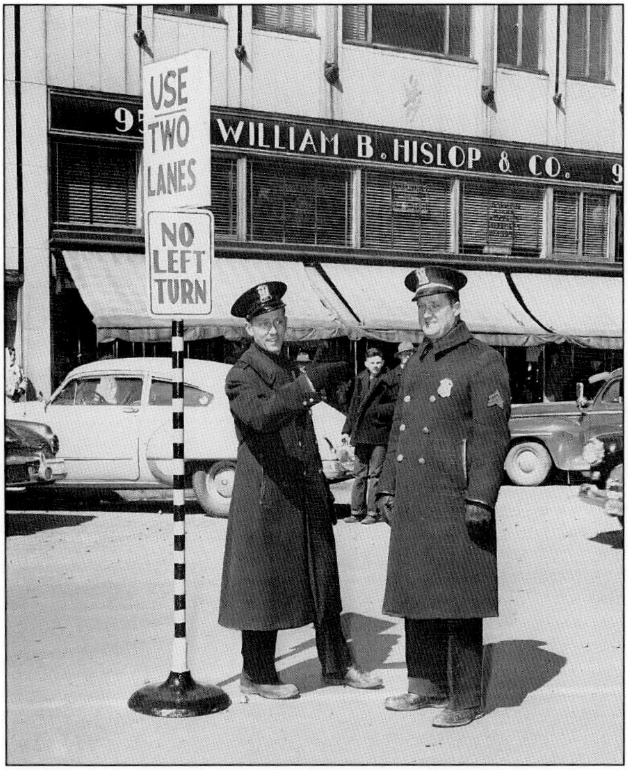

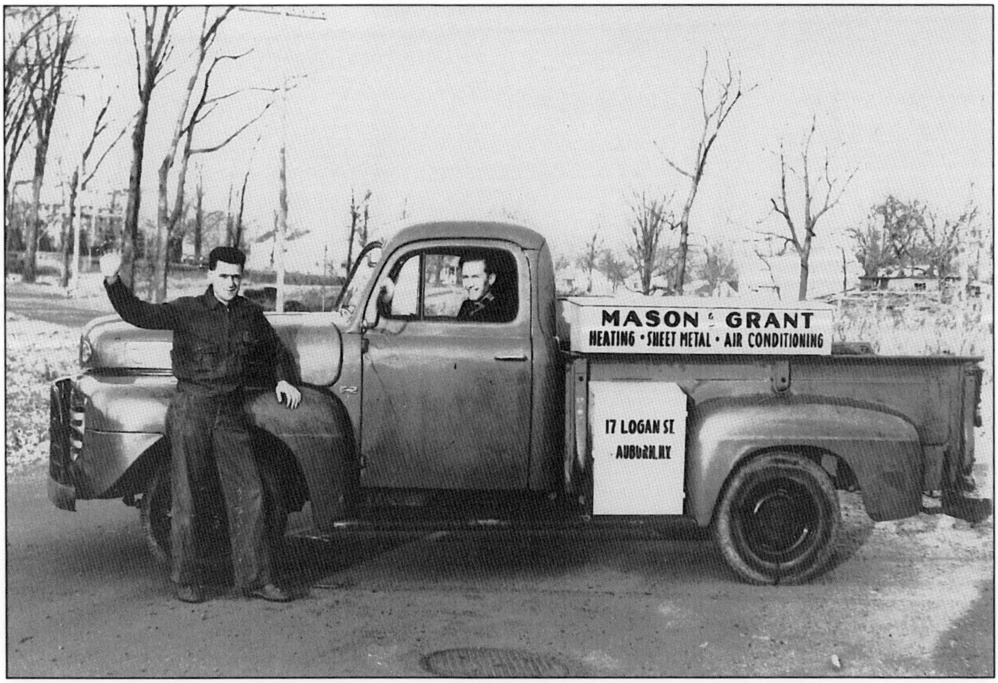

Ready to Service All Repair Needs, December 1952. George Grant and Jay Mason of Mason and Grant Heating and Air Conditioning posed in front of their saddlebag truck, which the company used into the 1960s.

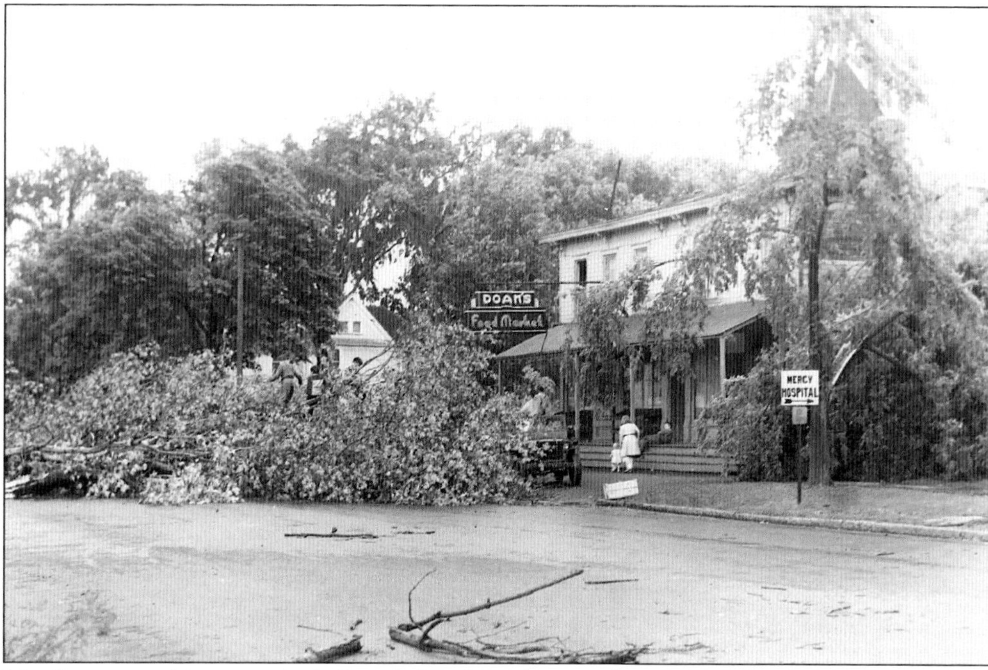

NO GROCERIES TODAY, 1946. Doan's Food Market, at the corner of Delevan and Genesee Streets, was one of many places faced with clean up in the aftermath of a memorable storm.

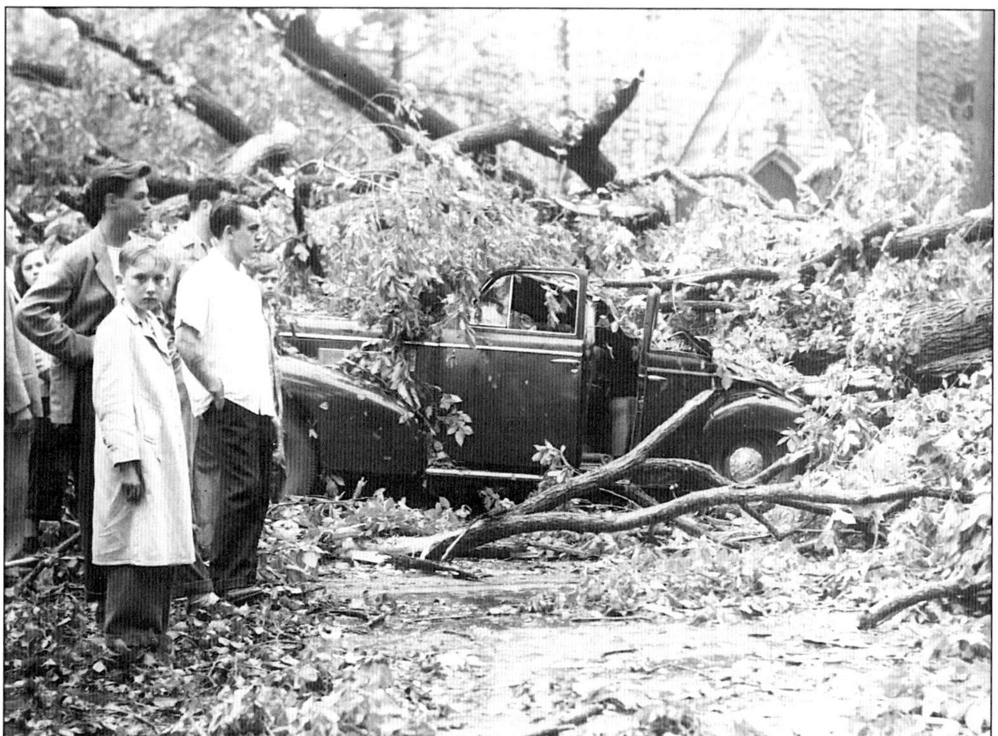

STORM DAMAGE, 1946. Who's the driver of this car? A crowd gathered to gawk at storm damage in front of St. Peter's Episcopal Church on Genesee Street.

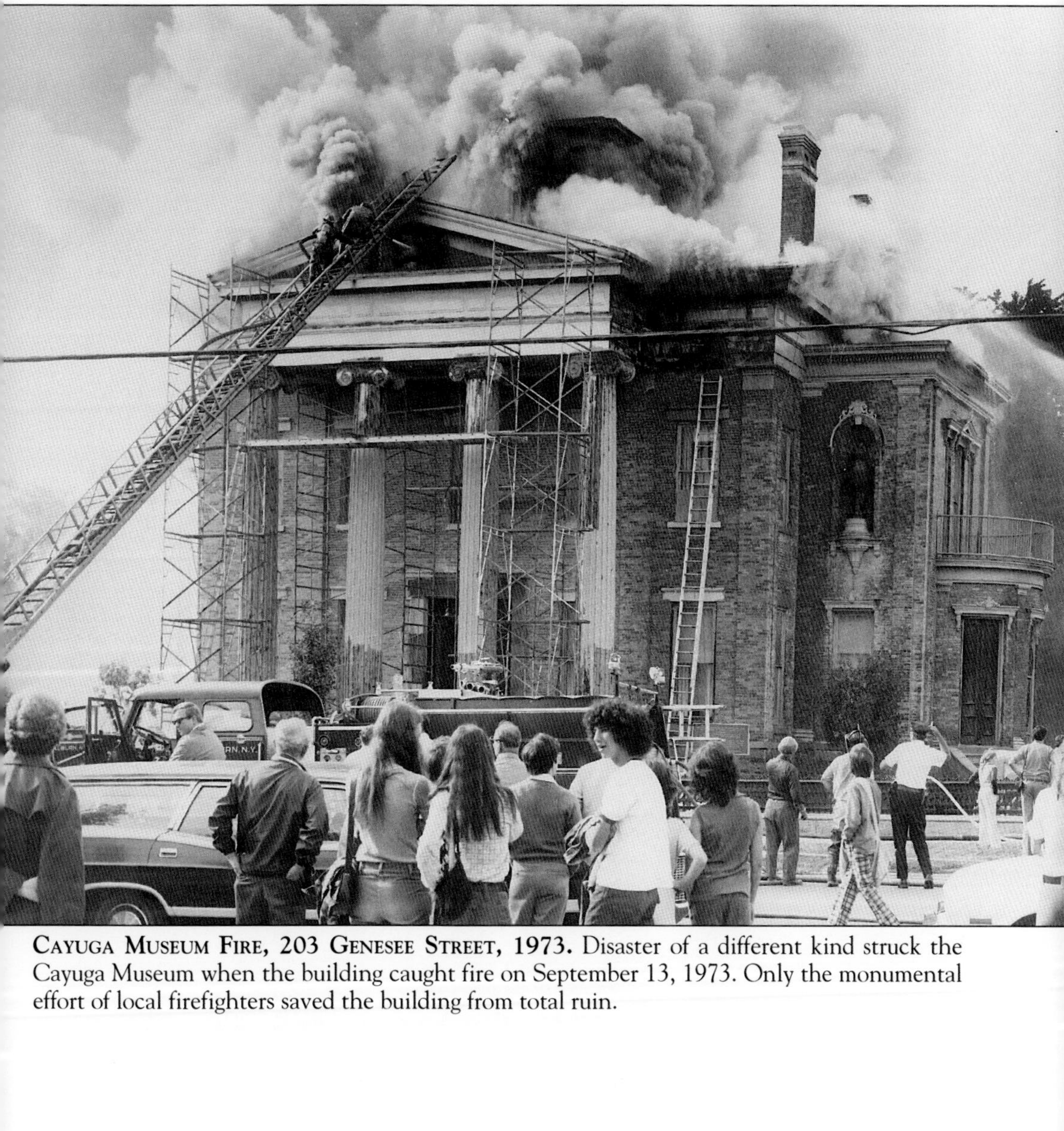

Cayuga Museum Fire, 203 Genesee Street, 1973. Disaster of a different kind struck the Cayuga Museum when the building caught fire on September 13, 1973. Only the monumental effort of local firefighters saved the building from total ruin.

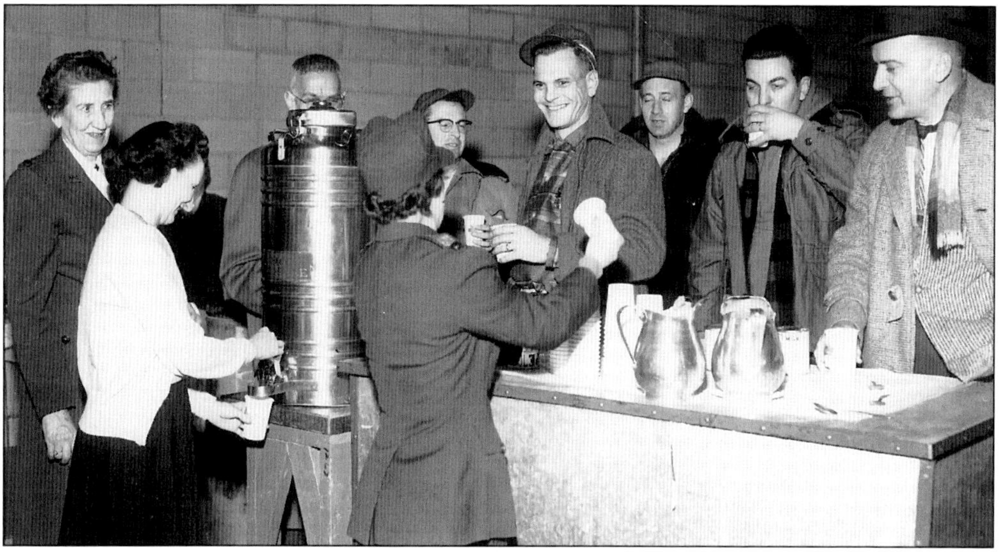

CANTEEN, CAYUGA COUNTY CHAPTER OF AMERICAN RED CROSS, 1944. The local chapter of the Red Cross has long served the varied needs of the community's residents.

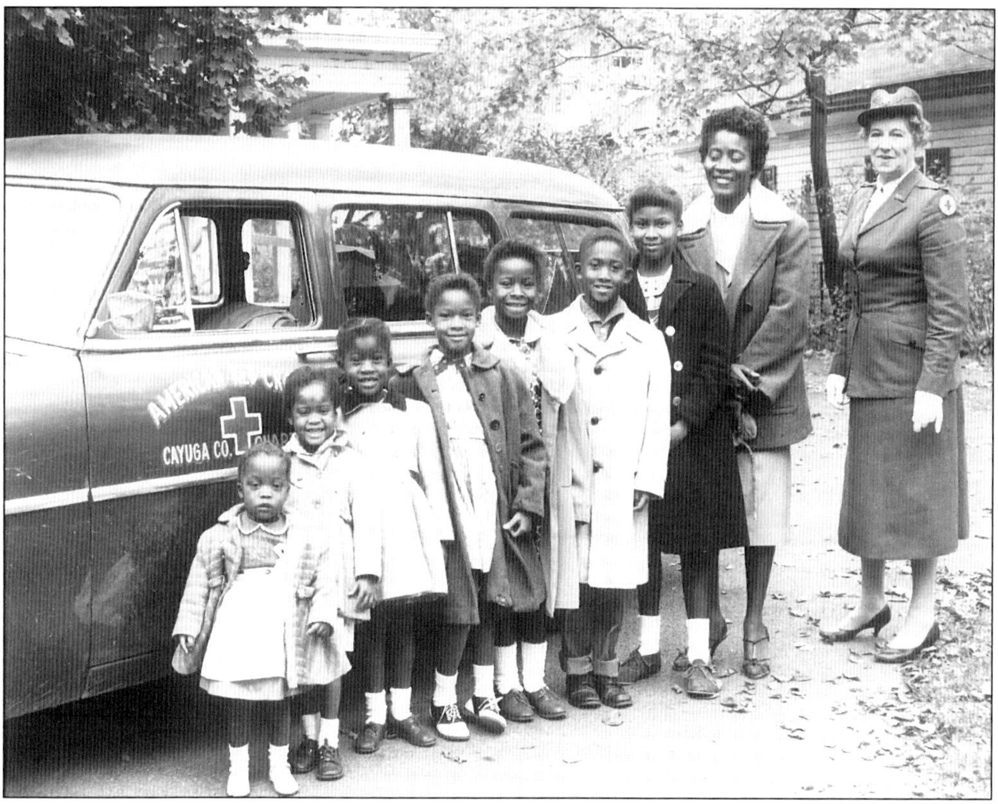

COPES FAMILY ON WAY TO AIRPORT, C. 1944. The Red Cross provided transportation for Mary Dean Copes and her children as they prepared to visit Mary's husband and the children's father, Bill. He was stationed overseas during WW II.

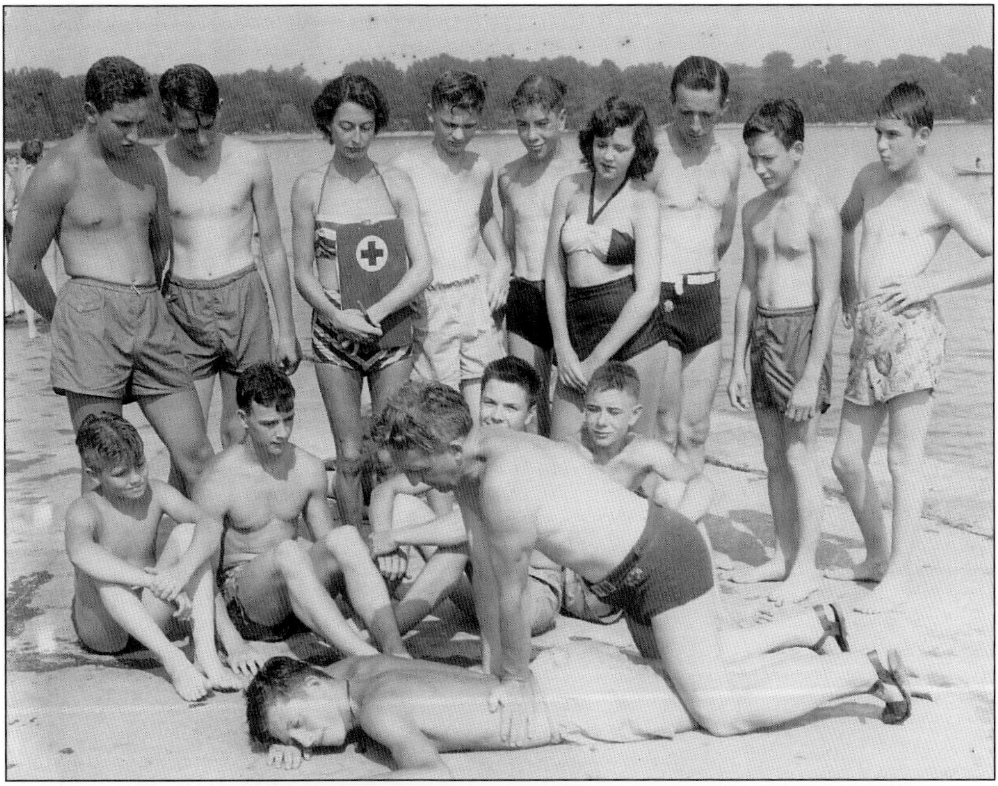

Ensuring Summer Safety, Emerson Park, 1947. Instructor Glen Mosher demonstrated proper techniques to students in a lifesaving class offered by the Red Cross at Owasco Lake.

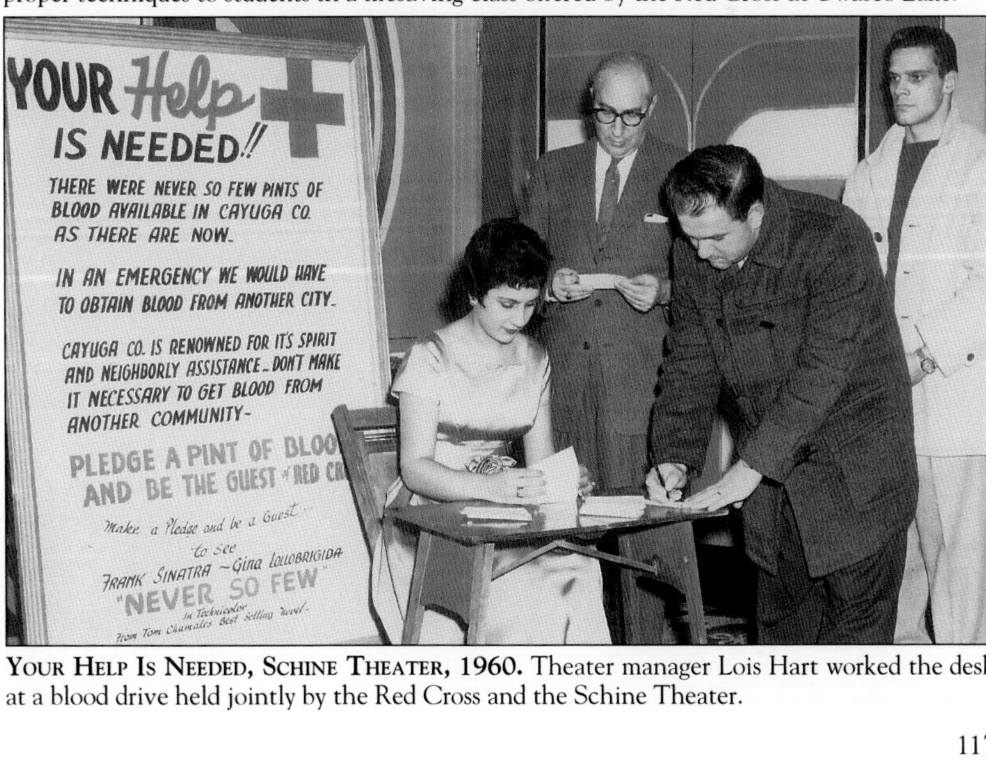

Your Help Is Needed, Schine Theater, 1960. Theater manager Lois Hart worked the desk at a blood drive held jointly by the Red Cross and the Schine Theater.

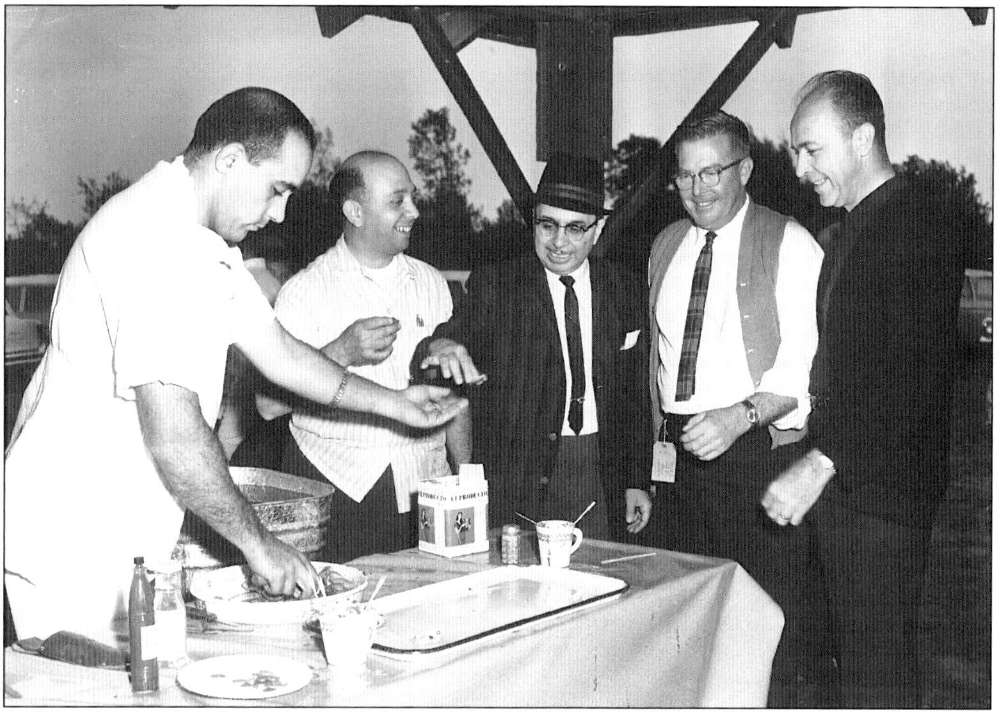

PASSING OUT CLAMS, 1960S. The Cayuga County Restaurant and Hotel Association held their annual clambake at the Polish Home Camp near Owasco Lake. From left to right are: Leo Tortorici, Vincent Dello Stritto, Joseph Cefaratti, Frank Inman, and Kenneth McClenathan.

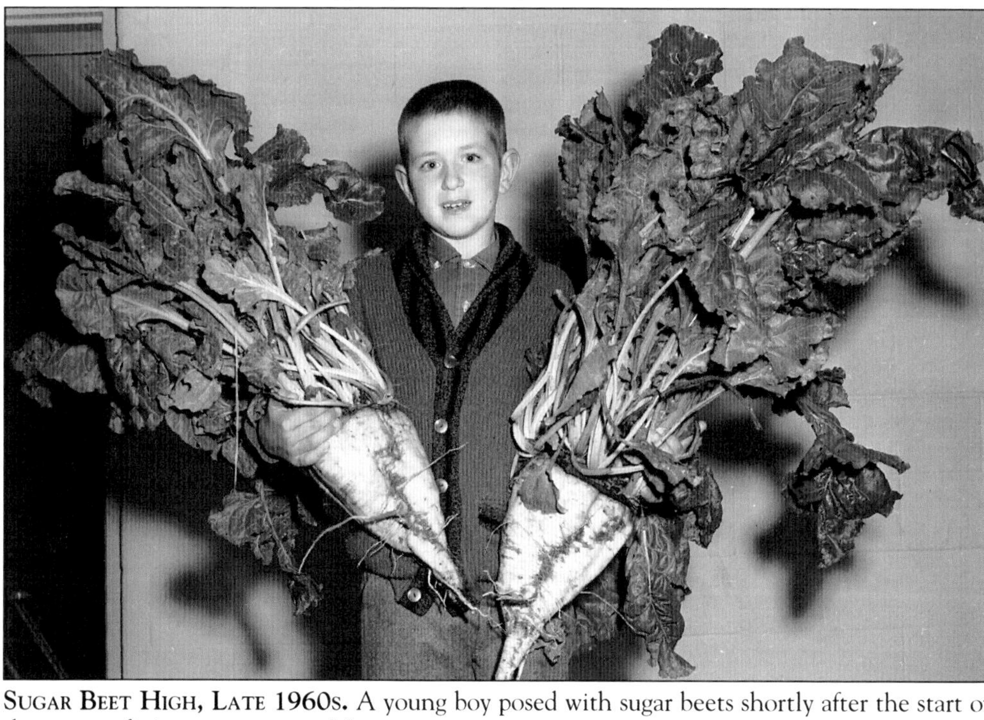

SUGAR BEET HIGH, LATE 1960S. A young boy posed with sugar beets shortly after the start of the sugar-refining venture near Montezuma.

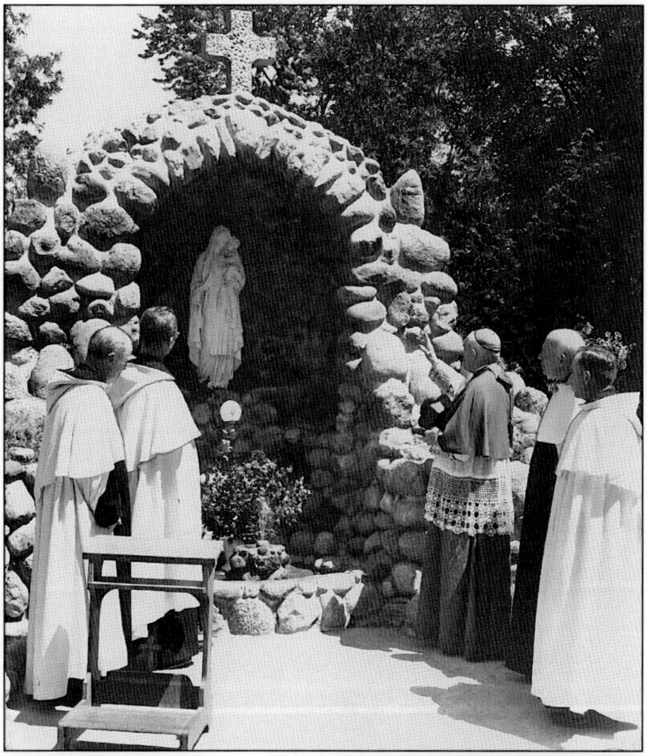

BLESSING THE SHRINE, CLARK STREET, 1960S. This small ceremony commemorated a shrine to the Virgin Mary at St. Francis Roman Catholic Church on Clark Street.

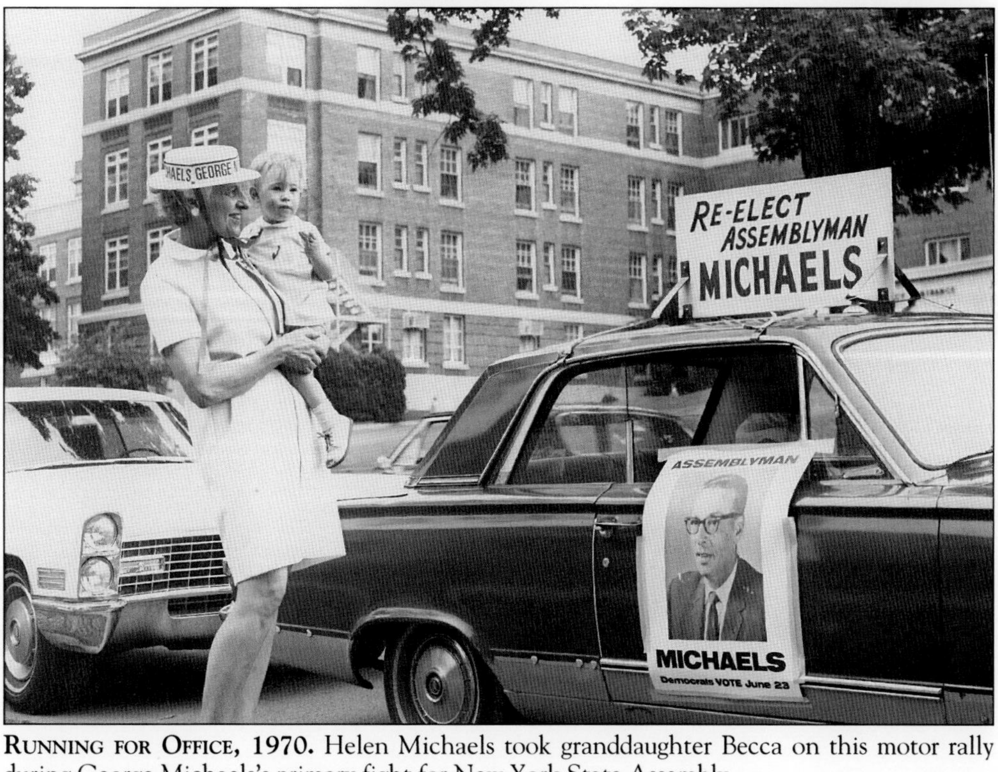

RUNNING FOR OFFICE, 1970. Helen Michaels took granddaughter Becca on this motor rally during George Michaels's primary fight for New York State Assembly.

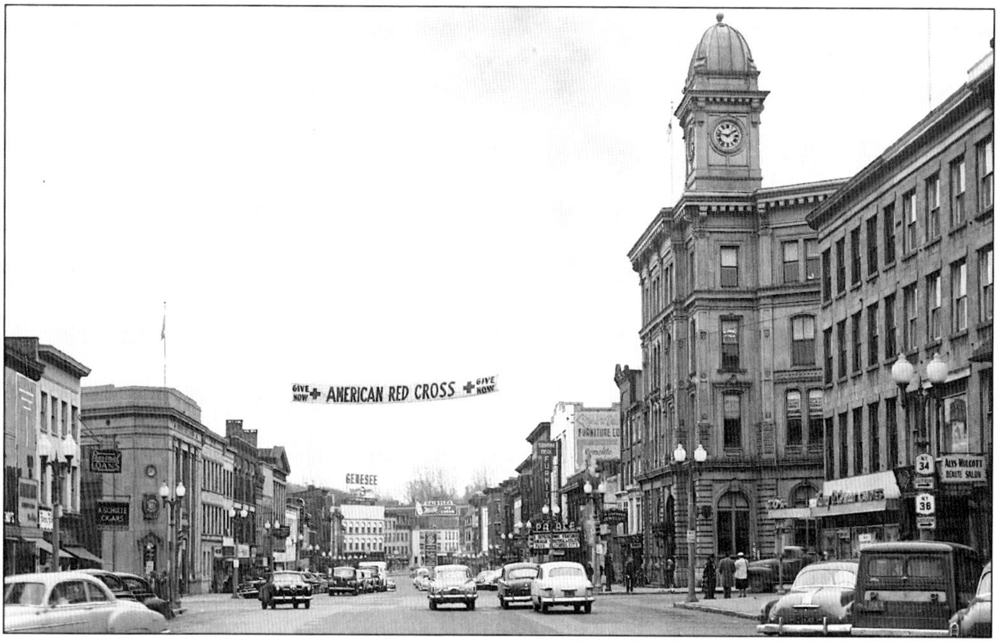

Genesee Street, March 1953. A Red Cross blood drive banner hung over Genesee Street while cars and pedestrians hurried about their business.

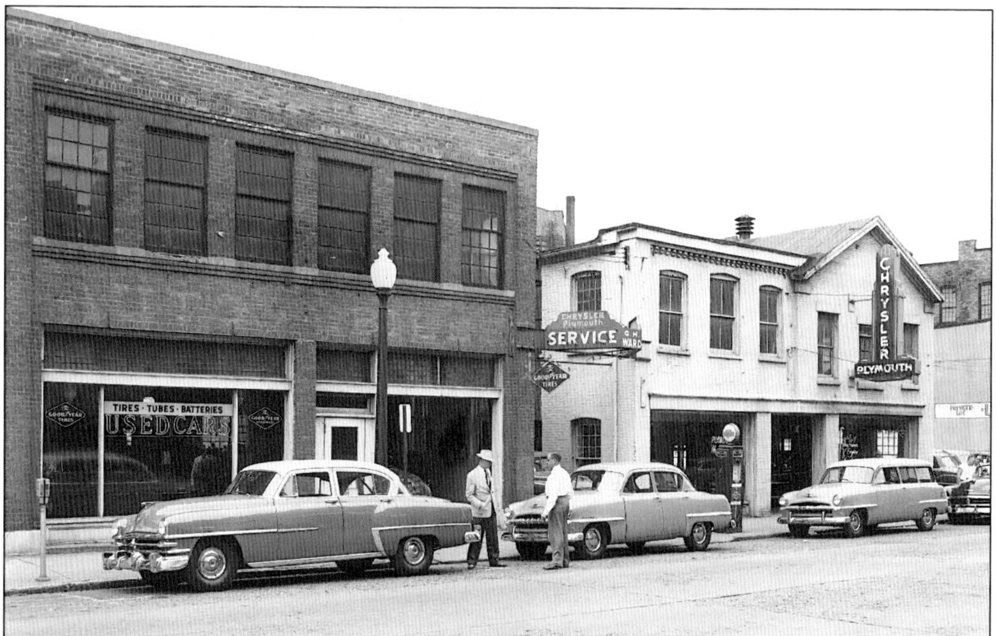

G.H. Ward Chrysler Plymouth Service Station, 20–26 Water Street, 1950s.

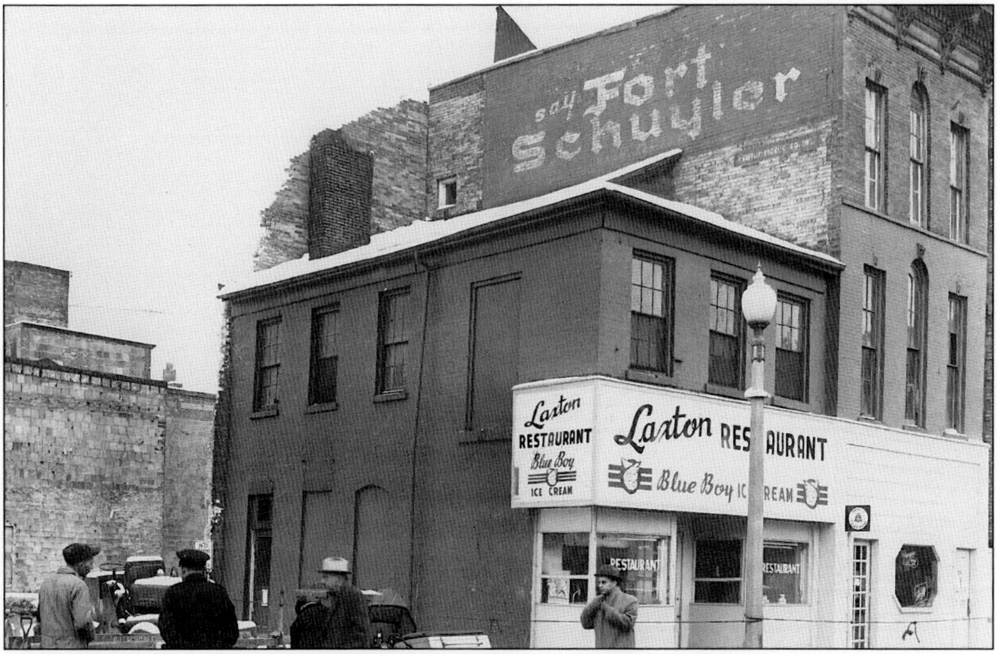

End of the Line for the Laxton Restaurant, 1957. The buildings at the corner of North and Market Streets were demolished in 1957.

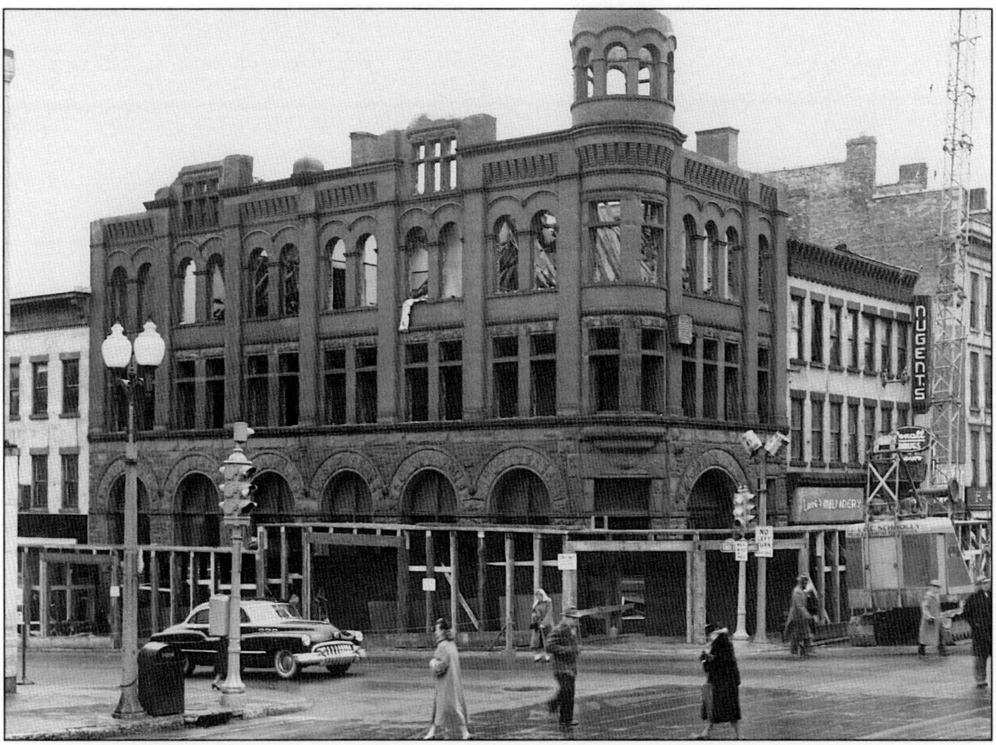

A Landmark Comes Down, c. 1954. The Cayuga County Savings Bank, a grand Richardsonian-style structure and Auburn landmark, stood at the corner of State and Genesee Streets until being razed in the mid-1950s.

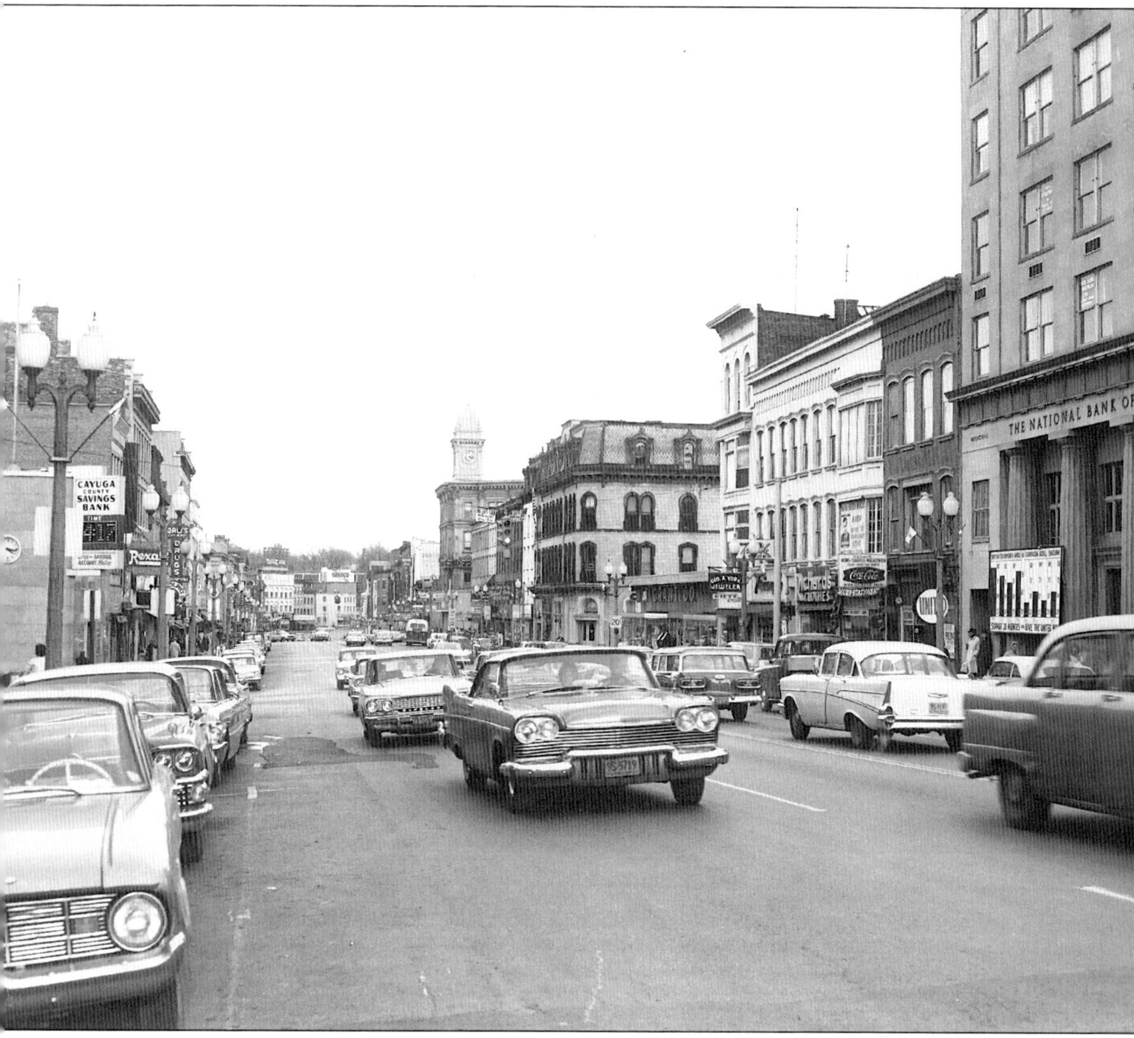

GENESEE STREET, C. 1963. This image conveyed the character of Genesee Street shortly before urban renewal profoundly altered the cityscape. (Image from collection of the Community Preservation Committee.)

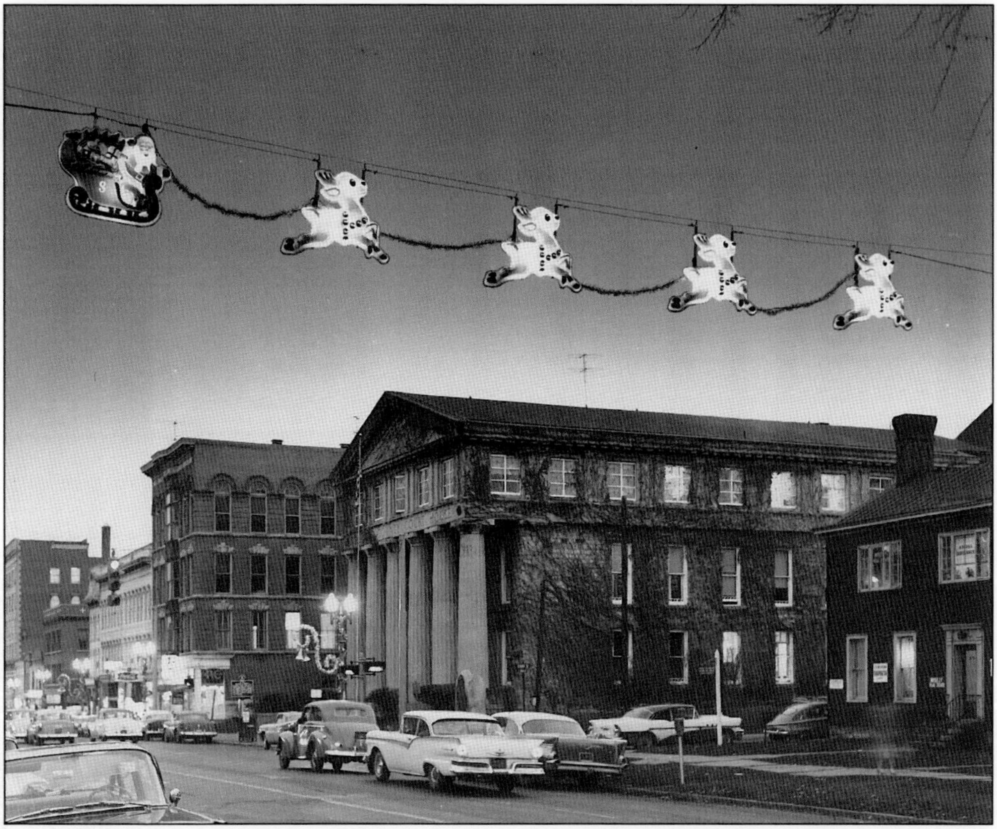

SANTA ARRIVES IN AUBURN, 1960S. Genesee Street displayed the latest decorations for the holiday season. (Image from collection of Community Preservation Committee.)

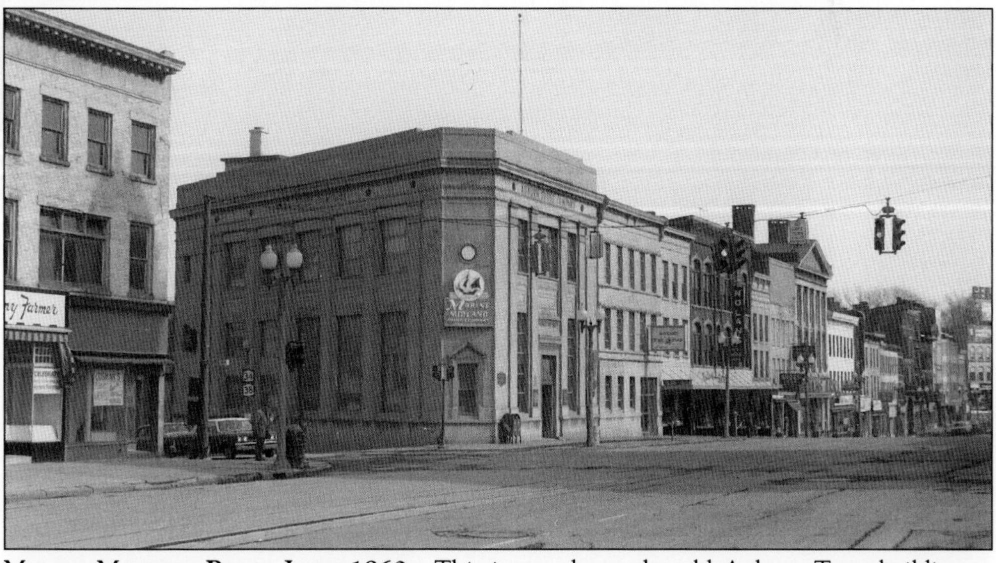

MARINE MIDLAND BANK, LATE 1960S. This image shows the old Auburn Trust building at the corner of Genesee and North Streets, shortly before it came down to make way for a more modern structure.

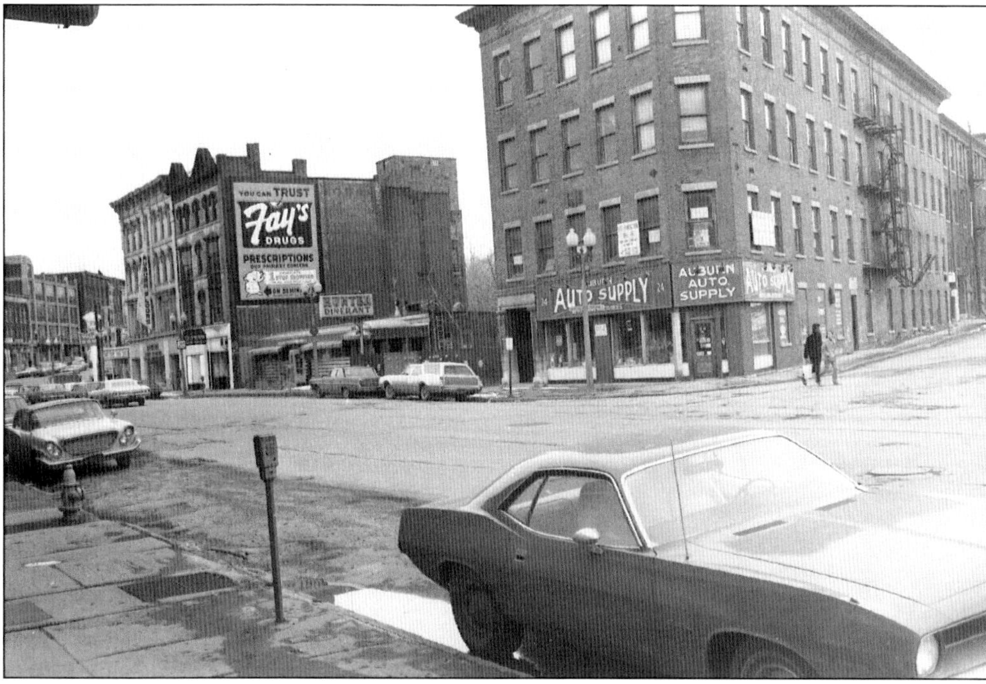

LOOKING DOWN THE WRECKING BALL, EARLY 1970S. An Auburn resident shot this image of Genesee Street, near the intersection of Osborne Street, a few days before demolition began.

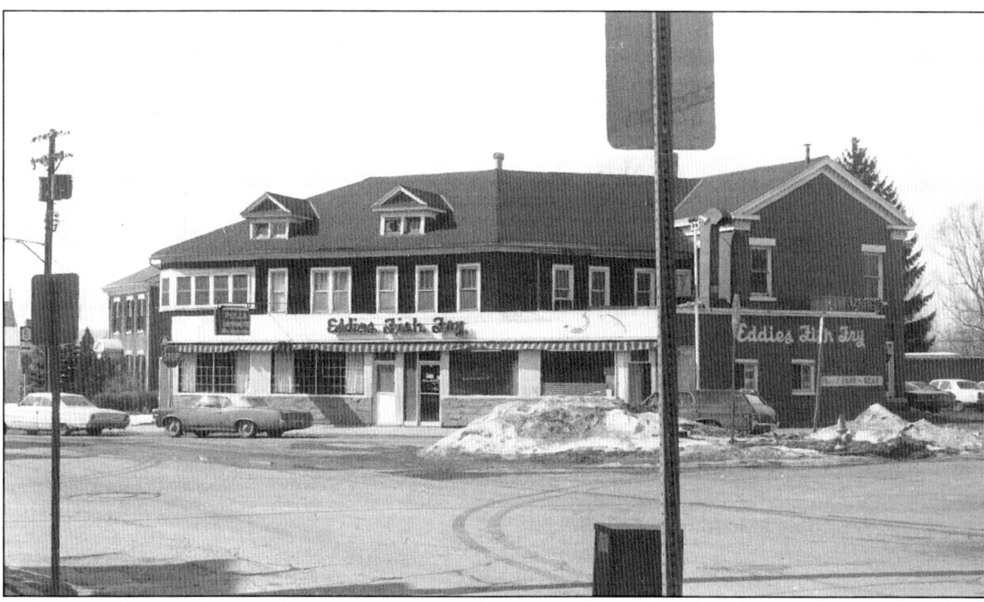

EDDIE'S FISH FRY, EARLY 1970S. This view shows Five Points, facing north, and the corners of Franklin and Lewis Streets. Eddie's burned in the early 1970s.

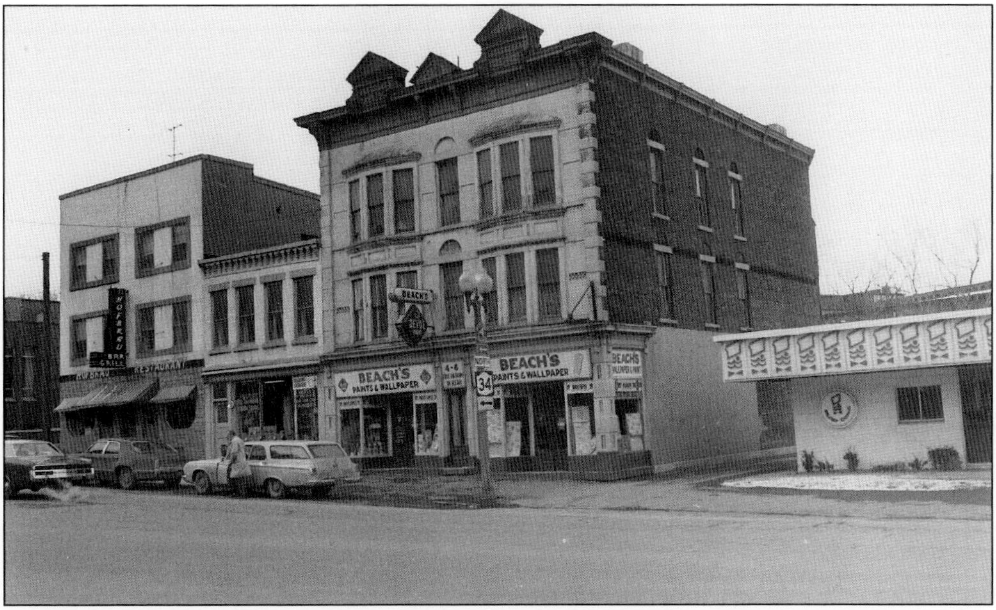

SURVIVORS, GENESEE STREET, EARLY 1970S. These buildings still stand on Genesee Street. The Hoffbrau restaurant is now Riordans. The neon sign, restored to reflect the new ownership, still glows in the evening hours.

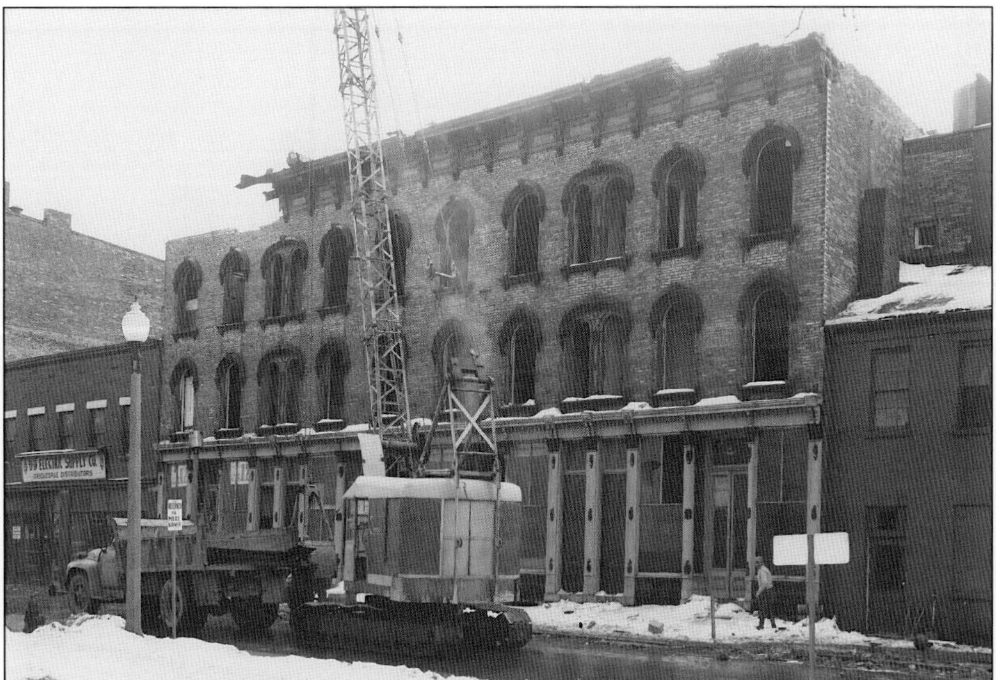

PROGRESS, JUNE 1972. A crane and wrecking ball demolished the buildings on the south side of Market Street, as urban renewal progressed.

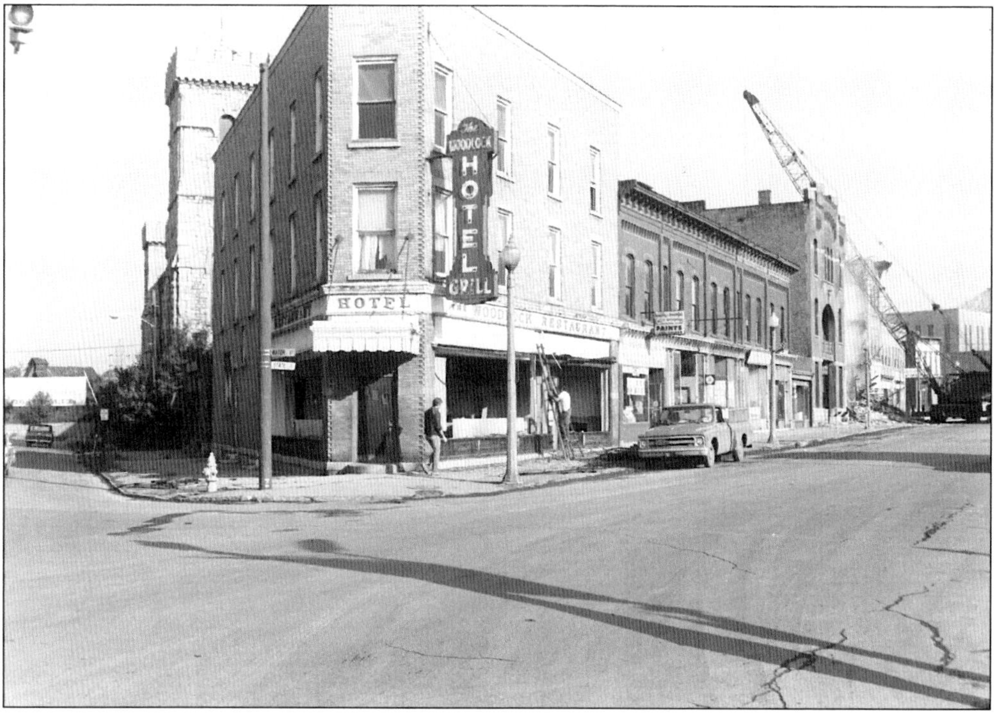

Woodlock Hotel, 1969–1970. Originally the Garrett Hotel, the Woodlock stood at the corner of Water and State Streets until it too was razed to make way for the arterial highway.

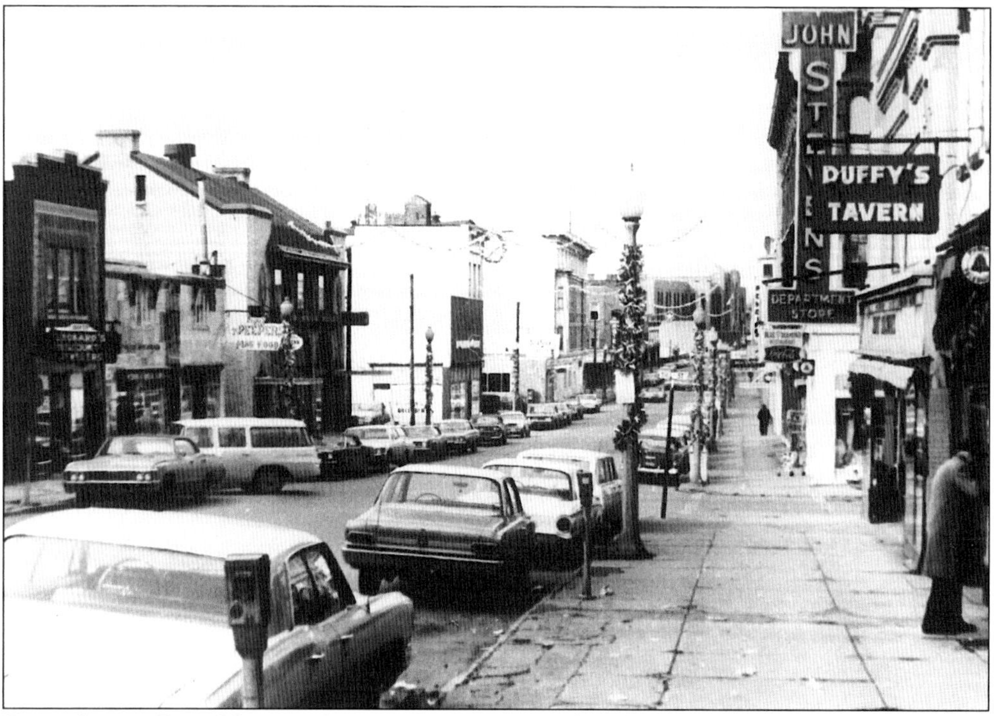

State Street Run, Holiday Season, 1969–1970. The John Stevens neon sign is one of the few recognizable landmarks in this image of the old State Street business district.

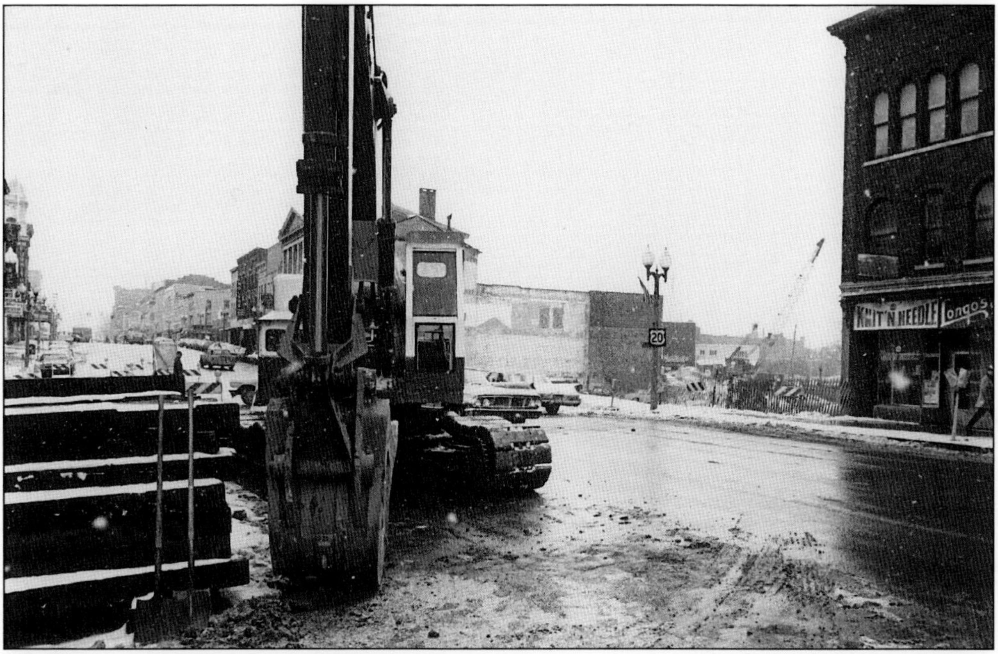

The Face of Progress, c. 1970. Construction equipment was a familiar sight to Auburn residents in the 1960s and 1970s.

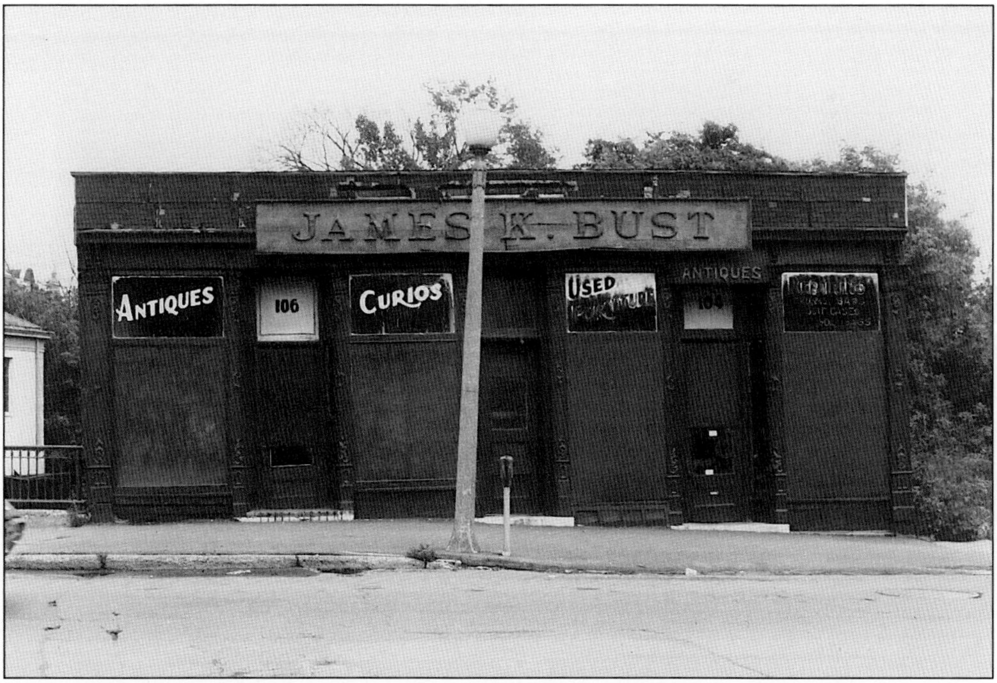

James K. Bust Antiques and Used Furniture, State Street, c. 1970. This purveyor of antiques and curios was consigned to memory by urban renewal. The sign now hangs in Curley's Restaurant on State Street.

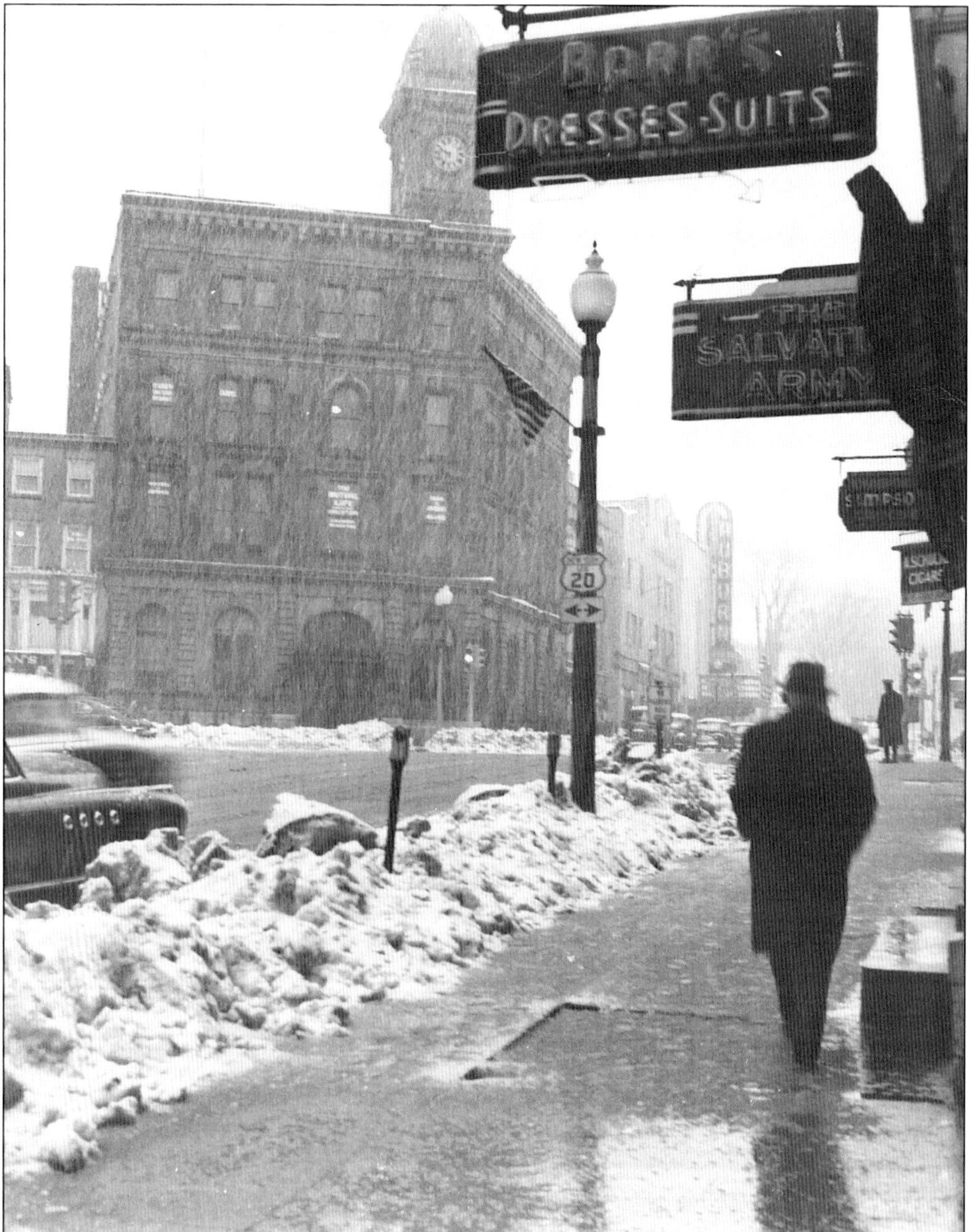

City in Winter, 1950s. Winter weather and the Auburn Savings Bank, now the Phoenix building, seem to be timeless elements of life in Auburn. (Image from collection of the Community Preservation Committee.)